S0-BOI-810

Also of Interest

oviet Union in the Third World: Successes and Failures, edited by Robert naldson

Soviet Union in World Politics, edited by Kurt London

Future of European Alliance Systems: NATO and the Warsaw Pact, edited Arlene Idol Broadhurst

ina, the Soviet Union, and the West: Strategic and Political Dimensions for e 1980s, edited by Douglas T. Stuart and William T. Tow

Communist Armies in Politics, edited by Jonathan R. Adelman

U.S. Defense Planning: A Critique, John Collins

* Managing U.S.-Soviet Rivalry: Problems of Crisis Prevention, Alexander L. George and Associates

* Red Flag Over Afghanistan: The Communist Coup, the Soviet Invasion, and the Consequences, Thomas T. Hammond

Nuclear Deterrence in U.S.-Soviet Relations, Keith B. Payne

* The Foreign Policy Priorities of Third World States, edited by John J. Stremlau

Arms Control and Defense Postures in the 1980s, edited by Richard Burt

* The Third World and U.S. Foreign Policy: Cooperation and Conflict in the 1980s, Robert L. Rothstein

Thinking About Defense: National Security in a Dangerous World, Harold Brown

Strategy, Doctrine, and the Politics of Alliance: Theatre Nuclear Force Modernization in NATO, Paul Buteux

Soviet Allies: The Warsaw Pact and the Issue of Reliability, edited by Daniel N. Nelson

* Available in hardcover and paperback.

Con
Milh

* The S
H. Do
* The
The
by
* C
t

Westview Special Studies in International Relations

Communist Nations' Military Assistance
edited by John F. Copper and Daniel S. Papp

This book looks at the military aid given by communist bloc countries to other bloc countries and to Third World nations. The authors analyze the military aid capabilities of communist donor nations, their specific motivations for offering military aid, and the policies and guidelines that govern arms assistance. They also discuss competition with Western weapons purveyors, especially the United States. Finally, the authors evaluate the general successes and failures of military aid programs, examining their effects on recipients and their impact on crisis situations and regional power balances. The book makes it possible to compare the military aid activities of the major communist nations, points to trends in these activities, and suggests implications for U.S. foreign policy.

Dr. John F. Copper is an associate professor in the Department of International Studies, Southwestern University at Memphis. He is the author of *China's Global Role: An Analysis of Peking's National Power Capabilities in the Context of an Evolving International System* (1980). Dr. Daniel S. Papp is director and associate professor, School of Social Sciences, Georgia Institute of Technology. He is the author of *The Net of International Relations* (1983).

To Harrison Blair, Elizabeth Allison, and Anne Devona Copper

J.F.C.

To William Stephen and Alexander Stephen Papp

D.S.P.

That our children may grow up
in a world more aware of the realities of war and peace

Communist Nations' Military Assistance

edited by John F. Copper
and Daniel S. Papp

Westview Press / Boulder, Colorado

Westview Special Studies in International Relations

All rights reserved. No part of this publication may be reproduced or transmitted in any form or by any means, electronic or mechanical, including photocopy, recording, or any information storage and retrieval system, without permission in writing from the publisher.

Copyright © 1983 by Westview Press, Inc.

Published in 1983 in the United States of America by
  Westview Press, Inc.
  5500 Central Avenue
  Boulder, Colorado 80301
  Frederick A. Praeger, President and Publisher

Library of Congress Catalog Card Number 83-60505
ISBN 0-86531-296-6

Composition for this book was provided by the editors
Printed and bound in the United States of America

10 9 8 7 6 5 4 3 2 1

Contents

List of Tables. ix
Preface. xi

1   Communist Military Assistance:
    An Overview, *Daniel S. Papp* 1

2   Soviet Military Assistance to Eastern Europe,
    Daniel S. Papp. 13

3   Soviet Military Assistance
    to the Third World, *Roger E. Kanet*. 39

4   Eastern European Military Assistance
    to the Third World, *Trond Gilberg*. 72

5   China's Military Assistance, *John F. Copper* 96

6   Cuban Military Assistance
    to the Third World, *W. Raymond Duncan* 135

7   Vietnam's Military Assistance, *Douglas Pike*. 160

8   North Korean Military Assistance,
    Nack An and Rose An 169

9   Conclusion, *John F. Copper and Daniel S. Papp*, ... 178

List of Abbreviations. 187
Index 188
Contributors 200

Tables

1.1   Communist Arms Exports, 1969–1978 3
1.2   Ratios of Communist Arms Exports,
      1969–1978, Compared to Total World Arms Exports 4
2.1   NSWP Armored Vehicles, 1968–1974 20
2.2   Arms Imports by Non-Soviet Warsaw Pact
      Nations as Compared to Total Soviet
      Arms Exports, 1969–1978 23
2.3   Eastern European Arms Imports and Defense
      Expenditures, 1974–1978 25
2.4   Eastern European and Soviet Arms Transfers,
      1974–1978 26
2.5   Evolution of Non-Soviet Warsaw Pact Force
      Structures, 1975–1982 28
2.6   Evolution of Non-Soviet Warsaw Pact Force
      Structures by Country, 1975–1982 29
2.7   Evolution of Non-Soviet Warsaw Pact Force
      Structures by Tier, 1975–1982 31
3.1   Soviet Military Relations with
      Noncommunist Developing Countries, 1955–1979 45
3.2   Soviet Military Relations with Developing
      Countries by Region, 1956–1979 48
3.3   Deliveries of Soviet Armaments to Noncommunist
      Developing Countries, 1967–1978 49
3.4   Major Recipients of Soviet Economic
      and Military Aid and the Existence
      of Soviet Basing Facilities 58
3.5   Relationship of Military Sales to the Hard
      Currency Balance of Payments of the Soviet Union 62
4.1   Communist Military Agreements with LDCs:
      Agreements Concluded and Equipment Delivered 77
4.2   Communist Military Technicians in LDCs, 1978 78

ix

x

4.3   Military Personnel from LDCs Trained in
      Communist Countries, 1955–1978 79
6.1   Cuban Armed Forces Structure, 1982 142
6.2   Cuban Military Personnel in Africa, 1980 144
6.3   Cuban Economic and Technical Personnel (E&T)
      Compared to Military Personnel (M) in
      the Caribbean and Central America, 1978–1980 145
6.4   Modern Weapons in Guerrilla Inventory,
      El Salvador, 1981 146

Preface

In this generation the United States and its allies have been involved in two major wars -- in Korea and in Vietnam. In the former the United States fought its first indecisive war. The latter was the first war the United States ever lost.

In both wars the United States engaged a communist enemy that was receiving military assistance from other communist nations. And in each instance this support was crucial in determining the outcome of the conflict. In the first it was sufficient only to force a stalemate and a negotiated end to the war. But that was something new and different for the United States. In the second case it contributed significantly to, indeed caused, a humiliating defeat for the United States -- the effects of which are still being felt.

Yet the military assistance programs of the communist bloc countries have not been systematically studied. Not even a monograph or scholarly article on the military assistance of several communist nations can be found in the literature. Although some communist nations such as Cuba, North Korea, and Vietnam have only recently given military assistance worthy of concern, China has been in the arms assistance business for more than three decades, as have several Eastern European nations. Soviet arms assistance has been the topic of a large number of studies -- but these studies have not compared Soviet assistance to the assistance of other communist nations.

In short, our lack of understanding about the military assistance of communist nations is a serious shortcoming. And it is not just a shortcoming in itself. It contributes to our inability to comprehend the problems of foreign-policymaking, the issues of war and peace, and the condition of world politics in general.

Some other facts are also relevant: Since World War II more casualties have resulted from civil wars than from wars between or among nations. Many wars of both types have been proxy wars. Some have been designated revolutions or wars of national liberation, but most have been fought with outside help in the form of arms, equipment, and training. In almost all of them conflict was either made possible or, in fact, decided by foreign arms assistance. It seems likely that this trend will continue into the foreseeable future, playing a central role in many conflicts and wars to come.

This is not to say that the East-West struggle will increasingly take the form of proxy battles or wars fought because of competing military assistance. The situation is much more complicated than that. Communist nations have given and are giving arms assistance to other communist nations locked in struggles against each other. Since the middle 1960s, most of China's arms exports have gone to nations or liberation groups unfriendly to or hostile toward the Soviet Union. Such assistance has often been used against the Kremlin's friends and protégés and on occasion even against Soviet advisers and bases.

At the same time, Eastern European countries are demonstrating their independence, or lack thereof, through their military aid programs to Third World countries and insurgency or liberation groups. Cuba, North Korea, and Vietnam are also playing new roles in world affairs -- in large part by providing military assistance to one side or regime in a vital area caught in a conflict situation.

It is with a sense of recognition of the importance of communist nations' military assistance and with awareness of the absence of understanding in the West of the importance of this factor in world politics that this volume was undertaken. We seek to make the reader aware of the relevance of communist nations' military assistance to the increasingly close relationship between military assistance and conflicts and war; to the financial costs in arms races wherever they occur, but especially in the Third World; and finally to the rapid growth of military capabilities in many new and unstable countries made possible by outside help.

John F. Copper
Daniel S. Papp

1
Communist Military Assistance: An Overview

Daniel S. Papp

During the 1970s, military assistance and arms transfers reached unprecedented levels. In 1970, arms transfers alone totaled slightly less than $6 billion, and other forms of military assistance such as training and construction added considerably to this total. By the end of the decade the United States and the Soviet Union each had surpassed the $6 billion mark in official arms transfers annually. Meanwhile, total official world arms transfers had grown to more than $21 billion per year.[1]

Several distinct trends were evident in this growing international traffic in weapons, military supplies, equipment, and other support requirements. First, developing states, as might be expected because of the limited size of their industrial base and their real and perceived need for national military capabilities, imported more than 80 percent of the total value of world arms transfers. The Middle East alone received more than one-third of the world's total arms deliveries; Africa received one-fourth. Military assistance other than arms also flowed primarily to the developing nations.

Second, increasingly sophisticated weapons entered the international arms market and appeared in the arsenals of developing states. For example, the Soviet Union sold sophisticated MiG-23 and MiG-25 aircraft to several of its Third World clients shortly after the planes became operational; the United States followed suit with the sale of F-14 aircraft and the Phoenix missile system to Iran and the Airborne Warning and Control System (AWACS) to Saudi Arabia. In the past, neither the Soviet Union nor the United States exported its best weapons to Third World countries.

Third, although the United States remained the major exporter of arms and military supplies and equipment for most of the decade, it lost its position as the leading provider of arms to other countries to the Soviet Union. The U.S. share of the world arms export market dropped from 53 percent in 1970 to 33 percent in 1978.[2]

At least some of this reduced U.S. market share was attributable to domestic policy decisions within the United States. The years of U.S. involvement in Vietnam left many Americans uneasy at the thought of becoming militarily tied to other nations, and with Jimmy

Carter's accession to the presidency, a conscious effort was made to reduce U.S. arms aid and sales. Furthermore, U.S. military assistance and arms transfers were in some cases tied to the human rights records of recipient nations.

Notwithstanding these considerations, it is evident that one of the major trends in military assistance and arms transfers during the 1970s was an increase in non-U.S. exports of weapons, military supplies, and military equipment and non-U.S. provision of military training, construction, and other forms of assistance. Much of this surge originated in countries that had not, at the beginning of the 1970s, been significantly involved in the fields of military assistance and arms transfers, but that by the close of the decade had attained positions of prominence as purveyors of weapons. Austria, Belgium, Brazil, Bulgaria, East Germany, Egypt, Hungary, Israel, Italy, Japan, North and South Korea, the Netherlands, Romania, Sweden, Switzerland, and Yugoslavia all entered the 1970s with less than $20 million each in annual arms transfers. By 1978 each had increased the value of the arms, supplies, and equipment it exported annually to at least $60 million. These are paltry sums when compared to U.S. or Soviet figures, but they nonetheless serve to indicate that sources of arms proliferated during the 1970s.

An even more significant portion of the surge originated in countries that had been major suppliers in the international arms market at the onset of the 1970s and that expanded their participation in that market as the decade progressed. Included in this group were Czechoslovakia, France, Great Britain, Poland, the Soviet Union, and West Germany. This group of countries alone increased its share of the world arms transfer market from 38 percent to 56 percent between 1970 and 1978. Of particular note was the growth of Soviet arms exports from $1.5 billion in 1970, or roughly one-fourth of the world's arms exports, to $7.1 billion, or approximately one-third of the world's arms exports, by 1978. The USSR also increased its provision of other forms of military help to the extent that by the close of the 1970s, Soviet advisers and construction sites were seen throughout the world, the single exception being North America.

A fourth major trend in military assistance and arms transfers during the 1970s, and the trend to which this book owes its conception, was the growing share of the global arms and assistance market controlled by communist countries. Between 1969 and 1978, arms exports from communist countries climbed from 25.9 percent of the world total to 43.1 percent. Much of this growth was attributable to increased Soviet emphasis on military assistance, but it was also evident that other communist countries participated in the "arms transfer explosion" of the 1970s. Indeed, as it has been pointed out, Bulgaria, East Germany, Hungary, North Korea, Romania, and Yugoslavia all became significant arms exporters during the 1970s, while Czechoslovakia and Poland expanded their already major roles. Only Albania (which does not produce weapons of any significant quality or quantity), the People's Republic of China (PRC), Cuba, and Vietnam did not expand their arms exports. The latter two countries were themselves involved in major military operations outside their homelands. China during the period in question cut its economic aid drastically and began to give great emphasis to economic development at home. Table 1.1 illustrates the volume of communist arms exports through the 1970s. Table 1.2 presents the ratio of communist arms exports to world totals.

Exports are only one aspect of the arms transfer picture. Imports present still another aspect. During the same 1969-1978 period when communist arms exports rose from 26 percent of the world market to 43 percent, communist imports fell from 17 percent to 13 percent of total world imports.[4] It should be noted that with the exceptions of China, Romania, and Yugoslavia, all communist countries import arms exclusively from other communist countries.

TABLE 1.1 Communist Arms Exports, 1969-1978
(in current dollars x 10^6)

	1969	1972	1975	1978
Albania	0	0	0	0
Bulgaria	5	0	30	70
China	140	850	180	140
Cuba	0	0	30	0
Czechoslovakia	110	210	490	800
Germany (East)	10	50	50	60
Hungary	0	10	50	70
Korea (North)	0	0	10	70
Poland	150	140	170	350
Romania	0	50	30	70
USSR	1,100	2,900	4,000	7,100
Vietnam	0	0	0	0
Yugoslavia	0	10	90	140
Total communist	1,515	4,220	5,130	8,870
Total world	5,860	10,400	12,600	20,600

Source: Arms Control and Disarmament Agency, World Military Expeditures and Arms Transfers, 1969-1978 (Washington, D.C.: ACDA, 1980), passim.

Note: Kampuchea and Laos are excluded from this analysis because of the extreme uncertainty of available figures and because of government changes occurring during this ten-year period.

4

TABLE 1.2 Ratios of Communist Arms Exports, 1969-1978
Compared to Total World Arms Exports

	1969	1972	1976	1978
Albania	.000	.000	.000	.000
Bulgaria	.001	.000	.002	.003
China (PRC)	.024	.082	.014	.007
Cuba	.000	.000	.002	.000
Czechoslovakia	.019	.020	.039	.039
Germany (East)	.002	.005	.004	.003
Hungary	.000	.001	.004	.003
Korea (North)	.006	.000	.001	.003
Poland	.026	.013	.013	.017
Romania	.000	.005	.002	.003
USSR	.187	.279	.317	.345
Vietnam	.000	.000	.000	.000
Yugoslavia	.000	.001	.007	.007
Total communist	.259	.406	.407	.431

Source: Compiled from Arms Control and Disarmament Agency, World Military Expenditures and Arms Transfers 1969-1978 (Washington, D.C.: ACDA, 1980), passim

Particularly striking is the fact that, excluding the error caused by the arms traffic between and among communist countries, communist arms exports to noncommunist countries, most of which were Third World countries, have risen from roughly $500 million per year in 1969 (9 percent of the world's total arms exports) to more than $6 billion per year in 1978 (30 percent of the world's total arms exports). Again, much of the increase in communist arms exports to the noncommunist world is attributable to Soviet policy, as Chapter 3 shows, but as several of the other chapters illustrate, other communist countries have played and are playing roles in this growth.

None of this discussion, however, should be interpreted to mean that communist countries coordinate their arms transfer policies. To be sure, some do; but to be equally sure, some do not. In Chapter 4, on Eastern European military assistance, Trond Gilberg shows that even within the Warsaw Pact, different countries have adopted different levels of coordination with and independence from the USSR in their arms export policies. When the military assistance and arms transfer policies of non-European communist countries are examined, it becomes even more evident that communist governments as much as noncommunist governments use arms transfers to attain diverse national objectives. These objectives may even on occasion conflict; witness the Sino-Soviet struggle for influence with differing national liberation movements in Angola, where the Chinese supported Holden Roberto's National Front for the Liberation of Angola (FNLA) and Jonas Savimbi's National Union for the Total Independence of Angola (UNITA) while the USSR supported Agostinho Neto's Popular Movement for the Liberation of Angola (MPLA), and in Zimbabwe, where the Chinese supported Robert Mugabe's Zimbabwe African National Union (ZANU) while the Soviets supported Joshua Nkomo's Zimbabwe African People's Union (ZAPU).[5] An even more salient example is the brief 1980 Sino-Vietnamese border war, which was in part the result of Vietnam's military aid and assistance, including almost all the combat forces, to Heng Samrin's government in Kampuchea (Cambodia). The People's Republic of China supported Khmer Rouge forces, which were engaged in guerrilla warfare against Heng Samrin. China, in a clear effort to influence Hanoi to terminate or reduce its military aid and assistance to Heng Samrin, initiated hostilities with Vietnam.

This last example evokes a fundamental question: What is and should be included when military assistance and arms transfers are discussed? There is no simple answer to this question, whether one is discussing communist or noncommunist assistance or transfers. Arms transfers, according to the U.S. Arms Control and Disarmament Agency, represent the "international transfer under grant, credit or cash sales terms of military equipment...including weapons of war, parts thereof, ammunition, support equipment, and other commodities considered primarily military in nature."[6] Additional types of military assistance that one country may render to another such as training, provision of goods and services including food and medicine, construction, technical assistance, and support received by nongovernmental organizations, groups, or individuals are not, generally speaking, included in arms transfer statistics. Military assistance thus should be viewed as a more all-encompassing concept than arms transfers. Military aid, on the other hand, in common usage refers to military assistance, including arms transfers, under grant and occasionally credit terms. Additionally, given the different stages in any assistance or transfer program, ranging from tentative agreement through final delivery and payment, and given as well the differing modes of payment, ranging from cash and barter to grants and credit, it is not unusual for the same transfer to be interpreted and classified differently by different sources.[7]

Other reasons also exist for discrepancies in data among sources. Different exchange rates are often used when non-U.S. currencies are converted into dollars; this is an especially significant problem when dealing with the ruble and other communist currencies.[8] State secrecy provides yet another complicating factor that frustrates accurate data collection; indeed, transfers and assistance reported by one source are often denied by another or may be reported to be still pending by yet a third source. As a consequence, statistics on arms transfers and military assistance reported by the most prominent and reliable sources, the U.S. Arms Control and Disarmament Agency (ACDA), the U.S. Central Intelligence Agency (CIA), the Stockholm International Peace Research Institute (SIPRI),

...d the International Institute for Strategic Studies (IISS), are seldom, if ever, in full agreement. Omission presents another source of discrepancy, particularly in the case of China. Most of the PRC's arms assistance has not been reported by these official sources. Any conclusions that result from the use of such statistics, including some of the conclusions reached here, must of necessity be somewhat tentative.

With these methodological problems addressed, it is necessary to ask what systemic differences, if any, exist between the military assistance programs of communist countries and those of noncommunist countries. There is little doubt, as each of the chapters in this book makes clear, that military assistance programs are integral parts of the foreign policies of communist states. At one time, this fact constituted a significant difference between communist activities and noncommunist arms export policies, as in noncommunist countries arms transfers were formerly undertaken almost exclusively with an eye to profit by private entrepreneurs and businesses.[9] However, since World War II, noncommunist governments have enacted a variety of licensing requirements and other regulations for arms exports, and other forms of military assistance are generally provided by the government itself. Additionally, because of the political importance of military assistance and arms transfers, governments have increasingly become not only the controllers of such assistance and transfers but also the salesmen for these ventures. Military assistance and arms transfers have thus become tools of foreign policy in noncommunist as well as communist countries. Although profit remains a motive of the arms producers themselves, that objective in most cases in the West has been subordinated to government policy.[10] Thus, in the area of state use of military assistance and arms transfers as tools of policy, a convergence of systems has occurred, with the noncommunist systems having moved considerably closer to the models provided by communist systems.

This is not to say, however, that economic costs have not played a role in influencing communist military assistance and arms transfer programs. They have. As will be seen in Chapter 2, the USSR has regularly pressured its Warsaw Pact allies to assume a larger share of the Pact's defense burden, and one may assume that at least part of this pressure is generated by a Soviet desire to recoup a larger portion of the costs of the weapons it provides to its allies. Similarly, the USSR has increasingly favored cash sales and occasionally barter agreements as opposed to credits or grants as methods of payment for military assistance. This does not necessarily mean that the Kremlin is acting as a state monopoly capitalist and is seeking a profit as it extends military assistance, although that interpretation is certainly possible. It does, however, argue that at a minimum the Kremlin is cognizant of the economic costs incurred in its arms assistance programs and seeks to minimize those costs as it increases the volume of its assistance.

China's arms assistance policies in the present context are unique. In the past several years Beijing has reduced its military assistance to other states and movements with which it sympathizes.

Meanwhile, it has begun to concentrate more on its own internal development. Chinese leaders seem to be suddenly aware of the costs of arms assistance, although the decline in Beijing's arms exports may also be attributed to disputes with two former major recipients, Albania and Vietnam. North Korea, in contrast, has moved into the international military assistance and arms transfer markets at least in part to raise revenues to increase its foreign currency holdings and pay off some of its foreign debts. Yugoslavia, seeking to further develop its own arms industry to help it maintain its nonaligned posture, has also recently gone into the arms export business.

Although it is evident that communist nations, like capitalist nations, have diverse military assistance programs and policies, there is little evidence to suggest that communist nations have engaged in arms transfers for the purpose of increasing production runs of a particular weapon, thereby amortizing research, development, testing, and evaluation costs. Soviet exports of tanks and aircraft provide cases in point. As a rule, tanks that the USSR supplies to other nations are no longer first-line production models, and thus their export does not have an effect on cost per unit to the Soviet military.[11] When the USSR does supply modern tanks such as the T-64 and T-72, it does so in limited quantities; therefore no sizable reduction in cost per unit is achieved.[12] This is also true of aircraft. By 1970 the Soviet Union had exported about 1,600 MiG-15s, -17s, -19s, and -21s, while its own forces flew more than 8,000 of these aircraft.[13] Of the more modern MiGs, the USSR has exported some 400 MiG-23s. (including here the MiG-23D, sometimes called the MiG-27) while it operates 2,997 of the aircraft, and has exported 92 MiG-25s while it operates 540 of its own.[14] No significant reduction in cost per unit could be achieved by exporting such a small percentage of the total production run. This point is, of course, even more true of other communist nations.

It is often argued that the technical sophistication of weaponry exported, particularly to Third World countries, makes the recipient nation dependent on the donor nation for technical support services, personnel for maintenance and training, and spare parts.[15] With the exception of Soviet hardware, this observation is less true of communist military assistance and arms transfers than of capitalist assistance and transfers. The reason is straightforward. With the important exception of the USSR, communist arms exports are, generally speaking, more basic than those of noncommunist nations. Furthermore, even in instances in which a putative dependence on a supplier nation has existed, recipient nations have often not hesitated to demand that military advisory and training personnel leave. Witness the Egyptian, Nigerian, Somali, and Sudanese expulsions of Soviet personnel. It should further be noted that provision of spare parts has proved, even in the Soviet case, to be less of a dependency-creating factor in <u>situations other than wartime</u> than would generally be expected.

Three other policy issues need to be addressed in this overview: (1) communist attitudes toward transshipment of weapons and the role of third parties in arms deliveries or utilization; (2) the possibility of providing nuclear weapons to other countries; and (3) the role of communist military assistance and arms transfer programs in support of liberation struggles, guerrilla wars, coups, terrorism, and so on.

The first of these issues, communist attitudes toward the transshipment of weapons, is rarely discussed. Nevertheless, it may be expected that communist countries have different views on the question. It is evident, particularly in the Middle East and Africa, that the Soviet Union has used Eastern European and Cuban "intermediaries" to pursue its objectives. It is similarly clear that certain African states, such as Algeria and Libya, either have been used by the USSR as sites for the deposit of arms for later transshipment to locations of need or have themselves moved Soviet weaponry to third sites or third parties without objection or protest -- and indeed possibly even with encouragement -- from the USSR. Conversely, communist countries not close to the Soviet Union politically have rarely become involved in transshipment operations, with the exception of China in a few cases.

The second issue, that of nuclear weapons, pertains only to China and the USSR. The Chinese, despite their refusal to sign the Nuclear Non-Proliferation Treaty, have shown very little inclination to transfer nuclear know-how, nuclear weaponry, or nuclear-capable delivery vehicles to other countries. The Soviet Union, likewise, has been obdurate in its policy of not transferring nuclear know-how and has refused to export nuclear weapons.[16] Moscow has, however, supplied FROG and Scud missiles to Egypt and the USSR's Warsaw Pact allies. Both missiles are nuclear-capable. Nevertheless, the Kremlin has kept all nuclear warheads under its own control.

The third issue, the role of communist military assistance in support of wars of national liberation, guerrilla wars, coups, terrorism, and so on, must be approached on two levels. The first level is that of support for national liberation movements. There is no doubt, based on their own admissions, that every communist government has supplied some national liberation movements with military assistance. Most of this is definitionally precluded from inclusion in the statistical records compiled by ACDA, CIA, SIPRI, and IISS. Several of the following chapters gauge the significance of this assistance. Yet in most cases reliable figures on its value or cost are unavailable. Hence definitive conclusions are not possible. It must also be stressed that national liberation movements that communist governments support are often in conflict with each other. Moreover, on occasion, noncommunist governments, including the U.S. and Western European governments, find they are tendering arms and assistance to movements being supported by one or more communist nations against another communist-supported group. Thus, although the fact of communist support for various liberation movements is indisputable, the nature of that support necessitates close case-by-case scrutiny before any conclusions can be drawn.

The second level on which this third issue must be approached is that of the role of communist military assistance in support of terrorism. Here, a definitional problem exists. Put simply, at what

9

point does terrorism become revolution? When can it be defined as a national liberation struggle? There are, of course, no definitive answers to these questions, but it should be noted that although most communist governments officially oppose terrorism, they also claim that its underlying socioeconomic cause is exploitation that exists in noncommunist social systems -- the same root cause that leads to their support for national liberation movements. Thus, for most communist nations it requires only a limited dialectic shift to legitimate support for terrorist activities. Whether support for such activities should be analyzed in a volume devoted to more traditional forms of military assistance is a question that has been left to the chapter authors.

Finally, a few brief words must be said about the organization of this volume. For the most part, this is a donor-centered volume. Chapter 2, by Daniel Papp, is devoted primarily to an analysis of Soviet military assistance to the communist countries of Eastern Europe, including Yugoslavia and Albania; but it also assesses the flow of weaponry from certain of these countries to the USSR. In Chapter 3, Roger Kanet details the evolution of and motivation behind Soviet military assistance and arms transfer programs to the Third World; in Chapter 4, Trond Gilberg focuses on similar Eastern European programs for Third World countries. John Copper's analysis in Chapter 5 of Chinese military assistance views the PRC primarily as donor. W. Raymond Duncan, in Chapter 6, takes both the donor and recipient approaches in his discussion of Cuba. Douglas Pike's treatment in Chapter 7 of Vietnam's military assistance focuses on a region, namely Southeast Asia. Chapter 8, by Nack An and Rose An, gives particular emphasis to North Korea's assistance to national liberation movements (or, in the eyes of some, terrorists).

Given the increased global role communist nations have assumed in the realm of military assistance, it is clear that their activities will be a significant force in international politics throughout the 1980s, barring some unforseen policy changes in communist capitals. The editors and contributors hope that herein we provide a basis for understanding the similarities in and differences between the military assistance and arms transfer programs of communist countries.

NOTES

1.   These figures are in current dollars. In constant 1977 dollars, world arms transfers in 1970 totaled approximately $9 billion and in 1980 slightly more than $20 billion. The U.S. traffic in arms exports had meanwhile grown from slightly less than $5 billion to slightly more than $6 billion, with the USSR's arms transfers totaling about $2.3 billion in 1970 and $6.6 billion in 1978, again in constant dollars. Figures from Arms Control and Disarmament Agency, (ACDA), World Military Expenditures and Arms Transfers 1969-1978 (Washington, D.C.: ACDA, 1980), appropriate pages.

2.   Ibid.

3.   The following table has been developed from ACDA, World Military Expenditures and Arms Transfers 1969-1978; it well contrasts the limited value of the arms exported by the following countries at the beginning of the 1970s with the more significant values of arms they exported later. All figures are in current dollars x 10^6:

The Growth in Value of Arms Transfers
New Entries in the Arms Transfer Field

Country	1970	1978
Austria	0	120
Belgium	10	140
Brazil	0	90
Bulgaria	0	70
Egypt	0	80
Germany (East)	10	60
Hungary	0	70
Israel	5	100
Italy	20	600
Japan	10	70
Netherlands	20	70
Korea (North)	0	70
Korea (South)	0	60
Romania	0	70
Sweden	10	100
Switzerland	0	200
Yugoslavia	5	140

4.   Ibid.   See the following table:

Communist Arms Imports, 1969-1978,
in Current Dollars x 10^6

Country	1969	1978
Albania	5	0
Bulgaria	20	220
China (PRC)	5	70
Cuba	20	310
Czechoslovakia	80	110
Germany (East)	130	290
Hungary	40	260
Korea (North)	10	20
Poland	120	160
Romania	40	240
USSR	200	825
Vietnam	320	0
Yugoslavia	20	90
Total Communist	1,010	2,595
Total World	5,860	20,600

5.   See Daniel S. Papp, "The Soviet Union and Southern
Africa," in Robert H. Donaldson (ed.), The Soviet Union in the Third
World: Successes and Failures (Boulder, Colo.:   Westview Press,
1981), pp. 68-96; and Arthur Jay Klinghoffer, The Angolan War: A
Study in Soviet Policy in the Third World (Boulder, Colo.:   Westview
Press, 1980).

6.   ACDA, World Military Expenditures and Arms Transfers
1969-1978, p.28.

7.   For further discussion of these and related definitional
problems, see Richard H. Wilcox, "Twixt Cup and Lips: Some
Problems in Applying Arms Control," and Edward T. Fei,
"Understanding Arms Transfers and Military Expenditures: Data
Problems," in Stephanie G. Neuman and Robert E. Harkavy (eds.),
Arms Transfers in the Modern World (New York: Praeger Publishers,
1979), pp. 27-36, and pp. 37-47, respectively.

8.   See U.S. Central Intelligence Agency, National Foreign
Assessment Center, A Dollar Cost Comparison of Soviet and US
Defense Activities, 1967-77 (January 1978).   See also William Lee,
"Soviet Defense Expenditures in an Era of SALT" (US Strategic
Institute Report 79-1, 1979); and Franklyn D. Holzman, "Are the

Soviets Really Outspending the US on Defense?" International Security Vol 4, No. 4 (Spring 1980), pp. 86-104.

9.   For a discussion of earlier twentieth-century eras in the arms trade arena, see Cindy Cannizzo, "Trends in Twentieth Century Arms Transfers," in Cindy Cannizzo (ed.), The Gun Merchants: Politics and Policies of the Major Arms Suppliers (New York: Pergamon Press, 1980), pp. 1-17.

10.   For further discussion of this point, see John Stanley and Maurice Pearton, The International Trade in Arms (New York: Praeger Publishers, 1972), pp. 6-10. See also George Thayer, The War Business: The International Trade in Armaments (New York: Simon and Schuster, 1969), which contrasts private and governmental roles in military assistance and arms transfer activities in the post-World War II era.

11.   It must be pointed out that providing recipient nations with dated equipment does, however, provide the donor nation with useful opportunities to dispose of equipment it no longer wants or needs and provides an option, in certain cases, for keeping production lines in being.

12.   By 1980, the Soviet Union had roughly 10,000 T-64s and T-72s in its inventory. It had exported somewhere in the vicinity of 500 of these tanks. See International Institute for Strategic Studies, The Military Balance 1981-1982 (London: IISS, 1981), appropriate pages.

13.   Stockholm International Peace Research Institute, The Arms Trade with the Third World (New York: Humanities Press, 1971), pp. 182.

14.   IISS, Military Balance 1981-1982.

15.   See Neuman and Harkavy, Arms Transfers in the Modern World, for further discussions of this point, as well as Anne Hessing Cahn and Joseph J. Kruzel, "Arms Trade in the 1980's," in Anne Hessing Cahn and Joseph J. Kruzel, Controlling Future Arms Trade (New York: McGraw-Hill, 1977), pp. 27-105.

16.   Soviet restraint in providing nuclear know-how to China has been listed as one of the precipitants of the Sino-Soviet dispute, as has the Soviet refusal to provide the PRC with a "sample" atomic bomb. It must also be remembered that in 1962, when the Soviet Union was deploying IRBMs in Cuba, the nuclear warheads as well as the IRBMs themselves were to remain under Soviet control. Put simply, when viewed from this perspective, neither know-how nor weapons nor missile delivery vehicles were actually "transferred" during the Cuban Missile Crisis in anything other than a locational sense.

2
Soviet Military Assistance to Eastern Europe

Daniel S. Papp

During the 1970s, military assistance became a significant segment of the Soviet Union's foreign policy. Between 1974 and 1978, Soviet military assistance totaled $27 billion, more than $19 billion of which went to non-European recipients. Most of the remaining $7.7 billion worth of arms exported by the USSR went to Eastern European socialist states.[1]

Soviet military assistance to Eastern Europe has been provided in a variety of forms. In addition to equipment, the USSR has provided support for Eastern European military and paramilitary institutions in the areas of training and education, doctrine and organization, and military operations and production. To be sure, there is no monolithic pattern of practice either in Soviet policy toward the Eastern European militaries or in those militaries' adherence to or acceptance of policy preferences. However, the militaries of Eastern Europe are to a great extent dependent upon the USSR for a wide variety of their military needs. It is the purpose of this chapter to examine the scope, purposes, and trends of Soviet military assistance to the USSR's Eastern European neighbors.

THE HISTORY OF SOVIET MILITARY ASSISTANCE TO EASTERN EUROPE: AN OVERVIEW

Soviet military assistance to Eastern Europe has gone through several distinct periods since the end of World War II. The first period ended in 1955 and may be described as an era of consolidation of Soviet dominance in Eastern Europe. The second period began with the formation of the Warsaw Pact in 1955 and ended in approximately 1960, when a decision was reached by Moscow to convert the Warsaw Pact into an effective military organization. The third period may be categorized as the "Khrushchev buildup," which marked the implementation of the 1960 decision. The fourth is the early Brezhnev era, extending from 1964 through 1974. The final period is the contemporary era, characterized by continual although differentiated enhancement of the fighting capabilities of the non-Soviet Warsaw Pact militaries.[2] A brief overview of the first four periods is presented below.

At the outset, it should be noted that the Soviet Union has rarely followed a single policy at any particular time in its military assistance programs toward Eastern Europe. Rather, the USSR has fashioned policies on assistance as local conditions demanded. This phenomenon became apparent even during the era of consolidation of Soviet dominance in Eastern Europe.

Period 1: 1945-1955 Consolidation and Control

As World War II drew to a close, the Soviet Union was militarily in control of Eastern Europe. The debate has long raged in the West whether the Soviet decision to consolidate its position and maintain its influence in Eastern Europe was a product of an expansionistic mentality or a defensive paranoia. This is not the place to continue that debate. Suffice it to say that even before 1945, the Soviet Union had extended considerable military assistance to selected groups and organizations in Eastern Europe. This assistance was vital to the extension and growth of Soviet influence there.

Soviet sources identify three types of groups that received military support from the USSR during World War II. Guerrilla detachments operating in Yugoslavia, Bulgaria, Poland, Czechoslovakia, and Albania received Soviet support, as did so-called people's liberation armies formed in Yugoslavia, Poland, and Bulgaria. People's liberation armies were defined as more highly organized and larger in size than guerrilla detachments and were "component parts of emergent revolutionary states ."[3] For the most part, the command and control of these armies was to remain outside the Soviet Union. In the case of Yugoslavia, this fact was to have lasting significance.

The third type of group that received military assistance from the USSR during World War II was the Eastern European national military unit formed in the USSR. For example, the First and Second Polish armies, the First Czechoslovakian Army Corps, and two independent Romanian divisions were formed in the Soviet Union during World War II under the immediate command of pro-Soviet officers from the respective countries.[4] In all cases, these units were ultimately subordinate to Soviet command. According to former Soviet Minister of Defense A. A. Grechko, nineteen infantry divisions, five artillery divisions, five airborne divisions, six infantry and airborne brigades, eight tank and motorized rifle brigades, twelve artillery brigades, and five engineering brigades of Eastern European origin had been armed and trained in the USSR by the conclusion of World War II.[5]

The units formed in the Soviet Union were to play integral roles not only in the fight against Nazi Germany but also in the creation of a socialist Eastern Europe. The Polish armies formed in the USSR, for example, were organized on Soviet lines, often with Soviet officers of Polish descent in command. These armies were to be the core of Poland's post-World War II military forces. Similarly, in Czechoslovakia, Czech units were organized in the USSR under Colonel Ludvik Svoboda, who would later become Czechoslovakia's postwar minister of defense. These units became the core of the postwar Czechoslovakian military. This pattern was also true for Romania, although the Romanian case was complicated by the fact that the Romanian National Army remained a force in being following Romania's August 1944 switch to the anti-Nazi cause. In Bulgaria, Hungary, and Germany, different strategies were of necessity pursued, as no national forces from these nations had been organized in the USSR.[6]

Following World War II, Soviet relations with Eastern European militaries followed a predictable course. Indigenous military establishments were reduced in size, suspect officers in Eastern European militaries were purged, Soviet officers and advisers were placed in positions of command, and what remained of the Eastern European militaries was Sovietized in organization, equipment, training, and tactics. Communist party control over all the local armed forces was strengthened. Finally, bilateral defense treaties were concluded between the Eastern European nations and the USSR.

Although differences remained in Eastern European armed forces, Soviet control predominated. Seventeen thousand Soviet officers filled the thirty-four thousand officer slots in the postwar Polish army alone,[7] and in 1949 Soviet Marshal Konstantin Rokossovsky was appointed Polish minister of defense and commander-in-chief of the Polish military. Additionally, the chief of the general staff, the commander of the Land Forces, and the commanders of four military districts in Poland were all former Soviet officers.[8] In Hungary, the reconstituted Hungarian army was controlled by Soviet officers.[9] The Bulgarian, Czechoslovakian, and Romanian armed forces were similarly officered, and the forerunners of the East German military -- the general police, the German Frontier Police, and the Barracked Alert Units — reported to Soviet general officers.[10]

Whether Soviet involvement with the armed forces of Bulgaria, Czechoslovakia, East Germany, Hungary, Poland, and Romania during the pre-1955 era should be termed aid and assistance or domination and control is an issue for semanticists. Regardless of terminology, these Eastern European military establishments were Sovietized during this period, although it should also be stressed that their military capabilities remained limited. Soviet unwillingness to provide these new socialist states, all of which had either been Soviet enemies during World War II or had territorial claims against the USSR, with significant military capabilities, was of course understandable. Thus, it came as no great surprise that the USSR did little to implement a request made at the August 1952 military conference in Prague attended by the USSR, Bulgaria, Czechoslovakia, Hungary, Poland, Romania, and China to reequip and expand socialist armies.[11] Political reliability needed to first be ensured, and by 1952, it had not been.

It should also be underscored that even during this early postwar period problems existed within the socialist commonwealth that complicated "military cooperation," as the Soviets would later term it. Albania and Yugoslavia both succeeded in averting Soviet or pro-Soviet control of their respective Communist parties, governments, and armed forces. The Albanian Communist party had come to power with no direct Soviet military intervention and with extremely limited Soviet support. Following World War II, the USSR extended some military assistance to Albania, developed a submarine base in Valona Bay, and sent a limited number of military advisers to Albania. With such limited aid and no domestic arms industry to speak of, the small and ill-equipped Albanian military remained small and ill-equipped but free from Soviet control. In 1955, with the onset of deterioration in Soviet-Albanian relations, Soviet military aid was further reduced, and in 1961 Soviet submarines and advisers were withdrawn.

The Yugoslavian aberration was a more vexing problem to the Soviet leadership. Between 1945 and 1948 Yugoslavian military officers were trained in the USSR, and Soviet military advisers, at Tito's request, were in Yugoslavia. Structural reorganization of the Yugoslavian People's Liberation Army was begun to make it conform to the Soviet model but the reorganization was halted in 1948 as a result of sharp deteriorioation in Soviet-Yugoslav relations. Soviet advisers were also withdrawn at that time. The United States shortly thereafter began to extend limited military assistance to Yugoslavia.

Nonetheless, by 1955, with the exceptions of Albania and Yugoslavia, the Soviet Union controlled the countries of Eastern Europe and their militaries. The creation of the Warsaw Pact in 1955, when viewed in conjunction with the effects of Khrushchev's 1956 de-Stalinizaton program, was to raise questions about the USSR's policies toward Eastern European armed forces that have not yet been fully answered.

Period 2:   The Formation of the Warsaw Pact

The Warsaw Pact was formally created in May 1955.[12] Operationally, the treaty obliged signatory nations "in event of armed attack in Europe on one or more of the Parties" to "come to the assistance" of the attacked nations "with all such means as are deemed necessary, including armed force."[13]

Practically speaking, the Warsaw Pact was little more than a political device for Soviet propaganda for the first five years of its existence.[14] No joint Warsaw Pact military exercises were held until the fall of 1961, and few concrete improvements were undertaken in non-Soviet Warsaw Pact forces between 1955 and 1960. Although the January 1956 meeting of the Warsaw Pact's Political Consultative Committee in Prague established a Warsaw Treaty Organization (WTO) United Command under Soviet Marshal Ivan Konev and integrated the National People's Army of East Germany fully into the WTO, the Warsaw Pact, with the exception of Soviet forces themselves, remained little more than a paper tiger.

Soviet hesitancy to arm Eastern European forces with significant quantities of modern weapons and munitions was if anything more understandable during the 1955-1960 period than it had been during the preceding five years. Some MiG-17 fighters and T-54 tanks were introduced to non-Soviet Warsaw Pact (NSWP) forces, but events in Hungary and Romania served to remind Soviet leaders that their control of Eastern Europe was not as absolute as they had hoped. Khrushchev's de-Stalinization program fostered the growth of nationalistic sentiment within Eastern European armed forces. With the 1956 Hungarian revolution, the Soviet position in Eastern Europe became even more tenuous. Given these difficulties, Khrushchev and his comrades undoubtedly reasoned that there was little logic in strengthening Eastern European military forces when those forces might turn against the USSR.

Shortly after the Kremlin's military intervention in Hungary, the Soviet Union moved to legitimate the presence of its forces in Eastern Europe. It concluded status-of-forces agreements with Poland, Hungary, Romania, and East Germany. This Soviet effort may at least in part be viewed as an alternative to strengthening Eastern European militaries for the purposes of providing a buffer between the Soviet Union and the West and of enhancing its political conrol in Eastern Europe. Its efforts were less than fully successful. Within two years, Romania had prevailed upon the USSR to withdraw its forces. In other Eastern European countries, particularly Poland, resentment toward the continued Soviet military presence mounted.

In part because of this resentment, some Soviet leaders felt it would be wise to withdraw forces from Eastern Europe. In his memoirs, Khrushchev detailed four reasons why he believed these forces should be withdrawn. A Soviet withdrawal would help to refute the argument that these societies had to be forced to be communist, was wise because of lingering anti-Russian sentiment within these countries, and would, it was hoped, lead to reciprocal action regarding forward basing by the United States. It would also save money, as, according to Khrushchev, the USSR had to pay NSWP nations for barracks construction and compensate them by transferring "the latest weapons and high-technology industrial equipment."[15] Regardless of the legitimacy of the first three of Khrushchev's rationales, it is evident from the limited quantities and mediocre qualities of arms transferred to Eastern Europe that at least part of his fourth rationale for Soviet troop withdrawals was erroneous. Even by 1960, the Warsaw Pact was more a political tool of the Kremlin than a military alliance, and the Soviet record of military assistance to Eastern Europe was not impressive. The assistance sent had been clearly delivered for Soviet purposes, namely the extension and maintenance of Soviet power in Eastern Europe.

Period 3: Khrushchev Build-Up

During the last four years of the Khrushchev era, Soviet military assistance to WTO nations increased quantitatively and improved qualitatively. Greater numbers of T-54 and T-55 tanks found their way into NSWP arsenals, as did increased quantities of MiG-21s and SU-7s. Antitank missiles, self-propelled artillery, and nuclear-capable Scud missiles (without their nuclear warheads) were also provided to

NSWP military forces. Joint Warsaw Pact maneuvers were held for the first time during the fall of 1961, and occasional maneuvers were held by WTO forces under the command of NSWP officers.[16] It is also likely that the Soviet home air defense system and the air defense systems of other Warsaw Pact nations were integrated during this period.[17] Clearly, Moscow had decided to upgrade the Warsaw Pact's military capabilities.

Several mutually supportive rationales have been advanced for this significant alteration in the Soviet Union's military assistance policies toward Eastern Europe, the least convincing of which was Marshal Grechko's assertion that Soviet-NSWP cooperation was the result of a "qualitatively new phenomenon which has naturally arisen as a result of the development of a world system of socialism."[18] Although Grechko's 1960 appointment as commander-in-chief of the Warsaw Pact was undoubtedly an organizational precursors of the upgrading of forces, there is no evidence to suggest that Soviet leaders had concluded that their Eastern European allies had suddenly become politically more reliable.

Khrushchev's own desire to downgrade the role of the Soviet Army and emphasize Soviet strategic rocket forces may also have played a significant part in the sudden surge in NSWP capabilities. With Khrushchev's oft-stated opposition to the "metal-eaters" and his desire to introduce some measure of efficiency into the Soviet economy, it may even be argued that the new Soviet attitude toward arms assistance to and military cooperation with its WTO allies was the first stage in a military version of an international socialist division of labor, with the Soviet Union destined eventually to concentrate on strategic rocket forces and NSWP countries on conventional land forces.[19]

A second convincing rationale for the changed Soviet policy was that the USSR, faced with resentment in Hungary, alienation in Albania, sentiment for independent policies in Romania, and disquiet in Poland, had opted for a new policy of cosmetic cooperation with Eastern Europe to foster cooperation in the military, political, economic, and ideological spheres.[20] From both the Eastern European and Soviet perspectives, however, closer integration brought mixed blessings. From the Soviet perspective, integration rendered less likely independent military action and planning on the part of NSWP militaries,[21] enhanced the fighting capacity of the Warsaw Pact, and conceivably would reduce the burden of defense costs if other WTO nations were both willing and able to increase their own defense outlays. Conversely, Moscow no doubt realized that unless integration was successfully kept under Soviet control, the improved military capabilities of Eastern Europe could make repeats of the 1956 Hungarian invasion costlier to the USSR. Khrushchev, with the historical lessons of Yugoslavian nonalignment, Hungarian military opposition, and Romanian rejection well in mind, had embarked on a potentially high-risk, high-benefit policy course.

From the NSWP perspective, costs and benefits were equally mixed. Access to more and more modern weapons and equipment would clearly enhance the prestige and capability of the military.

However, closer collaboration with the USSR was a quid pro quo for those weapons and equipment and would tie Eastern European militaries more immediately to Soviet policies and interests. With the gradual assumption of military command within NSWP forces by Soviet-trained indigenous Eastern European officers during the late 1950s and early 1960s, closer collaboration in return for improved forces may indeed have appeared a mixed blessing.

Yet a third rationale for the change in Soviet policy on military assistance to Eastern Europe may have been that Khrushchev, genuinely alarmed by deteriorating relations with the West in 1960, 1961, and 1962, and perhaps planning to renew pressure on Berlin, opted to improve NSWP capabilities simply to enhance Soviet security and the USSR's political bargaining position without incurring too great an economic burden for the USSR itself.

In any event, by the time Khrushchev fell from power in October 1964, the Warsaw Pact was in the process of being transformed from a political tool with limited non-Soviet military capabilities to a military alliance with much-improved capabilities in both its Soviet and non-Soviet forces. Khrushchev and Grechko had successfully altered Soviet policies on military assistance to Eastern Europe, and the Warsaw Pact was itself becoming a formidable military alliance.

Period 4: Continuity Under Brezhnev -- The First Decade

Khrushchev's removal did not lead to any immediate changes in Soviet military assistance programs to Eastern Europe. Modernization and force improvements begun during the last years of the Khrushchev era continued into the early 1970s as all but the most modern Soviet conventional weapons were sent to Soviet allies in Eastern Europe. Particularly noteworthy was the quantitative growth of Eastern European armored forces between 1968 and 1974, delineated in Table 2.1. All armored vehicles were either produced in the USSR and exported to NSWP countries or produced under Soviet-granted license by NSWP countries. In addition to weapons and equipment, the military infrastructure of the Warsaw Pact was improved as rail capacity was increased, a common pool of railroad cars was created, roads were improved, airfields were constructed, and pipelines were laid.

Some of the increased cost of the Warsaw Pact buildup was borne by the USSR, but a large portion was covered by NSWP nations. Thus, in 1968, Poland increased its military expenditures by 10 percent and the German Democratic Republic (GDR) by 60 percent.[22] Although it has never been clear how much of the cost of early NSWP force improvements was absorbed by the USSR, it has been evident since at least 1967 that the question of who would pay for the WTO's force improvements was a matter of concern in the capitals of the Warsaw Pact nations.[23]

Cooperative military activities such as joint training exercises and planning begun during the Khrushchev years continued under

TABLE 2.1   NSWP Armored Vehicles, 1968-1974

Country	1968	1974	Absolute Growth, 1968-1974
Bulgaria	2,000	2,250	250
Czechoslovakia	2,700	3,500	800
Germany (East)	1,800	2,400	600
Hungary	700	1,780	1,080
Poland	2,800	3,650	850
Romania	1,200	1,970	770

Source: IISS, The Military Balance, appropriate years (London: IISS).

Brezhnev.   Increasingly, however, the so-called Northern Tier countries — Poland, Czechoslovakia, and East Germany — received equipment both in larger quantities and of a more advanced nature.[24]

Improvements in the military capabilities of Eastern European armed forces evident by the early 1970s clearly resulted from Soviet arms transfers to NSWP countries, effective and continuing training procedures (most of which were based on Soviet models), and changed organizational structures within the Warsaw Pact.   With regard to the organizational structure of the Warsaw Pact, it is a matter of legitimate debate whether the Soviet Union or the NSWP countries benefited most from the changes,[25] and thus it is uncertain whether those changes should be included as military assistance.   However, the changes were significant and warrant further discussion.

Following the supression of Czechoslovakia's liberal experiment in 1968, three major changes occurred in the Warsaw Pact's organizational structure.   A committee of defense ministers was established, a Military Council was organized, and a staff of a Joint Armed Forces was created.[26]   For the purposes of our interest in Soviet military assistance, the third change is of greatest importance.

Despite denials by both Soviet and Eastern European sources, speculation mounted that a new integrated Eastern European armed forces of a supranational character had been created at the 1969 meeting of the Warsaw Pact's Political Consultative Committee in Prague.   It has since become clear that this "Joint Armed Forces" was considerably less than an integrated military organization, although the precise operational structure remains unclear.   The staff of the Joint Armed Forces was (and is) responsible for "the working out and conduct of joint maneuvers, exercises, and military games,"[27] and undoubtedly had (and has) contingency planning duties in the event of a war in Europe.   National forces devoted to the Joint Armed Forces include designated units of the Polish, Hungarian, Czechoslovakian, and Bulgarian armed forces (Romania refused to designate its forces to any non-Romanian command); all units of the East German army; all units of the groups of Soviet forces stationed in Eastern Europe; and undoubtedly some Soviet units stationed in the western military districts of the USSR.

With this formalization of a Joint Armed Forces, a question must again be asked concerning the nature of Soviet military assistance and arms transfers to NSWP countries. Given the fact that the Joint Armed Forces is directly subservient to Soviet command, to what extent is Soviet military assistance to Eastern Europe actually assistance, and to what extent merely an extension of the USSR's own military might? With the uncertainties inherent in the operational meaning of the Joint Armed Forces of the Warsaw Pact, a definitive answer is impossible. For the purposes of this chapter, Soviet military assistance to Eastern European militaries will be considered as legitimate assistance, although it must be realized that in the event of war in Europe many of those weapons, and much of the assistance and equipment, would undoubtedly revert to direct Soviet command and control.

On the basis of this historical record, one may conclude that the USSR has not been consistent in its military assistance programs to Eastern Europe. Local conditions within different Eastern European countries, changing Soviet domestic and international priorities, and differing Soviet perceptions over time as to how best to maintain Soviet power and influence in Eastern Europe have combined to yield a historical montage of changing Soviet military assistance policies vis-a-vis Eastern Europe. This is not to say Soviet assistance programs lacked purpose. Rather, it is to observe that the USSR exhibited flexibility in its dealings with military assistance questions as they relate to relations with Eastern Europe. The following section will illustrate that this pattern extends to the present day.

THE CONTEMPORARY RECORD

Contemporary Soviet military assistance to the socialist states of Eastern Europe may be divided into two categories: cooperation with socialist states not in the Warsaw Pact and cooperation with WTO members. The first category includes only Albania and Yugoslavia; it will be discussed only briefly.

Since 1961, the Soviet Union has not extended military assistance of any type to Albania. In 1968 Albania formally withdrew from the Warsaw Pact. It had been a number of the WTO in name only for the preceding seven years. The People's Republic of China extended limited military assistance to Albania (see Chapter 5), but that ended after Mao's death. Currently, Albania has no external source of military equipment or weapons. Thus, with almost no domestic military industrial capability, the Albanian military remains weak and ineffective.

Yugoslavia is a more interesting case. Following the deterioration in Soviet-Yugoslav relations in 1948, Soviet military aid and assistance to the Tito regime ended. In an effort to strengthen Yugoslavia's independent policies, the United States extended military aid to Yugoslavia -- $60 million in 1951 alone and a total of $703 million between 1951 and 1965, when U.S. military aid to Yugoslavia for all practical purposes ended.[28]

Soviet-Yugoslav relations improved in 1955, and since then have been marked by periodic rapprochements and coolings. Soviet military assistance followed the general course of Soviet-Yugoslav relations. Given this uncertain state of relations, it is perhaps surprising that 94 percent of the dollar value of arms imported by Yugoslavia between 1974 and 1978 came from the USSR (see Table 2.3). The USSR also licenced Yugoslavia to produce the AT-3 Sagger antitank missile. This does not imply, however, that Yugoslavia is exclusively dependent on Soviet arms for its defense. Yugoslavia has developed its own arms industry and is itself a mid-level arms exporter. Indeed, the $525 million in arms that Yugoslavia imported from the USSR between 1974 and 1978 was less than 6 percent of its total arms expenditures during that period, and was less than Yugoslavia's own arms exports to other countries.

Contemporary Soviet military cooperation with non-Soviet Warsaw Pact nations has several distinct aspects, including direct arms transfers, licensing and technical documentation for production, military training and education, joint exercises, and planning.[29] Direct transfers of weapons and equipment are the most important kinds of assistance, although Soviet licensing and technical documentation have permitted Poland and Czechoslovakia to add significant strength to their air and armored forces. Poland and Czechoslovakia have been licensed to produce the Mi-2 helicopter, MiG-21 and Yak-18 jet aircraft, the T-62 tank, and armored personnel carriers.[30] Hungary and East Germany have been licensed to produce smaller weapons, including in Hungary's case the FUG-70 scout car and OT-64 armored personnel carriers. Thus, as Grechko maintained, the USSR does play "a large role in the creation and development of the defense industry" in Warsaw Pact countries.[31] Standardization of weaponry is one objective of this Soviet support, and one may speculate that a certain interest in maintaining influence in Eastern European arms industries exists as well.

On an annual basis during the decade of the 1970s, Soviet arms exports to non-Soviet Warsaw Pact countries rarely exceeded one-third of total Soviet arms exports and in many years were significantly below 30 percent of total Soviet arms exports (see Table 2.2). There have been, of course, periodic rises and declines in the percentages received by NSWP members, but it should be stressed that that proportion fell every year between 1974 and 1978.

The reduced percentage of total Soviet arms exports to Eastern Europe may be explained in at least four ways. First, during the latter part of the 1970s, Moscow became more concerned with events in the Third World. There may well have been a corresponding de-emphasis on Soviet willingness and/or ability to transfer arms to its

TABLE 2.2   Arms Imports by Non-Soviet Warsaw Pact Nations
as Compared to Total Soviet Arms Exports, 1969-1978
(in current dollars x 10⁶)

Year	Total NSWP Arms Imports (NSWPI)	Total Soviet Arms Exports (SE)	$\frac{NSWPI}{SE}$
1969	430	1,375	.313
1970	430	1,770	.243
1971	430	3,360	.227
1972	1,040	3,360	.310
1973	1,860	5,875	.312
1974	1,790	4,800	.373
1975	1,680	4,820	.349
1976	1,810	6,080	.298
1977	1,650	7,540	.219
1978	1,280	8,520	.150

Source: ACDA, World Military Expenditures and Arms Transfers, 1969-1978 (Washington, D.C.:   ACDA, 1980), passim.

Note: Both the NSWP arms import totals and consequently the NSWPI/SE ratio are slightly inflated due to the inclusion of intra-NSWP arms transfer statistics and Romania's arms imports from the West within the NSWP arms imports total.   However, given the fact that, as Table 2.4 illustrates, 87 percent of total NSWP arms imports were from the USSR during the 1974-1978 period, this table is accurate within those limits.   The remaining 13 percent, again with the exception of Romania's Western imports, was almost totally intra-NSWP transfers.

Eastern European allies.   This view is supported by the fact that even in constant 1977 dollars, Soviet arms exports to NSWP countries dropped from roughly $2.6 billion in 1973 to approximately $1.3 billion in 1978.   Indeed, increased Soviet emphasis on arms transfers to developing countries may explain not only the diminution of exports to NSWP countries but also the reduction in quantity of armored forces in "Southern Tier" NSWP countries as older weapons systems were removed from the European environment where they might be expected to have a limited utility in the event of a crisis to less sophisticated Third World nations where they might be expected to have more utility.   There are few indications that the USSR uses its Eastern European allies for transshipment purposes.
     A second explanation for the reduced percentage of total Soviet arms exports to NSWP countries may have been the deteriorating economic conditions many Eastern European nations experienced in

the middle and late 1970s. Such an explanation would be consistent both with reduced expenditures in constant dollars and with Soviet pressures to force Eastern European states to step up their defense spending. Two final rationales for the reduced percentage of total Soviet arms exports to NSWP countries may be growth of production under license in Eastern Europe and a conscious decision to await availability of new front-line arms and equipment.

Much has been made of the NSWP countries' dependency on the USSR for their arms and equipment, particularly of major weapons systems, and with good reason. However, as Table 2.3 illustrates, a surprisingly small percentage of Eastern European military expenditures between 1974 and 1978 was devoted to importing arms from the USSR. A large portion of military expenditures, of course, was devoted to maintaining and operating forces already in existence. It must be cautioned, however, that mere analyses of expenditures presents a somewhat understated picture of actual NSWP military dependency on the USSR. Reduced prices for intra-WTO arms transfers enabled greater numbers of units of arms and equipment to be transferred per given dollar, and as previously noted, Soviet licensing and documentation practices have shifted actual production of some weaponry and equipment to NSWP countries. Weaponry and equipment produced in this manner do not appear in arms transfer statistics, yet it is clear that some degree of dependency does exist because of licensing and documentation. Additionally, in time of conflict, it may be assumed that much of the Soviet logistic, command, control, and communication infrastructure in place for the groups of Soviet forces in Eastern Europe will be used by Soviet Warsaw Pact commanders to deploy, employ, and support NSWP forces.

Several NSWP countries have developed arms industries apart from production licensed by the USSR. Czechoslovakia, for example, produces cargo aircraft, a multiple rocket launcher, and small arms. Poland produces similar weapons as well as engineering and chemical equipment with military utility. Romania, meanwhile, has sought to diversify its sources of weaponry as it pursues its own independent course within the Warsaw Pact and has even concluded licensing agreements with France and Great Britain to produce Alouette helicopters and Islander light transports.[32] Also, even though Romania has almost no indigenous arms industry, it has collaborated with Yugoslavia in efforts to develop the Orao and Jurom jet aircraft. East Germany, on the other hand, abandoned its effort during the 1960s to develop an independent small aircraft industry. Bulgaria and Hungary have extremely limited domestic industries and import nearly all of their major weaponry from the USSR (see Table 2.4).

As Table 2.4 illustrates, some arms traffic does exist between and among NSWP countries. For the most part, however, such traffic is small compared to arms transfers originating in the USSR. Moreover, almost all advanced military equipment, particularly

TABLE 2.3   Eastern European Arms Imports
and Defense Expenditures, 1974-1978
(in current dollars x 10⁶)

Country	Defense Expenditures	Arms Imports	Arms Imports from USSR	Arms Imports Defense Expenditures	Imports from USSR Defense Expenditures
Bulgaria	10,682	1,120	1,000	.105	.094
Czechoslovakia	17,846	1,290	1,200	.072	.067
Germany (East)	22,323	2,280	1,900	.102	.085
Hungary	8,088	1,010	950	.125	.117
Poland	30,573	1,630	1,400	.053	.046
Romania	14,997	880	700	.059	.047
Yugoslavia[a]	8,788	560	525	.064	.060

Source: ACDA, World Military Expenditures and Arms Transfers, 1969-1978 (Washington, D.C.:   ACDA, 1980), passim.
[a]Yugoslavia is included in this table solely for presentation purposes and should not be construed as being an ally of other nations included herein.

combat-effective aircraft, must be obtained from the USSR.

It must be stressed that at least part of the motivation behind Soviet willingness to license production relates to defense burden-sharing. The USSR has habitually pressured its NSWP allies to assume a greater share of the Warsaw Pact's cost of operation, for example during the November 1978 heads-of-state conference in Moscow.[33] At this meeting, the USSR demanded that its allies increase their defense expenditures by 3 percent to offset planned NATO increases. East Germany approved a 5 percent increase; Poland, after some delay, increased planned expenditures by 2.6 percent; Hungary hesitantly approved a 3 percent increase; and Romania, ever intransigent, flatly refused.[34]

As shown by the Kremlin's pressure on its allies to increase their defense spending, Soviet willingness to help the NSWP countries equip themselves is not unlimited. This is particularly obvious vis-a-vis Moscow's willingness to transfer first-line equipment to NSWP nations. In a number of instances, the USSR has been hesitant to furnish first-line equipment to its Eastern European neighbors or to grant production licenses for that equipment. Thus, for instance, T-72 tanks did not appear in the arsenals of all Warsaw Pact countries until 1981, even though the USSR had earlier exported them to Algeria, Iraq, Libya, and Syria. Similarly, Algeria, Libya, and Syria all received MiG-25 Foxbats, but no non-Soviet Warsaw Pact Pact

Poland didn't want T-72 because couldn't pay.

TABLE 2.4 Eastern European and Soviet Arms Transfers, 1974–1978
(in current dollars x 10⁶)

Importer	Exporter									
	Bulgaria	Czechoslovakia	GDR	Hungary	Poland	Romania	USSR	Yugoslavia[a]	Other[b]	Total
Bulgaria	—	20	x	x	50	x	1,000	x	50	1,120
Czechoslovakia	x	—	x	x	10	x	1,200	x	80	1,290
GDR	x	280	—	—	80	x	1,900	x	20	2,280
Hungary	x	20	x	—	40	x	950	x	x	1,010
Poland	x	180	x	x	—	x	1,400	x	50	1,630
Romania	x	20	x	x	60	—	700	x	100	880
USSR	x	1,500	x	x	625	x	—	x	115	2,240
Yugoslavia[a]	x	x	x	x	5	x	525	—	30	560
Other[b]	150	640	260	300	310	210	19,325	55	—	21,750
Total	150	2,660	260	300	1,180	210	27,000	555	445	32,760 GRAND TOTAL

Sources: Data compiled from IISS, ACDA, and CIA publications.
[a]Yugoslavia is included in this table solely for presentation purposes and should not be construed as an ally of other nations herein included.
[b]May include some limited unidentified arms transfers from countries specifically identified on chart.
Note: The symbol x denotes no significant arms transfers.

air force has yet received the high-performance aircraft.[35] Obviously, Moscow has not granted production licenses for such first-line equipment.

Any of several explanations for this differentiated Soviet policy on arms assistance and production licenses may suffice. The USSR continues to harbor doubts about the political reliability of its allies and therefore wishes to limit somewhat the capabilities of its allies' military forces.[36] Such an attitude on the part of the Soviet leadership lessens Warsaw Pact capabilities in the event of a conflict with NATO, but it also serves to confirm Eastern European military dependency on the USSR. This dependency, if not resented by Eastern Europeans, may have utility in enhancing the political reliability of the non-Soviet Warsaw Pact countries. Conversely, it may also be argued that a feeling of dependency may instill resentment, thereby decreasing political reliability.

Soviet chauvinism may provide a second explanation for the differentiated Soviet policy. As the senior socialist state and self-proclaimed leader of international communism, Soviet leaders may believe their forces need not only quantitative but also qualitative superiority over even their allies' forces, simply to preserve the primacy of the USSR.

Finally, ever-present defense economics may explain why first-line equipment is slow in appearing in NSWP inventories. Assuming that in socialist nations, as in capitalist nations, state-of-the-art and near-state-of-the-art technologies cost more than less advanced technologies, Eastern European defense decision makers may simply conclude from their cost-benefit calculus that the increased benefits of first-line equipment do not offset the increased costs. However, the persuasiveness of this rationale is somewhat diminished by the fact that by 1981 every non-Soviet Warsaw Pact army had acquired at least some T-72 tanks. Either the USSR had made T-72s available, or cost-benefit ratios had been reduced.[37] Reportedly, resentment had existed earlier within Eastern European militaries over the fact that other Soviet clients had received top-line equipment, but Eastern European militaries had not.[38] But given the persistence of reports that the USSR has operationalized a new T-80 tank, the appearance of T-72s in Eastern European arsenals may simply be a continuation of previous Soviet policy to permit the transfer of militarily effective but not state-of-the art weaponry to NSWP countries.

Since about 1975, as Table 2.5 indicates, the size of NSWP militaries and the number of tanks and combat aircraft they possess have remained relatively constant.[39] Qualitative improvements, particularly in type of tanks and aircraft, as well as artillery and armored personnel carriers have been emphasized instead. It may therefore be possible to conclude that the Soviet Union and other WTO nations will in the future emphasize qualitative as opposed to quantitative improvements in NSWP force structures. Similarly, it should be cautioned that before 1973 Soviet arms exports to the developing world were relatively limited, at least in comparison to the years since then. The relative constancy of the number of tanks in NSWP arsenals since 1974, for example, may therefore be a

function of a change in Soviet supply priorities as more weapons
have been directed toward Third World clients to support Soviet
policy priorities there.

A country-by-country breakdown of manpower and equipment
trends provides a more detailed view of the evolution of NSWP force
structures. It must be reiterated that capabilities of individual
weapons have improved; put simply, MiG-23s and T-72s are for most
purposes better weapons than MiG-21s and T-54s. Thus, even though
quantitative changes may appear limited, qualitative improvements
have been considerable.

TABLE 2.5 Evolution of Non-Soviet Warsaw Pact Force Structures,
1975-1982

	Manpower x 10^3				Equipment		
	Army	Navy	Air Force	Total	Tanks	Aircraft	Scud Missile Systems
1975	814	61	189	1,064	15,865	2,188	310
1976	800	61	212	1,073	15,665	2,416	315
1977	798	60	219	1,077	14,820	2,492	321
1978	813	60	222	1,095	15,445	2,580	329
1979	792	60	254	1,106	14,970	2,120	333
1980	775	60	267	1,102	15,410	2,226	351
1981	788	60	268	1,116	15,070	2,241	348
1982	793	53	269	1,115	14,650	2,251	348

Source: IISS, The Military Balance, appropriate years (London: IISS).

It is appropriate to interject here that all Bulgaria's tanks and
aircraft are imported from the USSR. This is also true for East
Germany, Hungary, and possibly Romania. Czechoslovakia and Poland
produce some of their own tanks and aircraft under license from the
USSR. All Scuds are transferred from the Soviet Union.

In addition to the fact of qualitative as opposed to quantitative
upgrading in the years since 1974, it is equally evident that the
Soviet Union has emphasized arms transfers and support for the so-
called Northern Tier states of Czechoslovakia, East Germany, and
Poland, particularly with regard to ground forces. Table 2.7 makes
this clear. It is also evident from the table that this process has
extended over a number of years. Different levels of transfer
between Northern Tier and Southern Tier of combat aircraft and
Scud and FROG missiles apparent in Table 2.7 are, in the opinion
of this author, too limited to have a definite significance. At a

TABLE 2.6   Evolution of Non-Soviet Warsaw Pact Force Structures
by Country, 1975-1982

Country and Year	Army	Navy	Air Force	Total	Tanks	Aircraft	Scud and FROG Missile Systems
Bulgaria:							
1975	120	10	22	152	2,200	253	50
1976	131	9	25	165	2,200	253	60
1977	115	9	25	149	1,900	270	56
1978	115	10	25	150	1,925	263	56
1979	115	10	25	150	1,800	166	56
1980	105	10	34	149	1,900	210	66
1981	105	10	34	149	1,860	248	66
1982	105	9	34	148	1,860	248	66
Czechoslovakia:							
1975	155	--	45	200	3,100	458	67
1976	135	--	45	180	3,300	458	67
1977	135	--	46	181	3,400	558	67
1978	140	--	46	186	3,400	613	67
1979	140	--	54	194	3,400	462	67
1980	140	--	55	195	3,600	471	67
1981	140	--	54	194	3,420	471	67
1982	143	--	54	197	3,400	471	67
GDR:							
1975	98	17	28	143	2,770	330	33
1976	105	16	36	157	3,115	441	36
1977	105	16	36	157	3,120	416	36
1978	105	16	36	157	3,220	362	36
1979	107	16	36	159	3,220	335	36
1980	108	16	38	162	3,200	347	42
1981	113	16	38	167	3,100	359	42
1982	113	15	38	166	3,100	359	42

Manpower x 10^3 / Equipment

TABLE 2.6. (continued)

Hungary:

1975	90	--	15	105	1,625	108	33
1976	80	--	20	100	1,475	140	33
1977	83	--	20	103	1,100	175	30
1978	91	--	23	114	1,100	180	36
1979	80	--	24	104	1,350	150	36
1980	72	--	21	93	1,410	170	36
1981	80	--	21	101	1,330	130	36
1982	85	--	21	106	1,300	140	36

Poland:

1975	210	25	58	293	4,100	785	79
1976	204	25	61	290	3,775	804	77
1977	220	25	62	307	3,800	745	82
1978	222	23	62	307	4,100	725	84
1979	210	23	85	318	3,700	679	88
1980	210	23	85	318	3,600	700	90
1981	210	23	87	320	3,560	705	87
1982	207	22	88	317	3,190	705	87

Romania:

1975	141	9	21	171	2,070	254	48
1976	145	11	25	181	1,800	320	42
1977	140	10	30	180	1,500	327	50
1978	140	11	30	181	1,700	437	50
1979	140	11	30	181	1,500	328	50
1980	140	11	34	185	1,700	328	50
1981	140	11	34	185	1,800	328	50
1982	140	7	34	181	1,800	328	50

Source: IISS, The Military Balance, appropriate years (London: IISS).
[a]Includes T-34s in storage.

policy level, however, the Kremlin no doubt considered the Northern Tier ground forces as worthy of upgrading. As the most likely scene of conflict in the event of a European war, and given the terrain in the area, this appears a logical decision.

It is worth noting at this juncture that the drawdown in armored forces in the Southern Tier occurred concurrently with an increase

TABLE 2.7 Evolution of Non-Soviet Warsaw Pact Force
Structures by Tier, 1975-1982

Area and Year	Manpower x 10^3				Equipment		
	Army	Navy	Air Force	Total	Tanks	Aircraft	Scud Missile Systems
Northern Tier (Czechoslovakia, GDR, Poland)							
1975	463	42	131	636	9,970	1,573	179
1976	444	41	142	627	10,190	1,703	180
1977	460	41	144	645	10,320	1,719	185
1978	467	39	144	650	10,720	1,700	187
1979	457	39	175	671	10,320	1,476	191
1980	458	39	178	675	10,400	1,518	199
1981	463	39	179	681	10,080	1,535	196
1982	463	37	180	680	9,690	1,535	196
Southern Tier (Bulgaria, Hungary, Romania)							
1975	351	19	58	428	5,895	615	131
1976	356	20	70	446	5,475	713	135
1977	338	19	75	432	4,500	773	136
1978	346	21	78	445	4,725	880	142
1979	335	21	79	435	4,650	644	142
1980	317	21	89	427	5,010	708	152
1981	325	21	89	435	4,990	706	152
1982	330	16	89	435	4,960	716	152
Cumulative Changes in Force Structure, 1975-1982							
Northern Tier	0	-5	49	44	-280	-38	17
Southern Tier	-21	-3	31	7	-935	101	21

Source: Compiled from Table 2.6.

in Soviet armored exports to the developing world. There is no
evidence of a direct link between most of the drawdown and increased
exports to the developing world.

Soviet arms exports to Eastern Europe and licensing and
documentation for production of arms in Eastern Europe are not the
only forms of military assistance the USSR extends to its Warsaw
Pact allies. Military training and education programs must also be
considered part of the Soviet assistance program, for it is through
training and education that the USSR hopes to instill cooperative
attitudes and political reliability in the officer corps of the NSWP
countries. Almost all the general officers in NSWP militaries have

attended Soviet service academies and speak Russian well, if not fluently. Eastern European military and postgraduate military academies teach military doctrine according to Soviet prescripts. In addition to professional training and education, NSWP cadres and officers undergo regular and extensive political indoctrination exercises that emphasize the central role of the Soviet Union in defending the socialist commonwealth and stress the "brotherhood in arms" concept as it relates to Warsaw Pact forces. Resolving the contradiction between the "closest unification" of socialist states and the maintenance of the "sovereignty and equal rights of socialist states and their armies" is a major goal of these political education activities.[40]

Joint military exercises may also be considered a type of Soviet aid to Eastern Europe. As already noted, no joint exercises were held before 1961. Since then, however, joint exercises have been held relatively frequently.[41] These exercises have involved land, air, and naval forces and have regularly had non-Soviet commanders.[42] The military and political advantages of having joint exercises is obvious if there is conflict with the West. What should not escape unnoticed is the fact that joint exercises as well as training and education may serve to complicate the efforts of individual Warsaw Pact nations to organize their own home-territorial defense and may also provide the psychological and organizational underpinnings for multi-lateral intervention in Eastern Europe, as in Czechoslovakia in 1968. Indeed, as the threat of Soviet intervention increased in Poland during the fall of 1980 and spring of 1981, joint Warsaw Pact exercises, including at one time or another troops from all Warsaw Pact nations save Romania,[43] were held, first in East Germany and then in Poland and the Soviet Union.

Planning for these exercises, and one may assume to a limited extent for contingencies in the event of conflict as well, was undertaken by the United Command of the Armed Forces of the Warsaw Pact.[44] The United Command, whenever it has been identified for a particular exercise, has always been multinational in composition.

Whether military training and education, joint exercises, and military planning should rightly be considered aspects of Soviet military assistance to Eastern Europe may be less obvious than in the case of direct shipments of arms and equipment, support for the military infrastructure, or licensing and documentation support. However, there is little doubt that as far as the Soviet Union is concerned, such efforts enhance the political reliability and therefore the potential military utility of NSWP countries. As discussed earlier in the section on the history of Soviet military assistance to Eastern Europe, political reliability is a needed adjunct for Soviet assistance to its neighbors. In the contemporary era, then, even with a new Soviet emphasis on Northern Tier states and an apparent stress on qualitative improvement rather than numerical growth in NSWP forces, at least that aspect of Soviet military assistance programs to Eastern Europe has not changed.

CONCLUDING OBSERVATIONS

Soviet military assistance programs toward Eastern Europe have varied tremendously. For the first fifteen years of the post-World War II era, including the first five years of the Warsaw Pact, Soviet military assistance to its putative allies and other socialist states in Eastern Europe was limited quantitatively and qualitatively. The few weapons that were supplied were primarily of World War II vintage, and what other assistance was extended was intended to further the primary Soviet objective in the area, the extension and consolidation of Soviet power and influence.

Since approximately 1960, Soviet assistance programs have substantially enhanced the military capability of NSWP armed forces. These programs began in the early 1960s as a quantitative buildup and continued during the middle and late 1960s and early 1970s as both a quantitative and a qualitative buildup. There were some indications during the late 1970s and early 1980s that future NSWP force enhancement efforts will be primarily qualitative in nature and primarily situated in the Northern Tier.

The purposes of Soviet military assistance to Eastern Europe are several. Strong Eastern European forces provide a defensive buffer ancillary to the groups of Soviet forces in Eastern Europe in the event of a Western invasion. The alleged "imperialist policy of forced confrontation" is thus frustrated,[45] in Soviet eyes, by a militarily strong Warsaw Pact. Additionally, the coordination and subordination of NSWP air defense systems to the Soviet home air defense (PVO Strany) provides the USSR with an aerial defense-in-depth under Soviet control. Standardization of weaponry is also for all practical purposes guaranteed.

Soviet forces themselves are designed and trained to seize the offensive in the event of a military conflict; NSWP forces are trained according to Soviet doctrine and thus would be expected in certain situations to provide added strength to Soviet forces if they were ordered to move west. Moreover, as illustrated in Czechoslovakia in 1968 and implied in Poland in 1980 and 1981, NSWP forces, in conjunction with Soviet forces, can serve as effective instruments for controlling each other and for maintaining a degree of discipline and political unity within Eastern Europe. The USSR can use and has used the Warsaw Pact and the capabilities that the USSR has provided it through its military assistance programs to exert psychological and military pressures on other WTO states.

This is not to say that the USSR since 1960 has willingly armed Eastern Europe without reservations. As we have seen, the USSR has exhibited a certain hesitancy to provide first-line weaponry to NSWP nations, and some NSWP officers are alleged to spend much of their time trying to convince their Soviet colleagues of a need for more and better weapons.[46] Furthermore, Soviet military assistance and Soviet military presence have not guaranteed the political reliability of Eastern European armed forces. Indeed, before the imposition of martial law in Poland in December 1981, there had been seven known cases in which Eastern European governments had asked their militaries to subdue internal disturbances and the armed forces had refused.[47] The political reliability of NSWP forces has not been guaranteed, and the Soviets realize this.[48] The declaration of martial law in Poland did not necessarily alter this picture.

Issues other than political reliability also affect Soviet military assistance programs to Eastern Europe. Soviet pressures on NSWP members to increase their share of the defense burden extend back to the mid 1960s. Eastern European nations, for their part, allege that the terms of trade for Soviet weaponry are unfair.

Soviet military assistance to Eastern Europe, then, is fraught with both dangers and opportunities when seen from the Soviet perspective. NSWP countries are heavily dependent on the USSR for such assistance but are not "Finlandized" by their military dependence to the point where their militaries may be considered only extensions of the Soviet armed forces. Throughout its nearly forty-year history of extending military assistance to Eastern Europe, the USSR has maintained a flexibility of implementaton that allowed it to change the thrust of military assistance programs either from one country to another or within the same country. Even with this flexibility, maintaining Soviet preeminence in Eastern Europe remains the basic objective of these programs. In the future, these programs will undoubtedly continue to be altered in whatever manner the Soviet elite believes will be most likely to maintain that preeminence.

NOTES

1.   Depending on which source is used, the dollar value ascribed to arms transfers will vary. Variances may be attributed to a number of factors, including differing dollar/ruble exchange rates, disagreement as to the cost of a particular munitions or weapons system transferred, and uncertainty over the precise quantity and type of arms transferred.

2.   For other interpretations of the stages of Soviet military relations with Eastern Europe, see A. Ross Johnson, "Has Eastern Europe Become a Liability to the Soviet Union? (II) The Military Aspect," in Charles Gati (ed.), The International Politics of Eastern Europe (New York: Praeger Publishers, 1976), pp. 38-52; and John Erickson, "The Ground Forces in Soviet Military Policy," Strategic Review (Winter 1978), pp. 64-79.

3.   Marxism-Leninism on War and Army (Moscow: Progress Publishers, 1972), p. 256.

4.   Ibid., p. 258.

5.   A. A. Grechko, The Armed Forces of the Soviet State (Moscow: Voenizdat, 1975), translated by the U.S. Air Force (Washington, D.C.: Government Printing Office, n.d.), p. 336.

6.   For an excellent detailed analysis of Soviet military relations with Eastern Europe in World War II, see Raymond L. Garthoff, Soviet Military Policy (New York: Praeger Publishers, 1966), pp. 133-148. See also J. M. Mackintosh, "The Satellite Armies," in B. H. Liddell Hart (ed.), The Red Army (New York: Harcourt, Brace and Company, 1956), pp. 439-51.

7.   Zyciei Mysl, No. 10 (October 1964), as quoted in Garthoff, Soviet Military Policy, p. 136.

8.   Mackintosh, "Satellite Armies," p. 441.

9.   Istvan Szent-Milkosy, Political Trends in the Hungarian Army (Santa Monica, Calif.: Rand Corporation, 1957).

10.   For an excellent discussion of the development of East Germany's army, see Thomas M. Forster, The East German Army (London: George Allen and Unwin, 1967). For East Germany's later role in the Warsaw Pact, see N. Edwina Moreton, East Germany and the Warsaw Alliance: The Politics of Detente (Boulder, Colo.: Westview Press, 1978).

11.   Zbigniew Brzezinski, The Soviet Bloc (Cambridge, Mass.: Harvard University Press, 1967), p. 457. There is disagreement among

36

military historians as to the extent of Soviet arms transfers to Eastern Europe in the pre-1955 era.

12.   For a good account of the forces that led to the creation of the Warsaw Pact, see Robin Alison Remington, The Warsaw Pact (Cambridge, Mass.:   M.I.T. Press, 1971), pp. 3-27.

13.   For the complete text of the treaty, see ibid., pp. 201-206.

14.   See Thomas W. Wolfe, Soviet Power and Europe 1945-1970 (Baltimore: Johns Hopkins Press, 1970), p. 148; John Borawski, "Mutual Force Reductions in Europe from a Soviet Perspective," Orbis, Vol. 22 (Winter 1979), pp. 845-874; and Dale R. Herspring, "The Warsaw Pact at 25," Problems of Communism, Vol. 29 (September-October 1980), pp. 1-15.

15.   Nikita Khrushchev, Khrushchev Remembers: The Last Testament (Boston: Little, Brown and Company, 1974), p. 226.

16.   For a discussion of these changes, see Thomas W. Wolfe, "The Warsaw Pact in Evolution," in Kurt London (ed.), Eastern Europe in Transition (Baltimore: Johns Hopkins Press, 1966), pp. 207-235.

17.   In 1964, Commander-in-Chief of Soviet Air Defenses V. Sudets was publicly identified as commander-in-chief of the Warsaw Pact Air Defense.

18.   Grechko, Armed Forces of the Soviet State, p. 324.

19.   See Roman Kolkowicz, "The Warsaw Pact: Entangling Alliance," Survey, No. 70/71 (Winter-Spring 1969), pp. 86-101.

20.   Dale R. Herspring and Ivan Volgyes, "Political Reliability in the Eastern European Warsaw Pact Armies," Armed Forces and Society, Vol. 6, No. 2 (Winter 1980), 287.

21.   See Christopher Jones, "The Warsaw Pact: Military Exercises and Military Interventions," Armed Forces and Society, Vol. 7, No. 1 (Fall 1980), 5-8.

22.   International Institute for Strategic Studies, Strategic Survey 1967 (London: IISS, 1968), pp. 19-20. Romania, meanwhile, increased its defense budget by only 3 percent.

23.   See John Erickson, Soviet Military Power (London: Royal United Services Institute, 1971), p. 103.

24.   For an excellent detailed study of Northern Tier militaries, see A. Ross Johnson et al., East European Military

Establishments: The Warsaw Pact Northern Tier (New York: Crane, Russak and Co., 1981).

25.   Christopher Jones has argued that the 1969 organizational reforms in the Warsaw Pact give the Soviets increased oversight capabilities on NSWP military forces; the International Institute for Strategic Studies, on the other hand, concluded that NSWP forces received more autonomy from the reforms.   See Jones, "Warsaw Pact," pp. 6-7, and IISS, Strategic Survey 1979 (London: IISS, 1980), p. 106. See also Lawrence T. Caldwell, "The Warsaw Pact: Directions of Change," Problems of Communism, Vol. 24 (September-October 1975), pp. 1-19.

26.   Johnson, "Has Eastern Europe Become a Liability?" p. 50.

27.   I. I. Yakubovskii, Boevoe sodruzhestvo bratskikh narodov i armii (Military Cooperation of Fraternal Peoples and Armies) (Moscow: Voenizdat 1975), p. 145.

28.   Dean Acheson, Present at the Creation (New York: W. W. Norton, 1969), p. 333; and T. N. Dupuy et al., The Almanac of World Military Power (San Rafael, Calif.:   Presidio Press, 1980), p. 703.

29.   Grechko, Armed Forces of the Soviet State, pp. 340-344.

30.   Stockholm International Peace Research Institute (SIPRI), World Armaments and Disarmament, various years (Cambridge, Mass.: M.I.T. Press).

31.   Grechko, Armed Forces of the Soviet State, p. 342.

32.   SIPRI, World Armaments and Disarmaments 1975, p. 180.

33.   New York Times, January 9, 1979.

35.   IISS, The Military Balance 1981-1982 (London: IISS, 1981), pp. 18-21, 49, 51, 54, and 57.

36.   The Polish crisis of 1980-1982 may have served to reinforce the wisdom of this perception in the minds of Soviet decision makers.

37.   In 1979, only East German forces had T-72 tanks.   By 1981, Bulgaria, Czechoslovakia, East Germany, Hungary, Poland, and Romania respectively had sixty, twenty, an unknown quantity, thirty, thirty, and an unknown quantity of T-72s.   IISS, Military Balance 1981-1982, pp. 18-21. See also New York Times, September 14, 1980.

38.   A. Ross Johnson, "Soviet-East European Military Relations: An Overview," in Dale R. Herspring and Ivan Volgyes

38

(eds.), Civil-Military Relations in Communist Systems (Boulder, Colo.: Westview Press, 1978), pp. 243-266.

39.   See also General David C. Jones, United States Military Posture for Fiscal Year 1981, Department of Defense Appropriations for Fiscal Year 1981, Hearings before a Subcommittee of the Committee on Appropriations, United States Senate. 96th Congress, 2nd Session, p. 282.

40.   Grechko, Armed Forces of the Soviet State, p. 327.

41.   For a listing of exercises between 1961 and 1977, see Graham H. Turbiville, Jr., "Soviet Bloc Maneuvers," Military Review, Vol. 58, No. 8, (August 1978) 19-35.

42.   Jones, "Warsaw Pact," pp. 15-16.

43.   Romania, as had been its policy for some time, sent staff officers. See New York Times, August 26, 1980; September 9, 1980; March 24, 1981; and April 8, 1981, for additional commentary on and description of these exercises, named "Brotherhood in Arms 1980" and "Unity 1981."

44.   P. A. Zhilin and E. Jadziak, Bratsvo po oruzhiiu (Brotherhood in Arms) (Moscow: Voenizdat, 1975), p. 352. See also I. I. Iakubovskii, p. 145; and Grechko, Armed Forces of the Soviet State, p. 341.

45.   TASS communique from Warsaw, May 15, 1980, following the conclusion of the May 14-15, 1980, Political Consultative Committee meeting.

46.   Dale R. Herspring, "Civil-Military Relations in Poland and Germany: The External Factor," Studies in Comparative Communism, Vol II, (Autumn 1978), p. 233.

47.   Herspring and Volgyes, "Political Reliability," pp. 278-279. Only three of the cases occurred following the change in Soviet assistance policy (Prague, 1969; Gdansk, 1970; and Lodz and Warsaw, 1976).

48.   In December 1980, as rumors of an impending Soviet invasion of Poland circulated, the BBC carried an undocumented report from Warsaw that more than 200 generals and colonels had agreed to use their forces to fight "external intervention" in Polish affairs.

3
Soviet Military Assistance to the Third World

Roger E. Kanet

Since World War II, the Soviet Union has been an active participant in the growth of military assistance worldwide. From 1969 to 1978 total Soviet arms exports increased by more than sixfold from $1.1 billion to $7.1 billion in total value.[1] Since 1960 the Soviet Union has ranked second to the United States as the major world supplier of arms, with Soviet exports accounting for 33.7 percent of total world exports as compared with 35.2 percent for the United States between 1974 and 1978.[2] In 1980, the USSR temporarily became the world's largest arms exporter.

One of the most distinctive characteristics of the growth of the international arms trade during the 1970s was the dramatic shift in the market. By far the most dynamic growth was among developing countries. The substantial increase in purchasing power among OPEC countries and the growing intensity of a number of regional rivalries among Third World states generated a new market for weapons, especially sophisticated and expensive ones. As a result, the developing countries' share of total world arms imports rose from an annual average of 56 percent in 1963-1966 to 73.2 percent in 1972-1976, 77.6 percent in 1977, and 81.0 percent in 1978.[3] During this period the Soviet Union expanded its share of this growing market for armaments in the Third World and for the period 1974-1978 provided 33.7 percent of all weapons shipped to Third World states ($20.8 billion of $61.7 billion dollars).[4]

An earlier version of this article was prepared for presentation at the international colloquium on "L'URSS dans les Relations Internationales," Talence, France, 14-15 November 1980. The colloquium was sponsored by Centre d'Analyse Politique Comparee of Universite de Bordeaux I, Centre d'Etudes et de Recherches sur les Civilisations Slaves of Universite de Bordeaux III, Maison des Sciences de l'Homme d'Aquitaine, and Institut d'Etudes Politiques de Bordeaux. The earlier version appeared under the title "L'Union Sovietique et les pays en voie de developpement: Le role de l'assistance militaire et des transfert d'armes," in L'URSS dans les relations internationales (Cahiers d'Analyse Politique Comparee, 1982).

Military assistance and arms transfers have been an integral part of Soviet policy toward developing countries ever since the shift in Soviet policy toward the nonaligned states in the mid-1950s. However, during the 1970s the military aspects of Soviet policy toward the developing world have far outstripped most other forms of contact. Military support, including the transfer of weapons systems and the provision of military training, has become the single most important element in Soviet relations with a large number of developing countries -- in particular, with those countries that the Soviets view as "progressive." The purposes of this chapter will be to examine the place of arms transfers and other forms of military support in overall Soviet policy toward the Third World -- especially in the countries of Africa and Asia -- to illustrate how the Soviet military aid and assistance program has developed over the past quarter of a century and how that program relates to other aspects of Soviet relations with the Third World. In addition, it is necessary to analyze what the Soviets hope to achieve by providing military equipment to Third World "clients" and "allies."

THE EVOLUTION OF SOVIET POLICY
TOWARD THE DEVELOPING COUNTRIES

When Stalin died in 1953 the Soviet Union was virtually isolated from the world outside those regions controlled by ruling communist parties. In contrast, the United States and its European allies were already engaged in a process of expanding a network of military bases from Europe through the Middle East to East Asia. While the Western opponents of the Soviet Union maintained political, economic, and military relations with all areas of the world -- much of which was still under European colonial control -- Soviet international contacts were limited primarily to the countries that formed their newly created empire in Eastern Europe and to their Chinese allies. The Western policy of containment of Soviet power had resulted in the creation of a system of alliances and a line of naval and air power, complemented by massive U.S. nuclear deterrence, that virtually surrounded the USSR. The Soviets, on the other hand, were limited in their ability to project military -- and in most cases political -- power to the region under the direct control of the Soviet army.

By the late 1970s the relative position of the two major power blocs had changed markedly. The collapse of the Western colonial empires and the ensuing rise of numerous anti-Western political regimes in the developing world, voluntary Western military retrenchment, and various other developments had resulted in the contraction of Western military presence and of Western political influence throughout most of Asia and Africa. At the same time the Soviets were able to establish a network of economic, political, and military relationships throughout much of Asia and Africa that permitted them for the first time to play the role of a global power.[5] The change in the relative position of the Soviet Union in the international political system stemmed in large part from the continued buildup of Soviet military power and the willingness and ability of the Soviet leadership to take advantage of the conflicts between the developing states and the major Western powers as well as among developing countries themselves.[6] By the 1970s the Soviets were able to employ their newly developed military power, including an oceangoing fleet and long-range transport aircraft, in conjunction with access to port and air facilities, to support distant and scattered political and strategic goals.

Soon after Stalin's death the new Soviet leadership sought to develop contacts with the nonaligned states of Asia and Africa. Khrushchev announced that the new states represented an integral part of a worldwide "zone of peace" and that the Soviet Union was willing to provide support both for national liberation movements struggling to achieve independence and for new states that had already acquired independence from the Western colonial powers.[7] The Soviets took the initiative in expanding contacts of all types with the new states of Asia and Africa, although the prime focus of that policy was the creation of economic links as a prelude to broader political contacts. Thus, while Soviet military assistance committed during the Khrushchev era, from 1955 to 1964, averaged approximatey $375 million per year, economic aid during the same period was greater, averaging more than $425 million annually. Moreover, the decade from 1955 to 1965 witnessed a fivefold expansion of Soviet trade with the noncommunist developing countries, from 304 million rubles (5.2 percent of total trade turnover) to 1,743.6 million rubles (11.9 percent of total trade).[8] In large part Soviet policy toward the developing countries was initially a response to U.S. efforts to create an alliance system in Asia as part of the policy of containment; the Soviets entered upon a policy of "denial" aimed at ensuring the neutrality of those developing countries -- especially Afghanistan, India, and Egypt -- that professed a nonaligned approach to foreign policy. The Soviets particularly sought to expand ties with these countries in order to prevent the uncontested growth of Western political and military influence, to guarantee that gaps would remain in the U.S.-sponsored alliance network, and to win the support of these nonaligned states for international political issues of importance to the Soviet Union.[9] As Soviet goals in the Third World now included the cultivation of the goodwill of developing countries, Third World leaders could no longer be depicted as reactionaries who should be swept away by the tide of revolution. In short, a contradiction existed between the imperatives of Soviet policy and the USSR's ideological assessments of these countries. The aid and political support provided to countries like Egypt and India in the mid-1950s signaled a shift in Soviet policy, but no change in doctrine at the top was made until Khrushchev's introduction of the concept of the zone of peace at the Twentieth Congress of the Communist Party of the Soviet Union (CPSU) in 1956. The nonaligned states from that time on were no longer regarded as mere outposts of Western imperialism but rather as independent proponents of peace and, therefore, were deemed worthy of Soviet support and assistance

-- despite continued Soviet criticism of domestic political and economic arrangements in most of the Third World.[10]

The regions of major Soviet involvement in the Third World during the decade of Khrushchev's leadership were those of special strategic concern to the Soviet leadership, i.e., the Middle East and South Asia. Measured in terms of political contacts, economic relations (including assistance), or military aid, Soviet involvement in the countries along the southern borders of the USSR expanded rapidly.[11] However, Moscow also attempted to take advantage of a number of opportunities in other areas, such as the civil war in Zaire (then Congo-Leopoldville) and the radicalization of the governments of Sukarno in Indonesia, Kwame Nkrumah in Ghana, and Sekou Toure in Guinea.

By the time of Khrushchev's overthrow in late 1964, Soviet policy toward the developing countries was in partial disarray. The optimism of the 1950s had waned and been replaced by realism concerning prospects for political and economic developments in most Third World countries. Although the Soviets had ended their hostility toward these countries, they had not succeeded in establishing significant influence relationships.[12] Where Soviet goals had been partially accomplished -- e.g., the reduction of the Western presence in the Middle East -- success came more from the initiatives of the developing countries themselves than from Soviet policy. Nevertheless, the foundations of future Soviet policy in the Third World had been laid prior to Khrushchev's departure from the Kremlin. In South Asia, India had already begun to depend heavily upon the USSR for both the military assistance deemed necessary for security vis-a-vis China and Pakistan and for support in the development of heavy industrial projects in the state sector of the economy. In the Middle East both Egypt and Syria were indebted to the Soviets for military and economic assistance, and Turkey and Iran had begun to expand ties with their northern neighbor as a means of lessening their dependence on the United States. Throughout Asia and Africa the Soviet Union had become a force to be dealt with by Western European countries and the United States, even though the West still commanded more influence and was able to exert more military capabilities in most areas of the developing world.

By the mid-1960s the Soviets already had recognized that the prospects for the introduction of socialism in the vast majority of the new states were bleak and that the instability of many developing societies meant that leaders who were favorably disposed toward the Soviet Union might well be overthrown by an alliance of "reactionary elements" and imperialists; witness the fate of Ben Bela, Nkrumah, and Modibo Keita. During the first few years of the regime of Brezhnev and Kosygin the reassessment of Soviet attitudes and policy continued. Confidence in the development of Soviet-type socialist systems and emphasis on economic "show projects" were replaced by efforts to establish firmly based relations with Third World countries that would provide the USSR with "bases of operation" from which it could expand contacts and attempt to increase activities and build influence. Even more than in previous years Soviet policy focused on countries and political groupings that had an inherent, immediate importance for the USSR's purposes. First, the Kremlin reemphasized close ties with those countries on or near the southern boundaries of the Soviet Union, from India in South Asia to the Arab countries of the Middle East. The importance of these countries for the strategic security interests of the Soviet Union was self-evident, as Soviet commentators repeatedly noted.[13] In contrast, support for minor revolutionary groupings and for activities in sub-Saharan Africa was generally downplayed in the late 1960s.

In the economic realm emphasis was now placed on projects that could do more than gain political favor. As Premier Kosygin stated in 1971, the Soviet Union would attempt to produce an "international division of labor" with the developing countries that would be mutually beneficial to both sides.[14] This policy meant, in practice, that the Soviets would evaluate potential projects for their economic feasibility prior to making any commitments of economic support. Another important shift in Soviet policy was the search for access to both naval and air facilities to provide an expanded reach for Soviet military capabilities.

Since about 1956, Soviet policy toward the developing countries has relied heavily on supplying economic and military assistance -- and more recently on sales of arms -- as means of developing and consolidating relations. From 1954 through 1979 the Soviet Union committed economic assistance valued at more than $18 billion to Third World states.[15] However, terms for Soviet assistance, contrary to repeated claims by Soviet political leaders and commentators, were and are not necessarily more generous to recipients than terms for Western assistance.[16] This is especially obvious if one contrasts the total amount of net aid actually dispersed. In 1978, for example, net development assistance from the USSR (i.e., current deliveries minus repayments on past assistance) totaled only $300 million; that provided by the West was almost $20,000 million. In recent years net economic assistance has averaged about 0.03 percent of GNP for the USSR compared with about 0.33 percent for Western industrial countries.[17]

Soviet trade with the developing countries continued to grow rapidly during the Brezhnev period. As we have already seen, trade with the Third World rose from a mere 300 million rubles in 1955 to more than 1,700 million rubles ten years later. By 1979 Soviet trade with the developing countries had reached 9,481 million rubles, although as a percentage of total trade it had remained stable at less than 12.0 percent during the prior fourteen years.[18] An important aspect of Soviet trade with Asia and Africa has been the degree to which it has been related to the provision of Soviet economic assistance. With few exceptions (e.g., the sale of military equipment to Libya and the purchase of rubber from Malaysia or grain from Argentina), trade has resulted from agreements between Soviet leaders and their Afro-Asian counterparts that include the commitment of Soviet economic and technical assistance. Such agreements have been especially attractive to those countries that have had problems obtaining the convertible currency necessary to purchase on the world market machinery and equipment needed for economic development projects. Economic contacts have been only one means employed by the Soviets in the expansion of relations with the countries of the Third World. Training of students and technicians from Third World states, the extension of various forms of cultural ties, political support in the United Nations and other international forums, and the establishment of close party-to-party ties with ruling revolutionary parties, especially in Africa, have all been employed by the Soviets in establishing and strengthening ties with Third World states. However, the most important development in Soviet policy toward the Third World during the 1970s was the increasing emphasis given to military relations with developing countries. The following sections of this chapter outline the evolution of military relations between the USSR and developing countries and assess the role that military assistance plays in overall Soviet policy.

THE EXPANSION OF SOVIET MILITARY
RELATIONS WITH DEVELOPING COUNTRIES

One of the most important changes in Soviet policy toward the Third World during the past decade has been the increasing emphasis on the expansion of military relations between the Soviet Union and individual developing states. During the period 1955-1967 the USSR delivered an average of slightly more than $300 million of military equipment per year to developing countries. From 1968 through 1971 the amount increased to about $700 million annually. After 1972, however, yearly deliveries increased substantially and by 1979 totaled more than $6,600 million (see Table 3.1).[18] Deliveries of Soviet economic assistance to developing countries have averaged about $515 million annually since 1972; deliveries of military equipment and supplies have averaged more than seven tims as much -- $3,553 million per year.[20] The major recipients of the increased Soviet deliveries have been Libya and Algeria (which pay for weapons with hard currency earned from oil exports), Iraq, Ethiopia, and Angola. Not only did Soviet sales and deliveries increase significantly during the 1970s, but the geographical distribution of deliveries was expanded. Until 1973 approximately 86 percent of all Soviet Military assistance and arms transfers (both committed and delivered) went to a few countries in South Asia and the Middle East. With the expansion of Soviet involvement in sub-Saharan Africa, especially in Angola and Ethiopia, during the 1970s, Africa also became a major recipient of Soviet military equipment, and the USSR replaced France as Africa's primary arms supplier. Between 1974 and 1979 new commitments of military support to sub-Saharan African and actual deliveries made up about 14 percent of total new commitments and deliveries, as the data in Table 3.2 demonstrate.

In spite of the expansion of the number of recipients of Soviet military equipment and support in recent years, the number of such

TABLE 3.1
Soviet Military Relations with Noncommunist
Developing Countries, 1955-1979 (in millions of current U.S. dollars)

	New Agreements Concluded	Deliveries
Total 1955-79a	47,340	35,340
1979a	8,365	6,615
1978a	2,465	5,400
1977a	8,715	4,705
1976a	5,550	3,085
1975a	3,325	2,040
1974a	5,735	2,225
1973	2,890	3,135
1972a	1,690	1,215
1971a	1,590	865
1970a	1,150	995
1955-69a	5,875	5,080
1969b	360	450
1968c	450	505
1967d	525	500
1966d	450	500
1965e	260	
1964e	875	
1963e	390	
1962e	415	
1961e	830	
1955-60e	1,285	
1960f	570	
1959f	40	
1958f	470	
1957f	240	
1956f	290	
1955f	110	

aData from CIA publication for 1979; see below.
bData from CIA publication for 1978; see below.
cData from CIA publication for 1977; see below.
dData from CIA publication for 1975; see below.
eData from State Department publication for 1972; see below.
fData from State Department publication for 1970; see below.
Sources: U.S. Department of State, Bureau of Intelligence and Research, Communist States and Developing Countries: Aid and Trade in 1970, Research Study, RECS-15, September 22, 1971, p. 17. Ibid for 1972. RECS-10, June 15, 1973, Appendix, Table 9. CIA, Communist Aid to Less Developed Countries of the Free World, 1977.

Table 3.1 (continued)

ER 78-10478U, p. 1. CIA, Communist Aid Activities in Non-Communist Less Developed Countries, 1978. ER-79-10412U, September 1979, p. 2. CIA, Communist Aid Activities in Non-Communist Less Developed Countries, 1979 and 1954-79: A Research Paper. ER-80-10318U, October 1980, p. 13.

N.B.: For substantially different estimates of Soviet military deliveries for the period 1956 to 1976, see Henrik Bischof, "Militarbeziehungen zwischen den kommunistischen Staaten und der Dritten Welt," Monatsberichte: Entwicklungspolitische Aktivitaten kommunistischer Lander (June 1977), p. 408. According to Bischof, deliveries for the period totaled $9,610 million.

countries is still relatively small. Of the twenty-four countries that reportedly received Soviet military support prior to 1967, fifteen received cumulative amounts of $40 million or less. Although the number of recipients of Soviet military supplies grew to thirty-five for the period 1974-1978, only seventeen received deliveries totaling $100 million or more,[21] of which two -- Egypt and Somalia -- have since broken relations with the Soviets (see table 3.3). Throughout the 1970s the major markets for Soviet military equipment have been Egypt (until 1976), Iran, Iraq, and Syria in the Middle East; Afghanistan and India in South Asia; Algeria, Angola, Ethiopia, Libya, and Somalia (until 1977) in Africa; and Peru in Latin America.

The arms export program of the USSR has differed in composition from that of the United States. Most important is the substantially greater role of military services such as training and military construction in the U.S. program. In recent years U.S. deliveries of such services have been nearly four times those of the USSR. On the other hand, Soviet deliveries of military hardware have been slightly larger than those of the United States and have made up a significantly greater portion of total Soviet arms exports than is the case in the U.S. program.[22] In 1978, however, Soviet military-related services, in particular training and technical assistance, grew markedly. In addition, this growth was complemented by the services provided by Soviet allies, in particular the German Democratic Republic and Cuba. In recent years the number of military personnel from developing countries being trained in the USSR has averaged about 1,900 per year. The largest numbers of these military personnel have received training on air defense systems or as pilots, tank operators, and maintenance technicians.[23] Finally, Soviet weapons are generally delivered to Third World customers much more rapidly than are those of the United States. The time elapsed between Soviet sales and deliveries has averaged twelve to eighteen months; U.S. lead times have averaged approximately three years.[24]

One of the most important modifications in the Soviet arms transfer program during the 1970s was the increasing commercialization of exports. From the beginning of the Soviet arms assistance program in the middle 1950s through the early 1970s, virtually all Soviet military equipment shipped to Third World states was provided on the basis of medium-term credits. These credits generally carried relatively low interest rates — when compared with private Western credit — and were repayable with traditional exports of the recipient country.[25] Moreover, the sale price of Soviet weapons was generally heavily subsidized. According to one estimate, approximately 40 percent of the value of Soviet military equipment was written off as grants. Even without discounts, the list price of Soviet weapons was usually below the price charged for comparable Western equipment.[26] Since the beginning of the 1970s, however, the percentage of Soviet exports paid for in hard currency has risen to the point that, by 1977-1978, hard-currency sales accounted for more than 40 percent of all military exports.[27]

The types of weapons that have been supplied by the Soviet Union to several of its major Third World customers should also be noted. During 1977-1978 Ethiopia received an estimated 550 Soviet tanks, 60 MiG-21 fighter aircraft and 20 of the more sophisticated MiG-23s, more than 300 armored personnel carriers, and large numbers of rocket launchers and 155mm and 185mm guns.[28] Libya during recent years has received immense amounts of Soviet military equipment (especially considering the size of the Libyan military) and is one of the very few countries to which the Soviets have sold the sophisticated MiG-27 fighter (also known as MiG-23D) and the modern air defense missile system, the SA-9.[29] Algeria, Iraq, and Syria have also received the most up-to-date Soviet equipment — often even before Eastern European Warsaw Pact states have received them.[30]

No matter how one measures the Soviet arms support program in the Third World, the evidence indicates its growing importance during the 1970s. In the following section the factors that have presumably influenced the Soviets in their various decisions to expand the sale of military equipment to Third World states and the benefits for their overall foreign policy position that they hope to gain from arms transfers will be examined.

THE PLACE OF MILITARY SUPPORT AND ARMS
TRANSFERS IN SOVIET FOREIGN POLICY

The earlier sections of this chapter surveyed the evolution of Soviet relations with the countries of the Third World. There it was argued that military assistance and arms transfers played an important role in Soviet-Third World relations. Now the precise function of military support in overall Soviet policy will be analyzed. First, however, it is important to understand a number of factors inherent in the Soviet economic-political system that affect the ability of the Soviet Union to engage in the type of military support operations that it has developed. First of all, the USSR has become the largest producer of conventional military equipment in the world. Exports have thus become the most effective method of disposing of a huge surplus of weapons and a supplementary method of earning hard currency.[31] Moreover, given the focus of the Soviet economy on

TABLE 3.2 Soviet Military Relations with Developing
Countries, by Region, 1956-1979 (in millions of U.S. dollarsa)

	Total 1956-79	1956-74	1975	1976	1977	1978	1979	Total 1975-79
AGREEMENTS	47,340	18,925	3,325	5,550	8,715	2,465	8,365	28,420
North Africa	10,960	2,805	535	0	4,650	770	2,200	8,155
Sub-Saharan Africa	4,635	715	220	840	1,510	980	370	3,920
East Asia	890	890	0	0	0	0	0	0
Latin America	970	205	70	335	110	0	250	765
Middle East	24,445	18,980	1,195	4,105	1,735	325	5,105	12,465
South Asia	5,410	2,330	1,305	220	705	390	410	3,080
DELIVERIES	35,340	13,495	2,040	3,085	4,705	5,400	6,615	21,845
North Africa	7,165	685	450	1,010	1,265	1,685	2,090	6,500
Sub-Saharan Africa	3,530	410	270	285	550	1,400	615	3,120
East Asia	885	885	0	0	0	0	0	0
Latin America	675	30	70	95	370	95	15	645
Middle East	18,675	9,375	1,080	1,235	1,720	1,890	3,375	9,300
South Asia	4,410	2,130	170	460	800	380	520	2,280

aValues are based on estimated Soviet prices in rubles converted into dollars.
Source: CIA, Communist Aid Activities in Non-Communist Less Developed
Countries, 1979 and 1954-79: A Research Paper, ER 80-10318U, October 1980,
p. 14.

TABLE 3.3   Deliveries of Soviet Armaments to Noncommunist Developing Countries, 1967-1978 (In millions of current U.S. dollars)

	Arms Imports from USSR, 1967-1976	Total Arms Imports of Country, 1967-1976	Soviet Percentage of Total, 1967-1976	Arms Imports from USSR, 1974-1978	Total Arms Imports of Country, 1974-1978	Soviet Percentage of Total, 1974-1978
SOUTHEAST ASIA:	25	2,951[a]	0.8	--	2,125[a]	----
Cambodia (pre '75)	5	720	0.7	--	625	--
Indonesia	5	240	2.1	--	290	--
Laos (pre '75)	15	701	2.1	--	220	--
MIDDLE EAST:	6,982	20,553[b]	34.0	7,500	29,000[b]	25.9
Egypt	2,365	2,801	84.4	430	1,200	35.8
Iran	611	5,271	11.6	310	8,700	3.6
Iraq	1,795	2,451	73.0	3,600	5,300	67.9
Kuwait	--	181	--	50	750	6.7
Lebanon	5	131	3.8	--	50	--
Syria	2,015	2,261	89.1	2,700	3,300	81.8
Yemen (Aden)	151	165	91.5	370	380	97.4
Yemen (S'ana)	35	80	43.8	50	180	27.8
SOUTH ASIA:	1,530	2,901[b]	52.7	2,000	3,100[b]	64.5
Afghanistan	100	131	76.3	330	350	94.3
Bangladesh	35	61	57.4	20	70	28.6
India	1,365	1,680	81.3	1,600	1,900	84.2
Pakistan	25	831	3.0	5	775	0.6
Sri Lanka	10	15	66.7	10	10	100.0
AFRICA:	2,051	5,131[b]	40.0	7,400	13,100[b]	56.5
Algeria	315	445	70.8	1,200	1,500	80.0
Angola	190	315	60.3	410	725	56.6
Benin	1	10	10.0	20	30	66.7
Burundi	--	--	--	5	10	50.0

50

Table 3.3 (continued)

	Arms Imports from USSR, 1967-1976	Total Arms Imports of Country, 1967-1976	Soviet Percentage of Total, 1967-1976	Arms Imports from USSR, 1974-1978	Total Arms Imports of Country, 1974-1978	Soviet Percentage of Total, 1974-1978
Cape Verde	--	--	--	20	20	100.0
Central Af. Rep.	1	5	20.0	--	--	--
Chad	5	10	50.0	10	10	100.0
Congo	10	20	50.0	30	40	75.0
Equatorial Guinea	5	5	100.0	10	10	100.0
Ethiopia	--	190	--	1,300	1,300	100.0
Guinea	50	55	90.1	50	50	100.0
Guinea-Bissau	5	5	100.0	10	10	100.0
Libya	1,005	1,835	54.8	3,400	5,000	68.0
Madagascar	1	5	20.0	20	30	66.7
Mali	25	25	100.0	100	110	90.9
Morocco	10	350	2.9	20	950	2.1
Mozambique	15	20	75.0	130	180	72.2
Nigeria	70	221	31.7	80	200	40.0
Somalia	181	185	97.8	300	500	60.0
Sudan	65	100	65.0	30	110	27.3
Tanzania	30	125	24.0	110	180	61.1
Uganda	65	81	35.9	110	120	91.7
Zambia	10	81	12.3	40	140	28.6
LATIN AMERICA:	165	3,095c	5.3	650	3,425c	19.0
Peru	165	655	25.2	650	1,000	65.0
TOTAL	10,753	34,631	31.1	17,550	50,750	34.6

aTotal includes all noncommunist countries of Southeast Asia except South Vietnam.
bIncludes all countries of the region.
cIncludes all countries except Cuba.
Sources: Data for 1967-1976: U.S. Arms Control and Disarmament Agency, World Military Expenditures and Arms Transfers 1969-1978 (Washington, D.C.: U.S. ACDA, 1980), pp. 160-162.
N.B. As the method of estimating data used by ACDA differs from that employed by the CIA, the figures in this table do not agree with those provided in preceding tables.

military production, weapons production has become the most efficient and competitive of all sectors of the Soviet economy. Soviet military equipment is generally qualitatively equal or even superior to comparable equipment obtainable from other suppliers.[32] Moreover, the Soviets have large stockpiles of surplus weapons of good quality and current vintage that they can make available to Third World states. The growing availability of such weapons has coincided with the phenomenal expansion of the market for weapons throughout Asia, Africa, and Latin America.

Another factor relevant to Soviet arms transfer policy has been the growth of the Soviet navy and its operation in waters far from Soviet territory. By the beginning of the 1970s this fleet was operational and required access to facilities throughout Asia and Africa.[33] Arms transfers to certain Third World states have been a "bargaining" factor in Soviet efforts to acquire access to such facilities.

Political Factors in Soviet Military Support

The major purposes of Soviet arms assistance and sales have been political. During the 1950s when the USSR was generally isolated from the developing world, the main purpose of military aid and assistance was to establish and solidify bilateral relations with countries such as Egypt. Later, particularly during the 1970s, the political nature of Soviet goals expanded to include an effort to strengthen the global policies of the Soviet Union. It should be borne in mind that it is not always possible to separate clearly the military-security aspects of Soviet objectives from the purely political. To a substantial degree the two are interrelated, inasmuch as the growth of military capabilities may well bring with it an enhanced ability to achieve political goals. It is also important to note that military aid and assistance is merely one of a number of instruments employed by the USSR in its effort to achieve foreign policy objectives. Diplomatic contacts, trade relations, economic and technical assistance, cultural policy and propaganda, and subversion are other methods employed by the USSR in its relations with Third World states during the 1960s, 1970s, and 1980s. In any particular set of circumstances one or another of these instruments may predominate. The focus on military relations in the present discussion should not be interpreted to mean that these relations alone constitute the totality of Soviet policy toward the developing countries.

Initially, the primary concern of the Soviet Union in extending military assistance to developing countries was the desire to undermine Western influence as well as strategic interests in regions of primary concern for Soviet security. The 1955 shipment of armaments to Egypt, valued at more than $250 million, as well as later agreements with Yemen, Syria, and Iraq,[34] were all aimed at undermining the attempts of the United States and its Western allies to create a unified anti-Soviet alliance system along the southern borders of the Soviet Union. Moscow was able to take advantage of growing antagonisms between the West and the revolutionary nationalist leaders of Egypt and other Arab countries as well as festering hostility between Israel and its Arab neighbors to gain a presence in the Middle East. The provision of weapons, although by no means the only policy instrument employed by the Soviet Union, was the most effective means at its disposal to make an impact on political developments in the region.

Elsewhere in the Third World in the late 1950s and early 1960s, the growth of anti-Western attitudes among nationalist leaders, the desire to gain a degree of independence from the weapons monopoly of the United States and its allies, and the expansion of regional hostilities provided the Soviet Union with additional opportunities to help undermine Western influence. By the early 1960s Indonesia, India, and a number of other Asian and African states had turned to the Soviet Union for military hardware.

Closely related to the Soviet goal of weakening Western dominance in Third World areas was the desire to establish or increase Moscow's own presence. In almost all cases where Soviet military equipment was supplied to developing countries, Soviet military technicians arrived along with the equipment to instruct the local military in its use. (India was and remains a notable exception.) As we have already seen, the corollary to this policy was the bringing of officers to the Soviet Union for extended periods of training. Probably the most extreme example of the growing role of the Soviet Union in the affairs of a client state prior to the attempted communization of Afghanistan -- at least the example that is most completely documented -- is provided by Egypt. After the disastrous Seven-Day War of June 1967, the entire Egyptian military was reorganized, largely by Soviet military advisers.[35] Prior to their expulsion by President Sadat in summer 1972, 21,000 Soviet military technicians were at work in Egypt.

More recent examples of large-scale Soviet presence in Third World states, generally in connection with military support to those states, are Angola, Somalia (until 1977), Ethiopia, and -- at a totally different level -- Afghanistan following the Soviet invasion of that country in late 1979. In all these cases the provision of military equipment and technical support has been one of the most important means employed by the Soviets in gaining a presence and in attempting to influence the course of political events in the recipient country.

Closely related to the goal of gaining political access through the supply of arms and equipment has been the effort to provide stability for countries that have turned to the USSR for support. During the 1970s this became an especially important element of Soviet policy in Africa, where the Soviets and their Eastern European and Cuban allies have provided not only military equipment but even the military personnel needed by revolutionary movements or regimes (as in Angola and Ethiopia) to seize power or to consolidate political control. Throughout Africa, for example, the East Germans in consort with their Soviet allies have been providing military and security training for revolutionary governments in a number of countries, e.g., Somalia, Angola, Mozambique, and Ethiopia. This emphasis on the training of elite "palace guards" and domestic security police has been motivated by the experience in the 1960s with "progressive" regimes favorably inclined toward the Soviet Union. The position of the Kremlin and its allies in Ghana, for instance, changed drastically with the overthrow of Kwame Nkrumah in 1966. The presence of well-trained and loyal security forces is now viewed by the Soviets as essential to stabilize the existence of "progressive" Marxist-Leninist governments in various African countries.

Although the initial focus of Soviet policy in the Third World was on the containment and reduction of Western influence, the break in relations with China in the early 1960s introduced new complications for that policy. The Soviets now found themselves competing for influence not only with the former Western colonial powers but also with the "maverick" Marxist-Leninists in Beijing. By the mid-1960s Soviet economic and miitary assistance to some developing countries was aimed at preventing the extension of Chinese involvement. Recent examples of the Soviet concern with China can be seen in both Angola and Southeast Asia. During the 1975 civil war in Angola, Soviet commentary made clear that the Kremlin was concerned with the possibility of China's gaining a presence were Jonas Savimbi's Union for the Total Independence of Angola (UNITA) to emerge victorious, as UNITA received substantial support from the Chinese. In Southeast Asia, Soviet support for Vietnam -- both before and after the Sino-Vietnamese War of 1979 -- was meant to counter the possible expansion of Chinese influence into the region. In addition, ever since the beginning of the 1960s Soviet military support for India had as one of its purposes the prevention of an expansion of Chinese activity in South Asia.

Throughout the 1970s Soviet policy in the Third World seemingly followed two paths: support for "progressive" regimes that were embarking on a path of socialist construction, and a more pragmatic approach in dealing with "nonprogressive" Third World states whose strategic location or raw materials makes them of potential strategic importance for the USSR. Military support was among the most important elements in both these sets of relationships. However, it appears most crucial in the case of those radical Third World states that have turned overwhelmingly to the Soviet Union for support. Among those states the Soviets have termed "progressive" in recent years, virtually all receive the vast majority of their military equipment from the Soviets.

So far three of the political goals for which military support has been important have been discussed: reduction of Western influence, attainment of a political presence for the Soviet Union, and support for clients and allies in the Third World. Related to this last objective is the military support provided by the Soviet Union to various national liberation movements, primarily in Africa. The Soviets and their Eastern European and Cuban allies became the major source of military support for rebel organizations in colonial Angola and Mozambique. In Zimbabwe they provided military equipment to Joshua Nkomo's forces before independence, and both the South West African People's Organization (SWAPO) in Namibia and the African National Congress in South Africa have received most of their military supplies from the Soviets and their allies. The "liberation" struggle in Oman was also supported, at least indirectly through South Yemen, by the Soviet Union.[36] Such military support, as in former Portuguese Africa, was expected to bring to power regimes not only favorably inclined toward the Soviet Union but also dependent upon it for their very security.

However, not only "progressive" or self-proclaimed Marxist-Leninist governments have been recipients of major Soviet military support. In fact, most Soviet military assistance and sales since the middle 1950s has gone to countries that, although often anti-Western (or at least anti-American), were hardly "progressive" in their domestic policies, at least in the Soviet sense of that term. Soviet military support to most of the Arab states in recent decades has had as its major focus the competition for political and military influence with the United States in the oil-rich Middle East. The continuation of the Arab-Israeli conflict has provided the Soviets with conditions favorable to their involvement. To date, however, there is little evidence that they have been able to translate this involvement, or presence, into influence. So long as the Soviets are willing to support Arab initiatives, relations remain cordial. When the interests of the Arab states and those of the Soviet Union diverge, however, the Soviets generally find themselves incapable of changing the policies of the Arab states.

One final political purpose of Soviet military policies in the Third World should be treated prior to the discussion of military and economic motives. Throughout the 1970s the Soviets stated repeatedly that the international environment had changed, that the role of the capitalist West in the international system was receding, and that a new international correlation of forces had emerged. However, only by playing a role in events on a global scale could the Soviets demonstrate to leaders throughout the world that their assessment of the changing international balance was indeed accurate. If nothing else, the Soviets have shown in recent years that they have both the ability and the willingness to provide support to their allies. The success of the MPLA in Angola, and, for the time being at least, of the central government in Ethiopia, is attributable only to Soviet and Cuban military support. The provision of various forms of military assistance throughout Asia and Africa has been among the most important means employed by the Soviets in demonstrating their claim that a changing balance of forces has already emerged. The image of the Soviet Union as equal — or even superior — to the United States may well influence leaders in Asia and Africa to work out a modus vivendi with Moscow and its clients, given the possibly dominant future role of the Soviet Union in the international system.

Military Security Considerations
in Soviet Military Support

Closely related to the Soviet desire to strengthen its global role is the continuing competition with the United States and with the People's Republic of China. During the Brezhnev era, Soviet policy in the Third World was based in part on the desire to expand its capabilities of projecting power abroad in support of Soviet state interests. These capabilities depended upon two separate but interrelated developments. First, there was and is the need for the Soviets to produce the military equipment needed to exert military power in regions beyond the territory under the control of the Soviet army. Throughout the 1960s and 1970s the Soviets launched construction programs that have given them a large and modern oceangoing navy and long-distance transport aircraft.[37] The second requirement was and is access to military facilities throughout the Third World at which to refuel, repair, and refurbish these ships and aircraft. Here Soviet military support to developing countries and the relationship between arms transfers and the Soviet acquisition of access to such military facilities will be demonstrated. In this discussion, it is necessary to distinguish between facilities over which the Soviets have exercised virtually complete, albeit often temporary, control and facilities to which they have had only limited access. Here the major concern will be the general relationship between access and the provision by the Soviets of military support to the host government.[38]

The evidence points to the acquisition of military facilities in areas of strategic interest to the Soviet Union as one of the primary factors motivating Soviet policy in the Third World.[39] The USSR has used both economic aid and (more important in recent years) military assistance as part of an overall policy of competition with the West for the acquisition and continued use of strategic access points. During the 1970s, Moscow has been especially successful in creating a network of such facilities throughout the Indian Ocean area, the Middle East, and various parts of Africa that now permits it to influence developments far from the territory of the Soviet Union. It must also be noted that the development of the Soviet network of facilities has depended upon the support that the Soviets have been willing to provide to host countries, either in local conflicts or in conflicts with the West.

Among the most important developments that have enabled the Soviets both to export military equipment and to acquire basing facilities has been the Arab-Israeli conflict. Initial direct Soviet involvement in the Middle East was related directly to the provision of military assistance to the Arab states. By the early 1970s the Soviets had developed a position in Egypt that appeared strong. Not only was Egypt almost totally dependent upon the Soviets for both developmental assistance and military equipment, but Soviet military advisers played a decisive role in revamping the Egyptian military. Meanwhile, Moscow gained access to port and air facilities throughout Egypt. These facilities, which were under complete Soviet command, provided the USSR with the opportunity to conduct air surveillance throughout the Eastern Mediterranean and to maintain its growing naval strength in the region.[40] Similarly, the Soviet Union was able to gain access to various types of military facilities in Syria and Iraq, although it has never exercised the type of control over these facilities that it maintained in Egypt prior to 1972. Moreover, disagreements between Moscow and the Syrian government concerning the latter's role in Lebanon and between the Soviets and Iraqis over the latter's war with Iran have cooled relations.

The conflict between Somalia and Ethiopia afforded the Soviets a dual opportunity: first, the acquisition of large-scale military facilities in Somalia; and later, after their decision to opt for support for the new revolutionary regime in Addis Ababa and the loss of the Somali military facilities, the acquisition of facilities in Ethiopia.[41]

The civil war in Angola in 1975 and, more recently, the war between Somalia and Ethiopia in the Horn of Africa have indicated both the extent of existing Soviet military facilities and their importance to the Soviet Union in supporting allies and clients throughout the Third World. Without access to air facilities in Algeria, Benin, Congo, Guinea, and elsewhere in West Africa, the rapid and large-scale shipment of Soviet military equipment and Cuban troops essential to the MPLA's victory would have been impossible.[42] More recently, Soviet access to facilities in Iraq, South Yemen, and Libya proved indispensable for the movement of massive amounts of Soviet military equipment and large numbers of Cuban troops to help the USSR's new friends in Ethiopia.

The apparent connection between Soviet arms transfers and the acquisition of military facilities has already been noted. All the countries that have provided the Soviets with facilities over which the Soviets exercised substantial control have been major recipients of Soviet military equipment, and most have also received substantial economic aid from the USSR, at least relative to the total population of the country. In addition, all the countries that have provided at least limited access to air and naval facilities have also received military supplies from the Soviet Union -- although in some cases the amounts have been quite limited (see Table 3.4). It should be noted, however, that not all major recipients of Soviet arms have provided the Soviet Union with major military facilities over which the USSR exercises some control. India, for example, has provided the Soviets with limited naval servicing and repair facilities equivalent to those provided to a number of other countries. In the case of Iran, it seems clear that the primary Soviet expectation at the time that arms were sold was to lessen Iran's dependence on the United States, not to acquire any type of military facilities.

A final point must be emphasized concerning the vulnerability of the Soviet position in many of the countries in which they have acquired military facilities. Both Egypt and Somalia expelled the Soviets when their goals and those of the Soviet Union clashed. During the 1976 civil war in Lebanon, Syria restricted Soviet access to naval facilities in that country in order to show its displeasure with Soviet opposition to Syrian intervention against the Palestine

57

Liberation Organization (PLO) and Lebanese leftists.[43] The Soviets have apparently been quite aware of the tenuous nature of their military presence in the developing countries and thus have usually sought parallel, or backup, facilities. For example, throughout the late 1960s and early 1970s the USSR simultaneously courted North Yemen, South Yemen, Somalia, and Egypt.[44] When Somalia expelled the Soviets as a result of the latter's military support for Ethiopia in 1977, the Soviets were able to "fall back" on the facilities in South Yemen. In West Africa as well, the Soviets seem to have developed parallel sets of facilities in Benin, Guinea-Bissau, Equatorial Guinea, Congo, and Mali.[45] This strategy can also be observed in the increased deliveries of military equipment to Syria imediately after the expulsion of Soviet forces from Egypt in 1972, which resulted in the extension of access to Syrian naval facilities. Later, during the deterioration of Soviet-Syrian relations that resulted from disagreements over policy in the Lebanese civil war, the USSR began to concentrate deliveries of arms to Iraq, and an agreement was concluded for the expansion of access to Iraqi air and naval facilities.[46]

To date, Soviet military capabilities in the Third World have been employed for a variety of purposes. First, they have been used to support allies or client states against a regional opponent -- e.g., the Arabs versus Israel, India versus Pakistan, and Ethiopia versus Somalia -- or to support one faction in a domestic civil war, as in Angola. Also, as has been noted, Moscow provided substantial military assistance to revolutionary movements committed to the overthrow of colonial regimes. Finally, Moscow's overseas military capabilities have provided an opportunity to monitor the activities of Western civil and military shipping in the major shipping lanes from the oil-rich Persian Gulf region through the Indian Ocean and South Atlantic to Europe and North America.[47]

Economic Factors in Soviet Arms Transfers

In an analysis published in 1976 of the economic costs to the Soviet Union of its arms supplies to the Middle East, Gur Ofer concluded that the delivery of these weapons constituted "a heavy and ever increasing supply burden," an increase that "creates even heavier claims on increments of new available resources."[48] Ofer based his conclusion on the fact that by the first half of the 1970s, military aid to the Middle East alone represented a total of 1.8 percent of total machinery production in the Soviet Union -- more than double the percentage for the years 1955-1966.[49] Yet, recent developments in Soviet arms transfer policy indicate that arms transfers cannot be viewed merely as an economic burden on the on the Soviet economy. For the period 1973-1978 an estimated 43 percent of all military deliveries were paid for in hard currency -- $7,390 million of a total of $17,200 million. This offset approximately one-third of the total hard currency deficit in Soviet merchandise trade experienced by the Soviet Union during those years (see Table 3.5).[50] Ever since the rise in OPEC oil prices and the

58

TABLE 3.4   Major   Recipients of   Soviet   Economic and   Military   Aid
and   the   Existence   of   Soviet   Basing   Facilities
(in   millions   of   current   U.S.   dollars)

Major   Recipients   of   Soviet   Economic   Assistance,
1954-1979

Rank	Country	Amount
1	Turkey	3,330
2	India[a]	2,280
3	Morocco	2,100
4	Egypt[b]	1,440
5	Iran	1,165
6	Pakistan	920
7	Syria[b]	770
8	Algeria[a]	715
9	Iraq[b]	705
10	Bangladesh	305
11	Ethiopia[b]	225
12	Indonesia	215
13	Guinea[b]	210
14	South Yemen	205
15	Somalia[b]	165

Table 3.4 (continued)

Major Recipients of Soviet Arms Exports
1967-1976   1974-1978

Rank	Country	Amount % of Total Arms Imports		Rank	Country	Amount % of Total Arms Imports	
1	Egypt[b]	2,365	84	1	Iraq[b]	3,600	67.9
2	Syria[b]	2,015	89	2	Libya[a]	3,400	68.0
3	Iraq[b]	1,795	73	3	Syria[b]	2,700	67.9
4	India[a]	1,365	81	4	India[a]	1,600	84.2
5	Libya[a]	1,005	55	5	Ethiopia[b]	1,300	100.0
6	Iran	611	12	6	Algeria[a]	1,200	80.0
7	Algeria[a]	315	71	7	Peru	650	65.0
8	Angola[a,c]	190	60	8	Egypt[b]	430	35.8
9	Somalia[b]	181	89	9	Angola[a,c]	410	56.6
10	N. Yemen	151	92	10	S. Yemen[b]	370	97.4
11	Afghanistan[b]	100	76	11	Afthanistan[b]	330	94.3
				12	Iran	310	3.6
				13	Somalia[b]	300	60.0

[a]Country that has provided limited access to air and naval facilities.
[b]Country in which the Soviet Union has had access to major military facilities.
[c]Most of the remainder of Angola's imports of military equipment has come from allies of the USSR.
Sources: U.S. Arms Control and Disarmament Agency, World Military Expenditures and Arms Transfers 1967--1976 (Washington, D.C.: ACDA, 1978), pp. 157-160; idem, World Military Expenditures and Arms Transfers 1969-1978 (Washington, D.C.: ACDA, 1980), pp. 160-162; Central Intelligence Agency, Communist Aid Activities in Non-Communist Less Developed Countries, 1979 and 1954-79: A Research Paper, ER-80-10318U, October 1980, pp. 18-20; Robert E. Harkavy, "The New Geopolitics: Arms Transfers and the Major Powers' Competition for Overseas Bases," in Stephanie G. Neuman and Robert

Table 3.4 (continued)

E. Harkavy (eds.), Arms Transfers in the Modern World (New York: Praeger Publishers, 1979), pp. 137ff.; and Michael MccGwire, "Patterns of Soviet Naval Deployment," in Michael MccGwire (ed.), Soviet Naval Developments, Capability and Context (New York: Praeger Publishers, 1973), p. 429.

resulting availability of large amounts of hard currency in a number of Arab countries, the Soviets have been receiving hard currency for weapons shipped to the Middle East. Libya, which became a major purchaser of Soviet weapons during the 1970s, now pays for all its purchases with dollars or other convertible currencies, and both Syria and Iraq have been able to cover the costs of most of their imports with foreign exchange provided by other wealthy Arab states.

In an interesting analysis of Soviet arms exports, Raymond Hutchings has maintained that the fluctuatons in Soviet arms sales abroad can be understood only in the context of internal Soviet economic forces. According to Hutchings, Soviet exports to Third World states during the 1960s and 1970s have followed a regular pattern of five-year cycles that are tied to the planning process of the Soviet economy.[51]

What is clear from the available evidence is that arms exports to Third World states have become an important source of hard currency for the USSR and that arms exports now play a major role in covering deficits in the USSR's balance of payments. Throughout the last decade the Kremlin substantially increased its imports of industrial equipment, including modern technology, in the effort to deal with problems facing the Soviet economy. However, in spite of increases in exports of raw materials, the USSR has continued to run a substantial deficit in its trade with the industrialized West. The one area in which the Soviet Union can compete effectively in the world market is in the sale of military equipment. As noted above, Soviet equipment is comparable to that produced in the West and, more important, the Soviets have the surpluses required to enable them to export arms to Third World customers.

Although the economic factor is not the most important influence determining Soviet arms transfers, it is conceivable that it comes increasingly into consideration as the Soviet leadership makes its decisions concerning the value of providing arms to various Third World customers.

AN ASSESSMENT OF SOVIET ARMS TRANSFERS
AND MILITARY SUPPORT POLICY

As a considerable portion of the discussion of Soviet involvement in the developing world that appears in the popular press tends to assume the virtually irrepressible implementation of a "grand design," it is necessary to put Soviet policy in perspective. Although the Soviets have indeed greatly expanded their role in world affairs in the Third World in particular, they have by no means been consistently successful in achieving their foreign policy goals. To a very great degree their policy initiatives and their successes and failures have depended on local developments over which they have exercised little or no control. Events such as the death of a Nasser or the seizure of power by a Mengistu have been extremely important for Soviet policy. The growth of arms transfers to the Third World and the ability to gain access to overseas military facilities have resulted far more from external circumstances than they have from Soviet policy initiatives. The expansion of regional conflicts -- such as that in the Horn of Africa or the periodic explosions in Arab-Israeli relations -- and the availability of surplus income in the oil-producing states have been major determinants that have enlarged the market for Soviet armaments as well as for those of the Western states. The acquisition of military facilities by the Soviets has often been viewed by the host country as a method of enhancing its own military security against a regional opponent. This was clearly the case in both Egypt and Somalia during the periods of their close relations with the Soviet Union. Yet, although the USSR has expanded its activities and capabilities in important areas of the developing world, it is still unable to dictate developments as it can, to some degree at least, in Eastern Europe.

To summarize, Soviet goals in the developing world have included (1) reduction of Western, in particular U.S., military and political influence; (2) containment of possible Chinese influence; (3) establishment of a network of military facilities that will enable Soviet military forces to project power; and (4) possible economic benefits for the Soviet economy. In large part these goals have been accomplished, often because of the failures of U.S. and Western European policy; at other times local developments have provided the Soviets with opportunities that they were able to exploit.

Soviet military assistance and arms transfer programs, as a part of overall policy toward the developing countries, are motivated primarily by political and strategic concerns. On the whole they have been related more to Soviet support for ideologically compatible allies, the search for strategic benefits, and the building of the foundations for future political influence than to economic motivations, even though the economic factor has grown in importance.

The expansion of the Soviet presence throughout much of Asia and Africa has increased the potential for Moscow to influence future political and military developments. However, it must be kept in mind that the Soviets still depend upon the goodwill of client states to maintain the network of facilities that they have constructed. As they become more involved in local affairs they will find that they cannot support two sides in a conflict and maintain favorable relations with both. As in the past, they are likely to opt for the stronger and potentially more important of the participants in a conflict. The possibility of becoming mired in local military conflicts also exists -- as the Soviets are learning in both Angola and Ethiopia, where Soviet-backed regimes are faced with serious internal opposition.

TABLE 3.5 Relationship of Military Sales to the Hard Currency Balance of Payments of the Soviet Union (in millions of current U.S. Dollars)

	1970	1971	1972	1973	1974	1975	1976	1977	1978
Exports, f.o.b.	2,201	2,630	2,801	4,790	7,470	7,835	9,721	11,345	13,157
Imports, f.o.b.	-2,701	-2,943	-4,157	-6,547	08,448	-14,257	-15,316	-14,645	-16,951
Balance of merchandise trade	-500	-313	-1,356	-1,757	0978	-6,422	-5,595	-3,300	-3,794
Receipts from military sales	100	87	122	1,345	1,000	793	1,108	1,500	1,644
Military sales as percentage of imbalance in merchandise trade	(20)	(28)	(09)	(77)	(102)	(12)	(20)	(45)	(43)

Sources: Adapted from data in Tables I and II in Paul G. Ericson and Ronald S. Miller, "Soviet Foreign Economic Behavior: A Balance of Payments Perspective," in U.S. Congress, Joint Economic Committee, Soviet Economy in a Time of Change (Washington, D.C.: Government Printing Office, 1979), II, pp. 212,214.

The future will probably witness a continuation of and perhaps further increases in military assistance to the developing world, policies that differ little from what evolved during the Brezhnev era. The festering of the Arab-Israeli conflict and the continuing unrest in southern Africa may well provide the USSR with greater opportunities for involvement in both of these regions. The fact that the Soviets, in spite of numerous setbacks, have been able to establish political-military relationships throughout much of the Third World means that they are now able to have an impact on events and to undercut Western political and economic interests in ways that would have been impossible only a decade ago. Arms transfers have played an important part in Soviet policy in the past and are likely to continue to represent the single most important Soviet instrument in relations with Third World states. As Franklyn Griffiths has argued, there is little either in Soviet political-ideological views or in Soviet perceptions of the world situation that is likely to result in voluntary limitations on the supply of arms to potential markets in the Third World.[52]

64

NOTES

1.   Arms Control and Disarmament Agency (ACDA), World
Military Expenditures and Arms Transfers 1969-1978 (Washington,
D.C.:   ACDA, 1980), p. 150.

2.   Ibid., p. 159.   See also Cindy Cannizzo, "Trends in
Twentieth Century Arms Transfers," in Cindy Cannizzo (ed.), The
Gun Merchants: Politics and Policies of the Major Arms Suppliers
(New York: Pergamon Press, 1980), pp. 10-11.

3.   ACDA, World Military Expenditures and Arms Transfers
1963-1973 (Washington, D.C.:   ACDA, 1974), p. 72; ACDA, World
Military Expenditures 1968-1977, p. 113; ACDA, World Military
Expenditures 1969-1978, p. 117.

4.   ACDA, World Military Expenditures, 1969-1978, p. 159.
This percentage should have risen during recent years, given the
cutoff of U.S. sales to its major Third World market, Iran (23.6
percent of total U.S. sales to Third World countries went to Iran in
1974-1978), and the massive shipments of Soviet military equipment
to Ethiopia and Afghanistan since 1978.

5.   For an excellent assessment of this aspect of Soviet
policy in the developing world, see Robert E. Harkavy, "The New
Geopolitics: Arms Transfers and the Major Powers' Competition for
Overseas Bases," in Stephanie G. Neuman and Robert E. Harkavy
(eds.), Arms Transfers in the Modern World (New York: Praeger
Publishers, 1979), pp. 131-154.   Other recent Western studies that
focus on Soviet efforts to establish a network of basing facilities
include Avigdor Haselkorn, The Evolution of Soviet Security Strategy,
1965-1975 (New York: Crane, Russak and Co., 1978); Walter F. Hahn
and Alvin J. Cottrell, Soviet Shadow over Africa (Washington, D.C.:
Center for Advanced International Studies, University of Miami, 1977);
and C. G. Jacobsen, Soviet Strategic Initiatives: Challenge and
Response (New York: Praeger Publishers, 1979).

6.   For a perceptive assessment of the Soviet concept of
"the changing correlation of forces" in international affairs, see
Vernon V. Aspaturian, "Soviet Global Power and the Correlation of
Forces," Problems of Communism, Vol 29, No. 3 (1980); 1-18.

7.   For a more complete discussion of Soviet policy toward
the developing counries during the Khrushchev years, see Roger E.
Kanet, "Soviet Attitudes Toward Developing Nations Since Stalin,"
in Roger E. Kanet (ed.), The Soviet Union and the Developing Nations
(Baltimore: Johns Hopkins University Press, 1974), pp. 27-50.

8.   For data on Soviet military aid, see U.S. Central
Intelligence Agency (CIA), Communist Aid to Less Developed
Countries of the Free World, 1977:   A Research Paper, ER 78-

10478U, p. 1; ER 76-10372U, p. 1; U.S. Department of State, Bureau of Intelligence and Research, Communist States and Developing Countries: Aid and Trade in 1972, Research Study RECS-10, June 15, 1973, Appendix, Table 9. For data on economic assistance, see U.S. Department of State, Bureau of Intelligence and Research, "The Communist Economic Offensive Through 1964," Research Memorandum RSB-65, August 5, 1965, p. 6.

9.   See Richard Lowenthal, Model or Ally? The Communist Powers and the Developing Countries (New York: Oxford University Press, 1977), pp. 185-186.   Chapters 3 and 4 of Lowenthal's book provide an excellent analysis of the interaction between Soviet ideology and Soviet foreign policy objectives in the developing countries.

10.   For a comprehensive treatment of the evolution of Soviet views concerning the developing countries, see Stephen Clarkson, The Soviet Theory of Development: India and the Third World in Marxist-Leninist Scholarship (Toronto: Toronto University Press, 1978).

11.   In 1964 more than 77 percent of Soviet exports to developing countries went to the countries of the Middle East and South Asia, and almost 64 percent of imports came from this region. Of all economic credits committed during the years 1954 to 1964, more than 76 percent went to South Asia and the Middle East.   See U.S. Department of State, Bureau of Intelligence and Research, Communist Economic Offensive Through 1964, p. 6; and idem, Communist Governments and Developing Nations: Aid and Trade in 1965, Research Memorandum, RSB-50, June 17, 1965, pp. 12-19.

12.   By "influence relationship" I mean the ability to cause other countries to behave in ways in which they would otherwide not have behaved.   Soviet military, economic, and political support did, however, permit individual developing countries to pursue policies that, without Soviet assistance, they would not have been able to undertake.   For a fuller discussion of influence in Soviet relations with the developing countries, see Alvin Z. Rubinstein, Red Star on the Nile: The Soviet-Egyptian Influence Relationship Since the June War (Princeton, N.J.:   Princeton University Press, 1977); and M. Rajan Menon, "India and the Soviet Union: A Case Study of Internation Influence," Ph.D. dissertation, University of Illinois at Urbana-Champaign, 1978.

13.   See, for example, the comments of Admiral S. G. Gorshkov, commander of the Soviet Navy, in an interview printed in Ogonek, No. 6 (February 3, 1968).   For a more complete presentation of Gorshkov's views see his Morskaia moshch' gosudarstva (Naval Power of the State) (Moscow: Voenizdat, 1976).   For a Western assessment of Gorshkov's major writings see James McConnell, "The Gorshkov Articles, the New Gorshkov Book, and Their Relation to Policy," in Micheal MccGwire and John McDonnall (eds.), Soviet Naval

Influence: Domestic and Foreign Dimensions (New York: Praeger Publishers, 1977), pp. 565-620.

14. For an excellent discussion of the changes in Soviet economic policy, see Elizabeth Kridl Valkenier, "New Trends in Soviet Economic Relations with the Third World," World Politics, Vol 22 (1970); 415-432; and idem "Soviet Economic Relations with the Developing Nations," in Kanet Soviet Union the the Developing Nations, pp.215-236.

15. Total commitments of Soviet economic assistance for the period 1954-1979 came to $18,190 million. See Central Intelligence Agency, National Foreign Assessment Center, Communist Aid Activities in Non-Communist Less Developed Countries, 1979 and 1954-79; A research Paper, ER 80-10318U (Washington, D.C., October 1980), p. 18. According to United Nations statistics, Soviet assistance totaled $17,712 million for 1954-1977. The figure for the comparable period in the CIA statistics is $13,381 million. See United Nations, Department of International Economic and Social Affairs, Statistical Office, Statistical Yearbook (New York: United Nations, various years).

16. For a collection of excellent studies of Soviet economic relations with developing countries, see Deepak Nayyar (ed.), Economic Relations Between Socialist Countries and the Third World (London: Macmillan, 1977).

17. Economic assistance provided by the Soviet Union and its Eastern European allies has been far smaller than that distributed by the West, both in absolute terms and as a percentage of gross national product:

Net Development Assistance Disbursed,
By Groups of Countries

Donor Group or Country	Billions of U.S. Dollars			Assistance as a Percentage of GNP		
	1973	1977	1978	1973	1977	1978
Western industrial countries	9.4	14.7	19.9	0.30	0.31	0.35
OPEC countries	1.3	5.9	3.7	1.41	1.96	1.11
Eastern Europe	.22	.20	.28	0.05	0.04	0.05
Soviet Union	.29	.31	.30	0.03	0.03	0.03

N.B. The figures are based on net disbursal of development assistance, which is determined by subtracting repayments on past development loans from current deliveries.

Source: Organisation for Economic Co-operation and Development, Development Cooperation: Efforts and Politics of the Members of the DAC: 1979 Review. (Paris: OECD, 1979.)

18. For data on Soviet trade, see SSSR Ministerstvo Vneshniaia Torgovli, Vneshniaia Torgovlia SSSR (Foreign Trade of the USSR) (Moscow: Statistika, various years.)

19. This chapter relies mainly on data on Soviet arms transfers that are provided by the Central Intelligence Agency. As those who have attempted to obtain complete and accurate data on arms transfers are aware, there exist serious problems with the data available. CIA data, which cover support facilities and services as well as weapons systems, are provided in current prices. Those included in the SIPRI Yearbook published by the Stockholm International Peace Research Institute are given in constant prices, but they include only major military equipment. Unfortunately, however, the divergence in the information provided by the two sources for individual years follows no pattern. The data provided by the U.S. Arms Control and Disarmament Agency (ACDA), which are also presented in current prices, differ even more from the CIA data than do those published by SIPRI. For the period 1967-1976, for example, ACDA data indicate a total of $10,753 million in arms exported by the Soviet Union to developing countries; the CIA gives the figure for deliveries for the period as $14,200 million. For the relevant sources see ACDA, World Military Expenditures and Arms Transfers 1967-1865 (Washington, D.C.: ACDA, 1977), pp. 157-160; Stockholm International Peace Research Institute, World Armaments and Disarmament: SIPRI Yearbook 1978 (Cambridge, Mass., and London: M.I.T. Press, 1978), pp. 256-257. For an excellent discussion of the discrepancies in the ACDA data, when compared with official French figures, see Edward A. Kolodziej, "Measuring French Arms Transfers: A Problem of Sources and Some Sources of Problems with ACDA Data," Journal of Conflict Resolution, Vol. 23 (1979); 195-227.

20. CIA, Communist Aid Activities in 1979, and 1954-79, pp. 13, 17.

21. It should be noted, however, that most of the recipients of small amounts of Soviet military support are sub-Saharan African countries. Even though the amounts of support are relatively small, they do make up, in most cases, a substantial percentage of total military imports for these countries, as the data in Table 3.3 show.

22. See Central Intelligence Agency, National Foreign Assessment Center, Arms Flows to LDCs: US-Soviet Comparisons, 1974-77, ER 78-10494U (Washington, D.C., November 1978), pp. 4-6. The following table exemplifies the differences in the two programs:

Composition of Soviet and U.S. Arms Sales and Deliveries,
1974-1977 (percentage of total)

	Deliveries		Sales	
	U.S.	USSR	U.S.	USSR
Total	100	100	100	100
Weapons				
Systems	39	58	35	60
Support	37	33	35	33
Services	24	9	30	7

Source: Ibid, p. ii.

23.   In 1979, 15,865 military technicians from the USSR and
Eastern Europe were working in the developing countries, up from
12,070, 10,250, and 9,080 in 1978, 1977, and 1976 respectively. In
1978, 60 percent of these military advisers were in the Middle East
and North Africa and an additional 32 percent were in sub-Saharan
Africa.   Cuban military "technicians," most of whom were actually
carrying out combat roles in Angola and Ethiopia, numbered an
estimated 38,650 in 1978 -- more than 96 percent in sub-Saharan
Africa. See CIA, Communist Aid Activities in 1979, and 1954-79, p.
6; CIA, Communist Aid Activities in 1978, p. 4; CIA, Communist
Aid to Less Developed Countries, 1977, p. 3; and CIA, Communist
Aid to Less Developed Countries, 1976, p. 4.

24.   CIA, Arms Flows to LDCs, p. 5.

25.   For a discussion of this point and the implications for
developing countries of mortgaging their exports to pay for weapons,
see Uri Ra'anan, The USSR Arms the Third World: Case Studies in
Soviet Foreign Policy (Cambridge, Mass.:   M.I.T. Press, 1969), pp.
161-163.

26.   See Roger R. Pajak, "West European and Soviet Arms
Transfer Policies in the Middle East," in Milton Leitenberg and Gabriel
Sheffer (eds.), Great Power Intervention in the Middle East (New
York: Pergamon Press, 1979), p. 155.

27.   See Paul G. Ericson and Ronald S. Miller, "Soviet Foreign
Economic Behavior: A Balance of Payments Perspective," in U.S.
Congress, Joint Economic Committee, Soviet Economy in a Time of
Change (Washington, D.C.: Government Printing Office, 1979), Vol
2, p. 214.

28.   International Institute for Strategic Studies, Strategic Survey 1978. (London: International Institute for Strategic Studies, 1979), p. 98.

29.   CIA, Communist Aid Activities in 1978, p. 20. See also SIPRI, World Armaments and Disarmament: SIPRI Yearbook 1978 (London: Taylor and Francies, 1980), pp. 146, 151.

30.   The Soviets delivered twelve MiG-27s to Syria in 1978. These planes were paid for by Libya in hard currency (SIPRI Yearbook 1979, p. 236. Iraq received 138 of these planes during 1977-1979) (SIPRI Yearbook 1980, p. 147).

31.   In recent years they have been producing about six times as many tanks as the United States, three times as many armored personnel carriers, eight times the artillery pieces, and twice as many combat aircraft. See Secretary of Defense Donald Rumsfeld, Annual Defense Department Report FY 1978 (Washington, D.C.: Government Printing Office, 1977), p. 11. See also Michael Checinski, "Structural Causes of Soviet Arms Exports," Osteuropa-Wirtschaft, Vol 23 (1977); 178.

32.   See P. R. Chari, "Indo-Soviet Military Relations: A Comment," India Quarterly, Vol. 33 (1977); 456. See also Gur Ofer, "Soviet Military Aid to the Middle East: An Economic Balance Sheet," in U.S. Congress, Joint Economic Committee, Soviet Economic Prospects for the 1970s (Washington, D.C.: Government Printing Office, 1973), p. 236.

33.   See James M. McConnell and Bradford Dismukes, "Soviet Diplomacy of Force in the Third World," Problems of Communism, Vol. 23, No. 1 (1979); 14-27. For case studies of the expanding role of the Soviet navy in the Third World see MccGwire and McDonnell, Soviet Naval Influence, expecially Part V; Michael MccGwire, Ken Booth, and John McDonnell (eds.), Soviet Naval Policy: Objectives and Constraints (New York: Praeger Publishers, 1975), especially Part II; and Bradford Dismukes and James McConnell (eds.), Soviet Naval Diplomacy (New York: Pergamon Press, 1979).

34.   The early agreements for the supply of arms to Arab states were negotiated by Czechoslovakia, which acted as a cover for the Soviet Union. For a discussion of these arms deals, see Mohamed Heikal, The Sphinx and the Commissar: The Rise and Fall of Soviet Influence in the Middle East (New York: Harper and Row, 1978), pp. 57-65; Ra'anan, USSR Arms the Third World, pp. 13-172; and Jon D. Glassman, Arms for the Arabs: The Soviet Union and War in the Middle East (Baltimore: Johns Hopkkins University Press, 1975), pp. 7-21.

35.   For an excellent discussion of the role of Soviet military advisers and of arms shipments in Soviet-Egyptian relations see

70

Rubinstein, Red Star on the Nile, passim. Rubinstein noted throughout his discussion both the efforts of the Soviets to use the arms relationship as a means of influencing Egyptian policies and the serious problems that arose periodically as Egyptian demands for support failed to be fulfilled. See also Heikal, Sphinx and the Commissar, passim.

36. For a discussion of Soviet support for national liberation movements, see Ian Greig, The Communist Challenge to Africa: An Analysis of Contemporary Soviet, Cuban and Chinese Policies (Richmond, Surrey; Foreign Affairs Publishing Co., 1977), especially pp. 135-210. See also Morris Rothenberg, The USSR and Africa: New Dimensions of Soviet Global Power (Washington, D.C.: Advanced International Studies Institute, in association with the University of Miami, 1980), especially pp. 163-255; and Hahn and Cottrell, Soviet Shadow over Africa, pp. 55-82.

37. For a discussion of the growth of Soviet conventional military capabilities see Jacobsen, Soviet Strategic Initiatives, pp. 51-72. See also William J. Durch, Michael D. Davidchik, and Abram N. Shulsky, "Other Soviet Interventionary Forces -- Military Transport Aviation and Airborne Troops," in Dismukes and McConnell, Soviet Naval Diplomacy, pp. 336-351; and Part IV: "Projection Capability," in MccGwire and McDonnell, Soviet Naval Influence, pp. 239-320.

38. For a careful discussion of the issue of military bases as they relate to Soviet policy, see Richard B. Remnek, "The Politics of Soviet Access to Naval Support Facilities in the Mediterranean," in Dismukes and McConnell, Soviet Naval Diplomacy, especially pp. 357-361.

39. See Harkavy, "New Geopolitics," p. 132. Harkavy's analysis suffers from a tendency to refer to even the most limited form of military access as a "base." However, he does present convincing evidence that arms transfers are related to the attempt to gain access to military facilities. See also the discussion of this point throughout Haselkorn, The Evolution of Soviet Security Strategy.

40. For an authoritative discussion of Nasser's motives in providing the facilities to the Soviet Union and of the fact that the Soviets exercised practically complete control over the bases, see Heikal, Sphinx and the Commissar, pp. 191ff. and 238.

41. For a discussion of Soviet efforts to obtain military facilities in the Red Sea region, see Nimrod Novik, On the Shores of Bab Al-Mandab: Soviet Diplomacy and Regional Dynamics (Philadelphia: Foreign Policy Research Institute, 1979).

42. For a discussion of the importance of these facilities see Hahn and Cottrell, Soviet Shadow over Africa, especially pp. 60ff.

43.   See "Syria-USSR: Soviets Asked to Leave Syrian Naval Port," Defense and Foreign Affairs Daily, January 14, 1977, cited in Harkavy, "New Geopolitics," p. 137.

44.   See Novik, On the Shores of Bab Al-Mandab.

45.   See the description of the Soviet basing network in "New Soviet Role in Africa Alleged," New York Times, December 10, 1975, p. 11.

46.   See Robert O. Freedman, "The Soviet Union and Sadat's Egypt," in MccGwire, Booth, and McDonnell, Soviet Naval Policy, pp. 211-236; and "Iraq: Defense Protocol with USSR," Defense and Foreign Affairs Daily, October 13, 1976, cited in Harkavy, "New Geopolitics," p. 138.

47.   For an excellent analysis of Soviet use of force in the developing world see James M. McConnell, "The 'Rules of the Game': A Theory on the Practice of Superpower Naval Diplomacy," in Dismukes and McConnell, Soviet Naval Diplomacy, pp. 240-280.

48.   Ofer, "Soviet Military Aid to the Middle East," p. 233.

49.   Ibid., p. 227. A more recent assessment of Soviet military assistance in the Middle East also concludes that Soviet arms exports can be viewed as an economic burden on the Soviet Union. See Mary Kaldor, "Economic Aspects of Arms Supply Policies to the Middle East," in Leitenberg and Sheffer, Great Power Intervention in the Middle East, p. 223.

50.   See Ericson and Miller, "Soviet Foreign Economic Behavior," p. 214.

51.   Raymond Hutchings, "Regular Trends in Soviet Arms Exports to the Third World," Osteuropa-Wirtschaft, Vol 23, No. 3 (1978); 182-202.

52.   Franklyn J. C. Griffiths, "De la justification des transferts d'armes par l'Union Sovietique," (The Justificatin of Arms Transfers by the Soviet Union) Etudes Internationales, Vol. 8 1977); 600-617.

4
Eastern European Military Assistance to the Third World

Trond Gilberg

During the 1970s, the nations of Eastern Europe became more active participants in global politics than had been the case in previous decades. The reasons for this increased activity were many and varied. First, the Eastern Europeans gained a measure of foreign policy autonomy in their relationships with the Soviet Union; no longer could (or would) the Kremlin dictate all foreign policy moves emanating from the capitals of Eastern Europe, and it therefore became more feasible for the political elites of that region to adopt semi-autoomous policies in areas they had not previously considered appropriate for direct involvement.[1] Eastern European countries, having been provided with the greater opportunity for semi-autonomous foreign policy activity, also acquired the will and the capability to carry out such activity. In fact, opportunity, will, and capability expanded hand in hand as the Eastern European states developed industrially and educationally, and local leaderships became more nationalistic and assertive. These developmental trends within Eastern Europe have been directly related to the modernization policies of the Soviet Union and the local communist leadership of the area ever since the late 1940s.[2]

Second, developments in the Third World made increased Eastern European involvement there more inviting in the 1970s. During that decade (as well as the decade preceding it) the trend toward national independence continued unabated, spurred along by fervent nationalists who were also, in many cases, revolutionaries. One of the hallmarks of this trend was anti-Westernism, often characterized as "anticolonialism". The socioeconomic policies of the emerging new elites fostered drastic changes in the class structure and a considerable redistribution of wealth, often undertaken by means of brute force. All these tendencies and developments produced conditions favorable to Eastern European involvement, as all the regimes in that area presumably were also anti-Western, anticapitalist, anticolonialist, and prorevolutionary, and theoretically possessed considerable experience in the redistribution of wealth and the creation of greater social and economic justice. Furthermore, the Eastern European states were small or medium-sized systems that presented no threat of new colonialism to the leaders of Africa, Asia, and Latin America. As a result, the Eastern Europeans avoided the charge of neocolonialism that was often leveled at the Soviet Union in its increased activity in the Third World.[3]

Furthermore, an increased understanding in the West of the complexities developing inside the Soviet bloc made it possible for the Eastern Europeans to conduct more active policies in the Third World without automatic negative reactions in Washington, Paris, London, and Bonn. New Western perceptions allowed for a more flexible policy vis-a-vis the Eastern Europeans, who found themselves in the vastly improved position of having room to maneuver rather than being hemmed in by the control mechanisms of the Soviet Union and the formerly undifferentiated anticommunist attitudes of the major Western powers.[4]

As the modernization process continued in Eastern Europe, the rapidly industrializing regimes of the area were placed in the difficult situation of needing at the same time both raw materials and export markets for finished goods. Therefore, both the input side and the output side of these managed economies became more dependent upon the outside world. The Soviet Union, of course, continued to provide most of the raw materials and fuels necessary for the Eastern European economies. Many of the finished products of Eastern European factories consequently found their way into the huge Soviet market. Meanwhile, the leaders in the Kremlin, faced with increasing demands for energy and raw materials domestically while requiring Western technology obtainable only through export of these same raw materials and energy made it clear to their allies in Eastern Europe that the latter must make increased efforts to find supplementary sources of resources. The Eastern Europeans, in turn, needed to loosen some of their dependencies on the giant to their east through a more diversified export policy. Given these constraints, and given the low quality of most Eastern European products which rendered them noncompetitive in Western markets, the choice of the Third World as a resource base and an export market for Eastern Europe was a logical one.[5] Within the parameters of these opportunities and needs, the stage was set for a much more active East European policy in the Third World.

FROM "HONEST BROKERS" TO "FAITHFUL AGENTS":
THE DIVERSIFIED NATURE OF EASTERN EUROPEAN
POLICIES IN THE THIRD WORLD

During the 1970s, Eastern European states implemented quite different policies toward the Third World. The level of activity also varied considerably by geographical region. Whereas Asia represented an area of great involvement during the early part of the decade, due predominantly to the Vietnam conflict, most Eastern European activity shifted to Africa and the Middle East during the second half of the decade as opportunities increased there and as this continent became more important both in terms of strategic location and raw materials supply. Toward the end of the 1970s, Latin America (especially Central America) became an area of increased focus for at least some Eastern European regimes as political developments in Nicaragua, El Salvador, and various Caribbean states seemed to invite such involvement.[6]

In the context of these improved conditions for Eastern European involvement in the Third World, the German Democratic Republic, Poland, Czechoslovakia, Hungary, Romania, Bulgaria, and Yugoslavia engineered new foreign policy goals. Albania, by contrast, increasingly isolated itself from the rest of the world, including after 1978, its erstwhile mentor China. It was not until the latter part of the decade that Tirana began a somewhat more active foreign policy, and when that finally happened, it also was directed more toward developed countries than toward the Third World. The analysis that follows will therefore for the most part exclude Albania, except for occasional references to specific events.[7]

Among the other socialist states and people's democracies, the variation in approaches to the Third World was rather astonishing, given the past uniformity of policy during the Stalin era. In the 1970s it became clear that the leaders of the various states in Eastern Europe perceived their roles in the Third World in drastically different ways, and these perceptual differences were reflected in actual policies. Basically, the Eastern European states can be divided into four major categories in terms of their policies in the Third World during the 1970s.

1. The "Faithful Agents." The "faithful agents" considered themselves as representatives of the Soviet Union in the Third World, and their activities there were designed to enhance the stature of the Kremlin and its power and influence in the developing countries in ideological, political, economic, and military-strategic terms. The German Democratic Republic, Czechoslovakia, and Bulgaria belong in this category.

2. The "Autonomist." Nicolae Ceausescu and the Romanian political leadership, on the other hand, saw the Third World as an arena in which Bucharest could continue and expand its quest for foreign policy autonomy, at the same time establishing favorable markets for Romanian exports as well as sources of raw materials for the expanding industries of this rapidly modernizing state. Part of this strategy involved close association with several countries of the Third World for the purposes of attaining the status of "developing country" in international forums, thus enhancing the chances for increased development aid for Romania. The high level of Romanian activity in the Third World, coupled with the continued quest for foreign policy autonomy conducted by Bucharest, meant that the Romanians occasionally adopted policies that were not in consonance with the Soviet Union's interests in the Third World.[8]

3. The "Neutralist." Yugoslavia continued its policy of neutrality during the 1970s, and Tito remained one of

the leaders of the nonaligned movement, which ensured him a special status in many Third World capitals. As Belgrade remained one of the staunchest critics of Moscow's quest for leadership of the international communist movement and was a persistent voice denouncing the increasingly "imperialistic" foreign policy of the Kremlin leaders, Yugoslav policies in the Third World often ran counter to Soviet interests there.[9]

4. The "In-Betweens." Poland and Hungary remained true to the principle of solidarity with the Soviet Union during the 1970s, but a careful reading of statements and actual policies emanating from Warsaw and Budapest in this period shows that this solidarity was adhered to with less enthusiasm than was the case among the "faithful agents." As the decade wore on and the internal political processes Poland produced demands for a "national path" for the country, the Polish leadership trod more carefully in foreign policy in order not to inflame public opinion through excessive demonstrations of pro-Soviet policies in the Third World. However, after the summer of 1980 the internal political and economic crisis in Poland precluded much activity by the Polish leadership in the Third World.[10]

These differentiations in general foreign policies by Eastern Europeans in the Third World in turn produced different policies in the field of arms transfers, economic assistance, and the establishment of various support mechaisms in this field. The East Germans have, in fact, become the most important asset of the Soviet leaders in many areas as Pankow supplies expertise and technical and monetary aid to a variety of political and military organizations in the Third World while supporting many of the regimes that have come to power in the decolonized areas since the early 1960s. Czechoslovakia maintains a role as a major manufacturer of arms, some of which are exported to a variety of movements and regions in the Third World. Bulgaria, the last of the "faithful agents," appears to have less of an impact, partly because of its lower level of economic development and consequent inability to supply the kinds of services and materials that flow from East Berlin and Prague. Sofia is, nevertheless, very active in a number of countries.[11] Hungary and Poland, although active in trade and other economic relations, have less of an impact in the military-strategic field. Romania and Yugoslavia, on the other hand, pursuing a very active policy in the Third World for their own purposes, have become suppliers of both military material and related services since the early 1960s.[12] Further details will be provided below.

SOVIET AND EASTERN EUROPEAN ARMS TRANSFERS TO THE THIRD WORLD: THE SCOPE OF THE PROBLEM

Considerable concern exists in the West to understand the scope and makeup of communist military assistance and arms transfers to the Third World. Such activity is of long standing, the amounts of money and material involved are substantial, and the political and military-strategic implications of these activities are enormous. In the late 1970s, the CIA estimated the value of communist arms transfers and economic aid to the Third World as follows: Pledges of military aid in 1977 totaled $5.7 billion; in 1978 they were $2.3 billion. Pledges of economic aid reached $5.4 billion in 1978. In 1978, the Soviet Union delivered $3.8 billion worth of military material to the Third World. In the same year, Moscow committed $3.7 billion of foreign aid through credit (most of this went to Morocco and Turkey). The CIA also estimated that in 1978, a total of 52,000 communist "military-related personnel" operated in the Third World.[13]

The key Third World importers of arms and related services during the 1970s were Iran, Libya, Syria, Vietnam, Saudi Arabia, Iraq, Jordan, South Korea, India, Egypt, Brazil, Taiwan, and Pakistan, in that order of magnitude. Israel and South Africa also imported sizeable quantities of arms. Iran imported 13.6 percent of all arms transferred to the Third World. For Libya, the figure was 6.2 percent; Israel, 6.1 percent; Syria, 5.7 percent; Vietnam, 5.6 percent; Saudi Arabia, 5.1 percent; Iraq, 4.5 percent; Jordan, 4.4 percent; South Korea, 4.4 percent; India, 3.8 percent; Egypt, 3.6 percent; South Africa, 2.4 percent; Brazil, 2.0 percent; Taiwan, 1.7 percent; and Pakistan, 1.7 percent. "Others" imported 2.2 percent of all arms exported to the Third World. The United States was the chief supplier to Iran, Israel, Vietnam (prior to 1975), Saudi Arabia, Jordan, South Korea, Brazil, and Taiwan; the Soviet Union held pride of place as a supplier to Libya (after 1975), Syria, Vietnam (after 1975), Iraq, and Egypt. France was the main exporter to Libya prior to 1975, to Pakistan after 1975, and to South Africa during the entire decade. China was the chief exporter to Pakistan prior to 1975.[14]

The involvement of the communist states in the Third World related above is, unfortunately, most frequently stated in terms of combined contributions, thus complicating any effort to distinguish Eastern European contributions from Soviet transfers. There are, however, some sources that attempt to disaggregate such figures, as shown in Table 4.1. Table 4.1 shows a considerable involvement by the states of Eastern Europe, even though their contributions were dwarfed by those of the Soviet Union. It is interesting that Eastern Europeans increased their activities in the 1970s despite occasional reductions such as occurred in 1970. The slowly but steadily increasing figures during the 1970s indicate the permanency of their commitment. One can expect that the 1980s will show a similar determination, barring any catastrophic economic or military developments in the Eastern European states themselves, significant changes in the global military balance, or internal changes in the recipient states of the Third World.

Just as the actual sale and transfer of arms have been substantial, the support activities required to maintain the flow of such equipment are likewise impressive. Table 4.2 examines the number of military technicians who accompanied this equipment in

TABLE 4.1 Communist Military Agreements with LDCs: Agreements
Concluded and Equipment Delivered

| | Agreements Concluded | | | | Equipment Delivered | | | |
	Total	USSR	Eastern Europe	China	Total	USSR	Eastern Europe	China
Total	33,825	29,655	3,255	910	28,675	25,310	2,605	755
1955-68	6,555	5,495	810	250	5,505	4,585	745	175
1969	485	360	125	negl	555	450	80	25
1970	1,265	1,150	50	65	1,105	995	80	30
1971	1,790	1,590	120	80	1,045	865	120	60
1972	1,865	1,635	150	80	1,360	1,215	70	75
1973	2,965	2,810	130	25	3,330	3,130	120	80
1974	4,840	4,225	530	85	2,500	2,310	165	25
1975	2,290	2,,035	215	40	2,190	1,845	255	85
1976	3,730	3,375	215	145	2,970	2,575	315	80
1977	5,710	5,215	450	50	3,910	3,515	325	70
1978	2,320	1,765	465	90	4,205	3,825	325	55

Source: CIA, Communist Aid Activities in Non-Communist Less
Developed Countries 1978 (Washington, D.C., 1979), p. 2.

1978, the latest year for which fairly complete data exists; Table
4.3 shows the number of Third World military technicians trained in
communist states in the period 1955-1978.

The data presented in Tables 4.2 and 4.3 suffer from the fact
that they are aggregated and thus can tell us little about the efforts
of any specific country in the field of arms transfer and related
military assistance. For this reason, other sources must be consulted.
The following information has been obtained from a careful reading
of the local press in each Eastern European country, as well as the
many translations of local newspapers and magazines that are
available.

Bulgaria

Bulgaria remained a "faithful agent" of the Soviet Union
throughout the decade of the 1970s, even though its own activity as
a supplier of arms and related services to the Third World remained
rather high and in fact increased. Some of the highlights and
important recent donations are cited below.

In December 1971, Premier Stanko Todorov led a delegation to
Hanoi that signed an agreement on free military aid for North
Vietnam in 1972. The amount, however, was not disclosed.[15] This
agreement was a continuation of military aid that had been given
since 1967; it may have represented an increase in arms help by the

TABLE 4.2   Communist Military Technicians in LDCs, 1978

	Total	USSR and Eastern Europe	China	Cuba
Total	51,400	12,070	680	38,650
Africa	44,655	6,575	590	37,490
North Africa	2,975	2,760		215
Algeria	1,105	1,000		15
Libya	1,950	1,750		200
Morocco	10	10		
Sub-Saharan Africa:	41,680	3,815	590	37,275
Angola	20,300	1,300		19,000
Equatorial Guinea	290	40	100	150
Ethiopia	17,900	1,400		16,500
Guinea	330	100	30	200
Guinea-Bissau	205	65		140
Mali	195	180	15	
Mozambique	1,130	230	100	800
Other	1,330	500	345	485
Latin America:	160	150		10
Guyana	10			10
Peru	150	150		
Middle East:	5,645	4,495		1,150
Iraq	1,350	1,200		150
North Yemen	155	155		
South Yemen	1,550	550		1,000
Syria	2,580	2,580		
Other	10	10		
South Asia:	940	850	90	
Afghanistan	700	700		
Bangladesh	50		50	
India	150	150		
Pakistan	40		40	

Source: CIA, Communist Aid Activities in Non-Communist Less Developed Countries 1978 (Washington, D.C., 1979), p. 4.

TABLE 4.3   Military Personnel from LDCs Trained in Communist
Countries, 1955-1978

	Total	USSR	Eastern Europe	China
Total	52,890	43,790	5,965	3,135
Africa	17,525	13,420	1,400	2,705
North Africa:	3,735	3,385	335	15
Algeria	2,260	2,045	200	15
Libya	1,330	1,265	65	
Other	145	75	70	
Sub-Saharan Africa:	13,790	10,035	1,065	2,690
Angola	60	55	5	
Benin	20	20		
Burundi	75	75		
Cameroon	125			125
Congo	855	355	85	415
Equatorial Guinea	200	200		
Ethiopia	1,640	1,190	450	
Ghana	180	180		
Guinea	1,290	870	60	360
Guinea-Bissau	100	100		
Mali	415	355	10	50
Nigeria	730	695	35	
Sierra Leone	150			150
Somalia	2,585	2,395	160	30
Sudan	550	330	20	200
Tanzania	2,855	1,820	10	1,025
Togo	55			55
Zaire	175			175
Zambia	130	85		45
Other	1,600	1,310	230	60
East Asia:	9,300	7,590	1,710	
Indonesia	9,270	7,560	1,710	
Kampuchea	30	30		
Latin America:	725	725		
Peru	725	725		

Table 4.3 (Continued)

	Total	USSR	Eastern Europe	China
Middle East:	18,115	15,630	2,485	
Egypt	6,250	5,665		
Iran	315	315		
Iraq	4,330	3,650	680	
North Yemen	1,180	1,180		
South Yemen	1,095	1,075	20	
Syria	4,945	3,745	1,200	
South Asia:	7,225	6,425	370	430
Afghanistan	4,010	3,725	285	
Bangladesh	485	445		40
India	2,285	2,200	85	
Pakistan	430	45	na	385
Sri Lanka	15	10		5

Source: CIA, Communist Aid Activities in Non-Communist Less Developed Counries 1978 (Washington, D.C., 1979), p. 5. In addition, the Eastern European states extended $9,086 million in economic credits and grants to the developing countries in the period 1954-1978 (ibid, p. 7).

Bulgarian government. To what extent this was done at the behest of the Soviet Union is uncertain. In any case the agreement also included economic assistance, part of which may have been military assistance in disguise.[16]

Further information on the extent of Bulgarian military and economic assistance to North Vietnam (since 1975, Vietnam) was provided during the visit of a Vietnamese delegation to Sofia and other Bulgarian cities in October 1975. In a speech at the reception following the signing of yet another agreement on economic intercourse, Todor Zhivkov, head of the Bulgarian Communist Party, revealed that in 1975, 2,000 Vietnamese technicians were receiving training in various Bulgarian plants. It was projected that this figure would rise to 5,000 by 1980. At the same time, 700 students from Vietnam were in Bulgaria. Although no details were provided as to the number who might be engaged in military training, it seems likely that at least some did, in fact, engage in such pursuits.[17]

Bulgaria has also been involved elsewhere in the military assistance game. A curious case of Bulgarian involvement as middleman for Soviet arms transfers developed in late 1975, when French periodicals charged that the Bulgarian firm KINTEX had been instrumental in transshipping Soviet T-54 tanks to Chile. Despite Soviet and Bulgarian denials, it appears clear that this transaction did in fact take place.[18]

In addition to these activities, Bulgaria has delivered small amounts of arms and advisers to a number of other countries in the Third World, such as Lebanon, Libya, Turkey, Yemen (both North and South), and Sudan. However, the size of the shipments and the number of advisers are not known.[19] Other Bulgarian activities in the Third World involving some form of military assistance include pledges of support for Ethiopia (no details of the size of this aid are known);[20] for Angola, which was visited by Todor Zhivkov in the fall of 1978; and for Robert Mugabe's Patriotic Front of the People of Zimbzbwe. It appears that some form of promise was given at the same time to Mozambique and South Yemen. Recent Bulgarian involvement in Mozambique appears to be somewhat more extensive than in the other Third World countries. In the fall of 1978 a clause on military cooperation between Bulgaria and Mozambique was inserted in a treaty of friendship signed between the two states.[21]

One of the main target states of Bulgarian military assistance in the Third World is Libya, partly because Sofia is acting as Moscow's proxy in this crucial country and partly because of growing needs in the Bulgarian economy for imported oil. One of the results of this involvement is a fairly large Bulgarian community in Libya, which in 1980 numbered approximately 3,000. Most of these are medical personel, but some have been engaged in military-related activities.[22]

Due to political developments in the People's Democratic Republic of Yemen, Bulgarian activities there picked up considerably during the latter part of the 1970s. Military delegations visited Sofia in 1971, 1976, and 1978 and in the spring of 1980 the Bulgarian defense minister paid an official visit to the People's Democratic Republic.[23] This high level of activity in a key area is consistent with reports on Soviet, East German, and other communist involvement there. Again the Bulgarian surrogate role seems to be confirmed.

In addition to Bulgarian support for various states in the Third World, Sofia has also been rather active in providing various forms of military assistance to a sizable number of liberation movements, particularly in Africa. Little is known about the size of these commitments, but they have been openly acknowledged by the Bulgarians. Included in this list are the MPLA in Angola, SWAPO in Namibia, and the Patriotic Front of the People of Zimbabwe. In fact, in the case of Zimbabwe, Sofia supported both Robert Mugabe and Joshua Nkomo. Bulgaria's military assistance treaty with Mozambique, mentioned above, merely formalized relations that had been established long before Mozambican independence.[24] Good relations exist with the PLO, whose leaders have repeatedly thanked Bulgaria for its material assistance.[25]

82

Czechoslovakia

Czechoslovakia has always been an active participant in the international arms trade. (The enormous Skoda works were known as one of the primary producers of weapons in the world in the 1920s and 1930s.) When, in the immediate post-Stalin era the Soviet leadership decided to try to gain a foothold in the Third World, Czech weapons figured very prominently as a source of influence. Various accounts of the weaponry used by Third World guerrilla units show that Czech arms constitute an important part of the arsenal of such groups. But details regarding the scope and size of the Czechoslovak involvement are hard to find, and the researcher must once again attempt to piece together a coherent picture from a variety of isolated accounts.

Czechoslovakia has maintained many links with the states of the Third World. As early as 1959 Czechs were training Egyptian military cadets. In 1967, an agreement on military cooperation was signed between the two governments. At the time Czechoslovakia openly admitted that Egyptian fighter pilots received training in Czechoslovakia.[26] In early 1973, high Czech officials visited Iraq, Syria, and Lebanon; agreements about various forms of economic and technical assistance were signed during these visits. It has since been rumored that Czech arms have become an important part of the Syrian and Iraqi arsenals.[27]

The many rumors of extensive Czechoslovak exports of arms are not without foundation. Radio Free Europe Research in 1975 published a report on this activity, quoting John K. Cooley of the Christian Science Monitor as saying that Czechoslovakia could be ranked sixth among all the world's exporters, immediately behind France. The same Radio Free Europe report cited Czechoslovak offers to sell arms in Latin America. Other reports have documented such sales to the People's Democratic Republic of Yemen, Biafra, Cyprus, Egypt, Ethiopia, Ghana, Indonesia, Iraqi Kurds, the Irish Republican Army (IRA), Morocco, Nigeria, Sudan, Syria, Uganda, Zaire, Thai insurgents, North Korea, North Vietnam, and Cuba. Czechoslovakia in several cases has supplied arms to both sides in a conflict, for example, the Nigerian government and Biafra, and the Ethiopian government and the Eritrean rebels. There is also evidence of the use of Czechoslovak arms by Japanese and West German terrorists.[28] Finally, the PLO has repeatedly received Czech assistance.[29]

Evidence of Czechoslovak arms assistance to Third World countries can be found elsewhere. For example, when Syrian President Hafez Assad visited Prague in September 1975, he was effusive in his thanks for shipments of Czechoslovak arms.[30] In July 1977, a delegation representing the Ethiopian government visited Prague to discuss economic and technical cooperation; "technical assistance" apparently included arms.[31] A similar interpretation seems fair for the visit by the Czech foreign minister to Libya in December 1977, a visit that had been preceded by many trips between Tripoli and Prague in the 1970s.[32] Similarly, the Czech foreign minister's tour to Ethiopia, Mozambique, and Zambia in the spring of 1979 included talks on arms transfers. According to earlier reports, Czechoslovakia had provided T-55 tanks, armored personnel carriers, artillery, and small arms to Ethiopia and had even provided support units in actual combat against the Eritrean secessionists. This arms assistance continued and perhaps increased after the 1979 visit.

In the same manner, recent Czechoslovak visits to Southeast Asia seemed designed to maintain the close relationships that were forged with the delivery of Czech arms to North Vietnam, the Khmer Rouge, and the Laotian insurgents during the Vietnam War. In early 1980 President Gustav Husak visited Vietnam, Laos, and Kampuchea. Technical aid, including arms aid, was once again on the agenda, although details were unavailable.[33]

The German Democratic Republic

The German Democratic Republic became during the 1970s one of the most important supporters of Soviet foreign policy in the Third World. During this period, the GDR emerged as a provider of sophisticated technology to "target states" that were considered likely to respond favorably to Moscow's Third World political-military offensive. Thus, the East Germans supplied large numbers of technical, medical, and administrative personnel to the newly established states of the world, particularly in Africa, and substantial economic and technical aid as well. All in all, the GDR has emerged as one of the most active Eastern European states in providing arms to the developing countries. It has been said that the Soviet Union, the GDR, and Cuba have emerged as a "tripod" in Moscow's Third World offensive. The Soviets provide most of the arms, the transportation facilities, and strategic clout; the Cubans provide the necessary manpower; and the East Germans supply the highly sophisticated technical and administrative expertise so desperately needed in the emerging states.[34] This is indeed a potent combination.

Elsewhere East Germany has been a direct purveyor of arms assistance. During the Vietnam War, Pankow was a significant supplier of arms to North Vietnam. In the second half of the 1970s considerable attention was given to East German arms involvement in Latin America. Arms assistance went to Cuba and also to Nicaragua and El Salvador. This pattern continued throughout most of 1982.

It is in Africa, however, that the GDR has been most heavily involved. Reports of this involvement vary, with one Western source estimating there were 3,000 East German military personnel in Africa in 1978. Another source claimed there were at least 15,000 East German military personnel in African states in 1979. Other sources put the figure at between a few hundred and ten thousand. Observers agree that the states in which the GDR is most heavily involved are Ethiopia, Congo, Angola, and Mozambique.[35] In addition, a substantial East German military advisory presence exists in Zambia, Algeria, and Libya. Reports indicated that the East Germans have been active in Egypt as well, engaged primarily in the training of the security police although this aid ended in the 1970s.[36] Finally, East German advisers have been reported at work in the People's Democratic Republic of Yemen.[37]

The East German involvement in the Third World is substantial, but the provision of arms does not appear to be as large as that by some other Eastern European nations. The GDR's primary emphasis is on the training of technical, administrative, and medical personnel, as well as the training (but not equipping) of military cadres. How many individuals are involved principally in military education cannot be established from existing sources. During the 1970s, at least 49,000 students from developing countries attended East German institutions of higher learning, and 55,000 to 60,000 individuals were trained in their own countries by almost 20,000 East German specialists in various fields. Hundreds, perhaps thousands, of students from Angola, Mozambique, Ethiopia, and Guinea-Bissau received military or paramilitary training from East German police specialists.[38]

The GDR thus maintains cordial and important ties with a number of states in the Third World. The East Germans also have a long tradition of supporting various national liberation movements there. The GDR supported the Front for the Liberation of Mozambique (FRELIMO) guerrillas in Mozambique prior to independence. A similar relationship existed with the MPLA in Angola. In early 1977, Joshua Nkomo, representing ZAPU, visited East Berlin. A SWAPO delegation visited the GDR in December 1977. The African National Congress sent a delegation to East Berlin in May 1978. In all three cases, official representation for these movements was established in East Berlin after the visit.[39] Another liberation movement with East German conections was the Katangan rebels who invaded Zaire's Shaba province in 1977. East German training of Libyan terrorist squads has likewise been reported by a variety of sources.[40] East German aid to the Sandinistas in Nicaragua and the rebels in El Salvador has been established, although the size and scope of the aid cannot be accurately determined.[41] Finally, the GDR has long had friendly relations with the PLO; there is a PLO office in East Berlin.[42]

Hungary

Compared to Bulgaria, Czechoslovakia, and East Germany, Hungary has maintained a rather low profile in the field of military assistance to Third World nations. In early 1972 a high-level Hungarian delegation to North Vietnam formally announced continued arms aid free of charge to Hanoi, aid that had been provided for several years prior to the visit.[43] Hungary was also able to render other assistance to North Vietnam through its participation in the Vietnam Supervisory Force, which was charged with the task of supervising the truce between North and South Vietnam after the Paris Accords.[44] A North Vietnamese delegation in Budapest in the summer of 1973 received pledges of continued "fraternal aid," which almost certainly included arms.[45]

As in the case of Germany, however, the most conspicuous Hungarian activity has been in Africa. In early 1978, the Hungarian foreign minister visited six states (Ethiopia, Angola, Mozambique, Congo, Tanzania, and Nigeria) and pledged extended "material aid" to all of them. Hungary's relationship with Mozambique seemed to involve the most military cooperation.[46] In the fall of 1980, high Hungarian officials visited Ethiopia, Tanzania, Mozambique, and Zambia. This visit was not accompanied by any new announcements of aid but rather underscored the fact that a substantial number of African students and other personnel trained in Hungary or were trained in their home countries by Hungarian personnel.

Hungarian support for the PLO is also strong and has been manifested in various visits and other ties. PLO statements about Hungarian "material assistance" indicate some arms assistance, although details have not been made available.[47]

Poland

Poland's interest in the Third World is substantial, although it focuses more on commercial relations than on arms assistance. Warsaw's involvement in Vietnam, at least in terms of arms transfers to that country, apparently came to an end after the unification.

In the early 1970s Warsaw may have been involved in helping Salvador Allende's leftist government in Chile with arms. Such aid, however, it was given, would not signify a larger or more widespread Polish commitment in military assistance to Western Hemisphere nations. Rather, it may have been related to a desire by Poland for more extensive economic relations with various parts of the Third World during the 1970s, including Latin America.

In terms of military assistance, Africa became the most important area of Polish activity during the 1970s. Poland augmented its ties to Algeria, which date back to the years of the Algerian independence struggle when unspecified amounts of aid, including arms, flowed from Poland to the insurgents. Polish ties to the Marxist regimes of Angola and Mozambique were enhanced, and economic aid to these states was given in part as a cover for military aid. Or, at least, aid relieved pressing economic needs so that other funds could be released for the purchase of military material elsewhere.[51] Polish support for the various liberation movements in Africa, such as SWAPO and ZAPU, was similar to support provided by other Eastern European nations. Training of political and administrative cadres from a variety of African states and movements probably included some military education. Similarly, numerous Polish specialists working in Africa (and elsewhere in the Third World) were enaged in some tasks that can only be classified as quasi-military.[52] Such activities were carried out in Ethiopia, Angola, and Mozambique. Of particular importance was Ethiopia, which received many Polish experts. Several important military delegations from Ethiopia also visited Poland and met with Polish officers.[53]

Even though the scope and size of these exchanges of personnel are difficult to gauge, official Polish sources have published figures that give some indication of Warsaw's commitment to Africa, and particularly to Black Africa. In 1960-1961, 740 undergraduates and 119 graduates from Black African states studied in Poland; in 1965-1966, 1,364 undergraduates and 110 graduates; in 1970-1971, 2,576 and 248 respectively; in 1975-1976, 2,438 and 439; and in 1976-1977, 2,472 and 428. The heaviest commitments were made to Sudan, Nigeria, Ghana, Ethiopia, Guinea, and Kenya, in that order.[54] These figures reveal an interesting mix of possible Polish motives. An educational commitment to Nigeria and Kenya was meaningful in economic terms, especially in the case of oil-rich Nigeria. Sudan, Ghana, Ethiopia, and Guinea, on the other hand, have much less to offer economically, although these states were led by leftist regimes friendly to the Soviet Union and the "loyalists" of Eastern Europe. Many of the students from these states probably received some form of military training in Poland.[55]

Romania

Romania's policy in Africa, Asia, and Latin America varies somewhat from that of most of the other states of Eastern Europe. Differences are attributable mainly to the fact that the Romanians have refused to follow policies that, in essence, support the designs of the Soviet Union in the Third World. They also stem from the Romanian quest for an autonomous policy in the developing countries, a policy that is designed to enhance the fortunes of "progressive forces" as well as the interests of Romania itself. At time, therefore, Nicolae Ceausescu and his colleagues have taken positions that differ rather sharply from those promoted by the Soviet Union and its faithful agents. Nevertheless, it should also be noted that the Ceausescu regime shares certain fundamental ideological views with the Kremlin. Insofar as the Romanian leaders attempt to implement such ideological preferences, then, there is a certain congruence between the goals of Bucharest and those of Moscow.

The activist nature of Romanian policy in the Third World is a phenomenon of the Ceausescu era, and particularly of the 1970s. During this period, Romania attempted to find new markets for its expanding industries (which are largely noncompetitive in Western markets) while enhancing its supply of vital raw materials, particularly oil. At the same time, Ceausescu saw himself as a spokesman for the "progressive forces" of the world, a protector of and advocate for the rights of small and medium-sized states in a world dominated by superpowers, and a true representative of the developing countries.[56] All this has led to a level of political and economic activity in the Third World unsurpassed by any of the other East European states, including weapons aid, training of military cadres in Romania and in the host country, and granting of fairly large credits for the purchase of various forms of goods, including military hardware.

Romania's activities in the military field have been particularly prominent in Asia and Africa. In Latin America, the Romanian involvement is primarily economic and occasionally political, as was the case in Chile during the Allende regime. There were unconfirmed rumors that Romania granted some military aid to Chile in this period.[57] Bucharest has been involved in Asia, primarily in Vietnam, but also in Laos and Kampuchea. Both Ceausescu and various Vietnamese leaders have repeatedly emphasized the importance of Romanian military aid during the Vietnam War.[58] Evidence on aid to the Khmer Rouge and the leftist forces in Laos is considerably more indirect and circumspect, but there are enough hints to warrant the conclusion that Romania's arms aid to them was also important.[59]

Elsewhere in Asia, there is no concrete evidence of active military assistance by Romania in the period under consideration, with the exception of a rather lively military relationship with the People's Republic of China -- a subject that is not under consideration here.

Africa became the major area of Romanian military involvement during the 1970s. Bucharest exchanged military delegations with Egypt, Angola, Congo, Ghana, Guinea, Mozambique, Zambia, and Zaire. Representatives of the police and security apparatus of the Central African Empire, Togo, Zambia, and Guinea also visited Romania or hosted their functional counterparts from Bucharest.[60] Weapons have been shipped to Egypt, Angola, Namibia, Rhodesia, and Mozambique. Reports that Romanian officers have been training tank crews in the latter country in the use of Soviet-made T-34 and T-54 tanks are particularly worthy of note.[61] There is also some evidence to support the contention that Romania has helped arm Zambia.[62]

The military aid supplied to several states in Africa often began as assistance for liberation movements there. Thus, early on, Romania supplied arms aid to ZAPU and ZANU in Zimbabwe-Rhodesia and to all three of the liberation movements in Angola, as well as FRELIMO in Mozambizue and SWAPO in Namibia. The commitment to the latter organization in fact appears to be increasing.[63]

Romania is also heavily committed to the training of a number of Third World cadres in various fields. There are now thousands of Third World students in Romania, a portion of them military and security personnel. Similarly, several thousand Romanian experts are enaged in fieldwork in the Third World. Once again, no definite evidence exists as to the number of these who can be classified as military and security personnel. But given the size and scope of the Romanian commitment in this field, such personnel must be fairly numerous.[64]

Yugoslavia

Yugoslavia was one of the founding members of the nonaligned movement and as such has had a great deal of influence in the Third World -- a position that may have been somewhat eroded since Tito's death due to attempts by Cuba to steer the movement in a more radical and pro-Soviet directon. Yugoslavia nevertheless remains a major actor in Third World politics.

Yugoslav policies have certain similarities with those implemented by the Romanians. The Yugoslavs have attempted to maintain their own position in the Third World, to enhance the political and military fortunes of "progressive elements," and to limit the influence of the major powers, including the Soviet Union. In this process, Yugoslav leaders have attempted to find profitable markets for their industrial goods while securing a steady source of fuels and raw materials from the developing countries.

Yugoslav military aid has generally focused on the same areas and states as other Eastern European efforts in the Third World, including sub-Saharan Africa, the Middle East, and during the first half of the 1970s, North Vietnam. In 1971, a number of leaders from the various Angolan liberation movements met with Yugoslav military officials; these meetings were followed by arms deliveries.[65] During the same year, the Sudanese defense minister visited Yugoslavia, and his Yugoslav counterpart toured several African states to discuss the possibility of arms delivery, the provision of expertise, and the training of military cadres, both in Yugoslavia and in Africa.[66] In 1973, Yugoslavia, having delivered small amounts of light arms to Egypt earlier, stepped up sales and delivery to this pivotal Middle Eastern state.[67] In the same year Belgrade held talks with Libyan leaders concerning the training of Libyan forces, but implementation of such agreements has been slow.[68]

Yugoslavia has also been a staunch supporter of various liberation movements in Rhodesia (Zimbabwe), Angola, Mozambique, and Namibia. Belgrade supported the PLO very consistently during the 1970s, and Yassir Arafat visited Yugoslavia on several occasions during the decade.[70]

Few details are known about the kind of equipment delivered by Yugoslavia. Indonesia has bought some Yugoslav artillery pieces.[71] In Libya, the Yugoslavs have established some small plants manufacturing light arms.[72] The Sudanese navy is equipped with Yugoslav-made boats and ships.[73] And a variety of weapons made in Yugoslavia or transshipped through that country have ended up in many African states, albeit in small numbers. Belgrade, therefore, has been a rather active element in the arming of Africa.

The Belgrade leadership has also been rather generous in its support of Third World educational efforts. Thousands of students from developing countries can be found in Yugoslav universities, and there are many Yugoslav experts working "in the field" in the Third World. Yugoslav economic assistance, which takes the form of loans, grants, and joint ventures, is also considerable.

CONCLUSION

The evidence presented above indicates a multifaceted Eastern European involvement in the Third World, with a fairly substantial military element as part of that involvement. As a supplement to the Soviet and Cuban military presence in the Third World, the efforts of the German Democratic Republic, Poland, Czechoslovakia, Hungary, and Bulgaria are most important. The GDR has become the chief auxiliary of the Soviet Union in many areas, particularly in Africa, and Czechoslovakia also acts as one of the most important arms suppliers in a burgeoning market. By comparison, Polish, Hungarian, and Bulgarian activities in the Third World are of lesser magnitude, but they nevertheless represent elements in a well-coordinated policy of expansion in areas that have hitherto been relatively immune from communist influence. The Soviet Union and its faithful agents are clearly major contenders in the struggle now under way for predominant influence in the vast, resource-rich, and populous countries of the Third World.

Romania and Yugoslavia, on the other hand, have maintained independent policies in the Third World. At times, these policies have run counter to the interests of the Soviet Union, either by accident or by design. But more often than not, the policies of these two states have corresponded, at least in part, to the needs and preferences of the Kremlin in the developing countries — a fact that should not be forgotten by Western policymakers.

This complementarity of needs and preferences can be seen in a number of areas. First, both Romania and Yugoslavia remain dedicated to the lessening of Western and "capitalist" influence in the Third World (even though both Bucharest and Belgrade would prefer to limit the influence of the Kremlin as well). Policies that reduce Western influence in strategic and resource-rich areas are beneficial to the USSR, even if they are not so intended.

Second, Romanian and Yugoslavian policies are designed to help overthrow certain existing regimes in the Third World while promoting leftist, sometimes violently anti-Western liberation movements. At some point, it is clear that the United States and its allies must face the reality of dealing with such movements, as neither the resources nor the inclination is available locally to suppress them. Such a task is not made easier by the policies of ideologues such as Ceausescu, who has on occasion advocated a military solution when the local rebels preferred negotiations.

Third, the leaders of Romania and Yugoslavia have maintained strong ties with established leftist regimes that are self-proclaimed adversaries of the West. A particularly relevant example here is the close relationship with Libya that has been cultivated by Bucharest and Belgrade. Such relationships are certainly maintained for economic reasons as well as ideological ones. But it is clear that these ties have helped foster the kind of militant policy that now characterizes Qaddafi's Libya. Tripoli today is one of the main arsenals for radical movements as well as terrorist organizations. The West faced major challenges in the Thid World during the 1970s, and part of this challenge stemmed from the willingness of the Eastern Europeans to transfer arms, related services, and necessary expertise to many of the volatile states and regimes in the developing world.

The challenge represented by Eastern European military activities in the Third World is likely to become even more dangerous during the 1980s, as it is honed and becomes more sophisticated. In the past, communist-sponsored revolutions often faded into insignificance once the battle for power was won and the struggle for political and socioeconomic performance started. The communists and their favorite liberation movements, it was said, were good at winning revolutions, but notoriously poor at maintaining themselves afterward. Hence the dramatic swings in Soviet influence in Black Africa in the 1960s and the willingness, indeed eagerness, of the Angolan leadership to do business with the West.

One of the primary reasons for this admitted deficiency was the Soviet and Eastern European penchant for shipping weapons and training soldiers for the liberation struggle without sufficient regard for the needs of the economy and the administrative structures that had to perform after liberation. This pattern is changing. Eastern European nations as a whole now expend a great deal of money and energy on the needs of the fledgling political, economic, and administrative systems that emerge from the military struggles of national liberation. This approach is designed to provide the new regimes with staying power and the ability to deal intelligently with the needs of new states in which virtually all human resources are in short supply. The provision of such expertise, backed by the proven ability of the Soviets and the Eastern Europeans to provide arms and related services, will make much of the Third World a battlefield for influence in which the West must become forcefully engaged.

NOTES

1.   Charles Gati, "From Cold War Origins to Detente," in Charles Gati (ed.), The International Politics of Eastern Europe (New York: Praeger Publishers, 1976), Chapter 1.

2.   See Trond Gilberg, Modernization in Romania Since World War II (New York: Praeger Publishers, 1975), Chapter 1.

3.   For a discussion of Soviet policies in the Third World and the perceptions of such policies among Third World leaders, see Elizabeth Kridl Valkenier, "The USSR, the Third World, and the Global Economy," Problems of Communism, Vol. 28, (July-August 1979), pp. 17-34.

4.   See Andrew Gyorgy, "Ostpolitik and Eastern Europe," in Gati, International Politics of Eastern Europe, Chapter 8.

5.   This choice was avidly pursued by all the Eastern European states during the 1970s.   One of the most active was Romania.   The phases of Romanian policy in the Third World and elsewhere were set forth in a variety of documents, e.g., Documente ale Partidului Comunist Roman: Politica externa a Romania socialiste (Romanian Communist Party Documents: The Foreign Policy of Socialist Romania.) (Bucharest: Editura Politica, 1972), pp. 13-29.

6.   This summary has been derived from a number of sources, e.g., the press of the Eastern European states, Radio Free Europe Research, and the Yearbook on International Communist Affairs.

7.   The foreign policy activity of Albania in recent years has been discussed by Louis Zanga in "Increased Number of Albanian Official Delegations Abroad," Radio Free Europe Research, RAD Background Report/242 (Albania), 9 October 1980.

8.   A rather outspoken discussion of some of the motivations behind Romanian foreign policy can be found in Silviu Brucan, Democratizaria relatiilor internationale: Premise se realitati (Bucharest: Editura Politica, 1975).

9.   Yugoslav policies in the Third World have been discussed many times in the news media of that country; for a recent exposition, which also deals with the Cuban challenge to the Yugoslav position in the nonaligned movement, see the weekly Nin (Belgrade), June 17, 1979.

10.   See Note 6 for specific references.

11.   For an excellent analysis of Bulgaria's activities in Black Africa, see "Bulgaria's Presence in Black Africa," Radio Free Europe Research, RAD Background Report/92 (Bulgaria), 20 April 1979.

12.   Some of these activities have clearly had a considerable impact in Africa. See, for example, the statement by Robert Mugabe thanking Romania for its assistance in the struggle for liberation in Rhodesia-Zimbabwe (Scinteia, September 17, 1980).

13.   Central Intelligence Agency, National Foreign Assessment Center, Communist Aid Activities in Non-Communist Less Developed Countries 1978 (Washington, D.C., 1979), pp. iii-iv, 1-2.

14.   Stockholm International Peace Research Institute, World Armaments and Disarmament. SIPRI Yearbook 1981, (New York: Crane, Russack, and Co., 1981) p. 10.

15.   Radio Free Europe Research, Bulgaria/1, 3 January 1972.

16.   The speeches made during Todorov's visit clearly showed such a military conection; see ibid.

17.   The joint communique that emanated from the meeting also discussed the close relationships between the two states; see Rabotnicheska Delo, October 16, 1975.

18.   Radio Free Europe Research, Bulgaria/31, 6 November 1975.

19.   Ibid.

20.   Such aid was pledged by Bulgarian party leader Todor Zhivkov on his visit to Ethiopia in October 1978; see Rabotnicheska Delo, October 29, 1978.

21.   Zhivkov's visit to Angola resulted in a Treaty of Friendship and Cooperation with that country; see ibid., October 22 and 25, 1978. The talks between Zhivkov and Mugabe were reported in ibid, October 29, 1978. The treaty with Mozambique also included a clause on military cooperation. This treaty was published in ibid., October 25, 1978.

22.   The Bulgarian news agency BTA reported this during a visit by Todor Zhivkov to Libya in March 1980. See also Radio Free Europe Research, Bulgaria/4, 26 March 1980.

23.   Ibid., Bulgaria/5, 18 April 1980.

24.   Bulgarian aid to the MPLA was officially acknowledged several times, e.g., Rabotnicheska Delo, October 14, 1976, and October 21, 1978.

25.   One recent meeting between Yassir Arafat and Zhivkov took place in Damascus in April 1980; see ibid., April 27, 1980.

26.   Tvorba, September 21, 1967.

27.   This visit was reported in Radio Free Europe Research, Czechoslovakia/7, February 14, 1973.

28.   Ibid., April 16, 1975.

29.   A strong statement of support for the PLO can be found in a speech by Prime Minister Lubomir Strougal during a visit by President Hafez Assad of Syria to Czechoslovakia in September 1975; see Rude Pravo, September 8, 1975.

30.   Ibid., September 9, 1975.

31.   A fairly detailed account of the economic agreements established during the meeting was published in Svet Hospodarstvi, August 9, 1977.

32.   For a discussion of the visit, see Radio Free Europe Research, Czechoslovakia/44, December 15, 1977.

33.   Rude Pravo, February 16, 1980, published a statement issued by the Czechoslovaks and the Vietnamese discussing such assistance.

34.   For details, see Woodrow Kuhns, "The German Democratic Republic in Africa," unpublished seminar paper, Pensylvania State University, Department of Political Science, Spring 1981.

35.   Ibid., especially pp. 9-11.

36.   Der Spiegel, March 2, 1980.

37.   Ibid.

38.   Ibid.

39.   The relations with the MPLA and FRELIMO have been discussed by Klaus Willerding in Deutsche Aussenpolitik, August 1979, pp. 5-19. Relations with SWAPO are discussed in Kuhns, "German Democratic Republic in Africa," pp. 15-16.

40.   Der Spiegel, March 2, 1980.

41.   The Reagan administration has repeatedly charged such involvement, but no figures have been published.

42.   For a thorough discussion of East German policy in the Middle East, see The New York Times, December 27, 1977.

43.   The visit was discussed in Nepszabadsag, February 9, 1972.

44.   Hungary's role in the force has been discussed in Radio Free Europe Research, Huungary/4, January 30, 1973.

45.   Ibid., July 24, 1973.

46.   See Magyar Hirlap, January 11, 1978.

47.   The Hungarian delegation's visit in Africa was reported in ibid., September 12, 1980, and in various other publications, e.g., Magyar Nemzet, September 25, 1980. As for material assistance to the PLO, it seems likely that this takes the form primarily of financial grants that are used to buy Soviet or Czechoslovak arms, as the Hungarian arms industry is negligible.

48.   Trybuna Ludu, January 29, 1972.

49.   Ibid., February 8, 1973.

50.   Ibid., November 13, 1975.

51.   In late 1978, for example, the Polish Workers' Party (PUWP) and the MPLA of Angola agreed to engage in cooperative relations, which involved the training of MPLA cadres in various fields (ibid., December 5, 1978).

52.   Support for the various liberation movements has been forcefully voiced in ibid., e.g., May 27 and 28 and November 21, 1978. A Radio Free Europe article estimates the number of Polish specialists in Black Africa at only 800 to 1,000 (Radio Free Europe Research, RAD Background Report/50 (Poland), March 1, 1979).

53.   Such visits took place in March 1977 and December 1978; see ibid.

54.   Calculated by the author from figures in Rocznik Statystyczny 1977, 1977.

55.   Poland most probably follows the general Eastern European tendency here. Furthermore, Polish experts may be active in some countries that utilize Eastern European military equipment, such as Uganda. For a discussion of this use, see John Keegan, World Armies (New York: Facts on File, 1979), p. 728.

56.   This attitude is demonstrated in virtually all the General Secretary's foreign policy statements. See, for example his speeches and statements concerning Romania as a developing country, e.g., interview in Le Monde, July 24, 1975.

57.   The strong Romanian ties with Allende's Chile were revealed in Bucharest's reaction to the coup there. See, for example, Agerpres, September 13, 1973.

58.   E.g., statement by Le Duan, first secretary of the North Vietnamese Communist party, in Bucharest; see Scinteia, November 18, 1975. A joint Romanian-North Vietnamese declaration, which stressed the same point, was published in ibid., November 19, 1975.

59.   Romanian-Kampuchean relations are discussed in Radio Free Europe Research, Romania/17, September 14, 1979.

60.   Ibid., May 23, 1979.

61.   Ibid.

62.   Ibid.

63.   President Kaunda of Zambia referred to a stepped-up role for Romania in the struggle for Namibian independence through SWAPO; see Scinteia, September 17, 1980; and broadcast by Radio Bucharest, September 16, 1980. See also Radio Free Europe Research, Romania/16, November 13, 1980.

64.   Nicolae Ceausescu himself detailed Romanian military aid to Africa in a speech to the Central Committee of the Romanian Communist party (PCR); see Scinteia, August 4, 1978.

65.   Richard F. Haan (ed.), Yearbook on International Communist Affairs 1972 (Stanford, Calif.: Hoover Institution Press, 1972), p. 114.

66.   Ibid.

67.   Yearbook on International Communist Affairs 1973, p. 106.

68.   The New York Times, November 19, 1973.

69.   The visit was mentioned in Yearbook on International Communist Affairs 1976, p. 105.

70.   E.g., a visit in 1976, reported in The New York Times, December 6, 1976.

71.   John Keegan, World Armies, p.. 323.

72.   Ibid., p. 446.

73.   Ibid., p. 658.

5
China's Military Assistance

John F. Copper

According to the official monetary value of its arms aid to Third World countries, China ranks somewhere below fourth or fifth place in the world. One U.S. government source put China's military assistance to Third World countries during 1967 to 1976 at $2.6 billion, giving China the ranking of the fifth largest arms supporter.[1] A later report of this same organization ranked China ninth in the world during the period 1974-1978.[2] Another U.S. government agency put China seventh during the period 1955 to 1979, with a ranking of eighth during the last seven years of that period.[3] According to the latter source, during 1955-1979 China's arms aid to less developed countries amounted to somewhat more than one-fourth of that of Eastern European countries, about one-fortieth that of the Soviet Union, and one-seventieth that of the United States.

These figures, however, understate the level of China's military assistance. First, using the designation "Third World" excludes much of China's assistance, inasmuch as a large portion of China's arms has gone to Second World countries, namely North Korea and North Vietnam. As will be seen below, for a number of years China's military help to these two countries was quite substantial. Inasmuch as Beijing is no longer aiding Vietnam, the reports on its military assistance to exclusively Third World countries are now at least more representative. Moreover, China's arms assistance has declined during the 1970s and 1980s, while many of its competitors -- especially the Soviet Union -- have increased their arms aid to other nations. On the other hand, China's military assistance is also underestimated because much of it has gone unreported, and most of it has been undervalued or has no price tag attached. And this remains true.

In one case, China must be given credit for supporting with military assistance two major wars -- in Korea and in Indochina. In the case of Korea, China's military assistance in the form of both weapons and "volunteers" virtually ensured North Korea's survival. Its aid to Hanoi during the Vietnam War was in large part responsible for the U.S. decision to end its involvement and suffer what many regard as its first defeat in war. This decision was followed by a decline of U.S. global influence, and according to some observers, a change in the structure of international politics from bipolarity to multipolarity. Although some would point out that the Soviet Union provided the arms assistance that led to the final victory for Hanoi, Chinese military assistance must still be seen as vital throughout most of the war. Clearly, without it the course of events, both in Southeast Asia and for the United States, would have been different.

China has similarly given sizable numbers of weapons to a number of friendly Third World nations that are generally unreported. In many cases this aid has affected relations with other countries and, almost as often, regional power balances. This support has included sophisticated weapons such as jet fighter planes, ships, submarines, tanks, and missiles. Few other nations have provided such a vast array of weapons. No other nation has done so in competition with both the United States and the Soviet Union.

China's military assistance has also had considerable influence in another realm. Beijing has given arms, supplies, and moral support to insurgency or guerrilla groups fighting "wars of national liberation" in more countries and regions of the world than any other nation. As we will see in subsequent pages, this aid has been relatively inexpensive, yet in many cases has had a major impact on political developments in the Third World. And it has been very costly for other nations to counter, especially early on for the United States and now for the Soviet Union.

China is unique as a supplier of arms aid in still another way: It is the only nation thought to have seriously offered nuclear weapons to another country. In the mid-1960s there were reports of Chinese plans to offer an atomic bomb to Indonesia. More recently it has been rumored that China has given Pakistan assistance in building a nuclear weapon.

Despite all of this, China must be seen as generally cautious in giving military assistance. There are a number of reasons for this. Chinese leaders are, in some fashion at least, opposed on principle to giving military assistance because they charge that such assistance is characteristic of "imperialism." Also Beijing generally seeks to avoid supporting right-wing governments or the military in Third World countries. Finally, Chinese leaders preach self-reliance as a trait essential to revolutionary movements and to friendly governments as well. A related and equally important factor (self-reliance may be only a rationalization) is China's lack of the capacity to give large amounts of military aid.

Besides North Korea and North Vietnam, which received arms and soldiers from China because Chinese leaders perceived a direct threat to Chinese territory, Beijing has been, or is, a major source of arms to only four other countries: Albania, Egypt, Pakistan, and Tanzania. Only Albania and Tanzania were in any real sense dependent upon China's arms assistance, and Albania clearly no longer belongs into this category. Thus Tanzania is the only nation in the world dependent upon China for arms, and its reliance on China is now diminishing.

98

A number of guerrilla or revolutionary groups have also relied upon Chinese weapons, but in most cases this has not been a permanent or lasting situation. Either the guerrillas win the struggle and come to power, in which case China must deal with them as a legitimate government, or they are defeated by the government or supplanted by competing forces. In addition, many liberation groups seek arms wherever they can get them, a factor that also limits Chinese influence.

In the following sections China's military assistance will be examined in the context of China's world view, its military capabilities, the state of its arms industry, and Beijing's global and regional military strategies. Chinese military assistance will be delineated and analyzed on three different levels: (1) arms support as it relates to China's own security needs and to proximate and threatening wars; (2) assistance to friendly or client states, usually reflecting regional objectives; and (3) support to insurgency or opposition groups that are defined as fighting "wars of national liberation." Finally, some conclusions are made which put China's military assistance in perspective and make possible some comparisons with other communist nations giving arms assistance. Here the author also makes some generalizations concerning the effectiveness and the impact of Chinese military assistance.

CHINA'S MILITARY ASSISTANCE AND ITS FOREIGN POLICY AND MILITARY STRATEGIES

The purposes of China's military assistance can be understood only in the context of examining China's world view, its foreign policy objectives and in some cases its military posture or strategy. China's world view has been influenced by both its communist ideology and by China's peculiarities in terms of its history, geography, culture, and population. It has also been influenced by China's perceived role in international politics -- which, notably, has changed markedly several times since 1949.[4]

When the Chinese Communists won control of China in 1949 they had been conditioned by more than two decades of war with enemies they defined as capitalist or supported by the forces of foreign capitalism and imperialism. Thus the new regime espoused a view of the world divided into two opposing camps: capitalism and communism. In 1949, Mao asserted that China must "lean to one side" and denied that a neutral stand was possible in a world characterized by a struggle between the forces of communism and capitalism. Thus, to Mao, the Third World referred simply to nations or people that had not yet decided; therefore, as a bloc it was not perceived as a major force in international politics.

In the mid-1950s, Mao's world view underwent a marked change. Suffering from a high degree of isolation caused both by China's attitude toward Third World leaders and by U.S. efforts after the Korean War to "contain China, Mao began to give more importance to the Third World in his global perspective. Not being able or willing to establish normal relations with pro-Western governments,

China began to direct arms assistance to communist parties and revolutionary movements in third World countries. Some assistance also went to socialist countries and even to friendly Third World governments.

By the 1960s Beijing began to give a lower priority to the struggle between communism and capitalism and placed the Third World in a special role in terms of world struggle. Reflecting this revised world view, Beijing increased its arms assistance to governments of Third World countries which were either anti-West or anti-Soviet, while continuing to aid revolutionary groups. In short, China maintained its anti-status quo stance, but began to direct its efforts against revisionism as well as capitalism.

In the 1970s China's view of the world evolved further. Beijing advanced the theory of a world made up of three camps or blocs: the first comprised of the two superpowers, the second the industrial, nonsuperpower nations, and the third the poor countries. China, of course, put itself in the latter category -- thereby justifying military assistance directed primarily toward the Third World aimed at promoting Third World unity and independence from superpower (i.e. U.S. and Soviet) influence. However, as relations with the United States improved, this "three world view" was amended or altered by giving emphasis to a "united front" doctrine which characterized the Soviet Union as the "worst" or "most dangerous" superpower and the United States as "less dangerous," having "learned a lesson" from the Vietnam War. Thus China sought to align with the United States, Japan, and Western Europe against the Soviet Union. In the process the Third World was given a less prominent role in China's global strategy.

This view still prevails in Beijing; indeed, it has been carried further. Beijing now seeks to align with the United States against the Soviet Union, even in its relations with Third World nations. Chinese leaders see most of Moscow's military assistance to the Third World in relation to the Kremlin's efforts to acquire influence and particularly basing rights abroad in order to "contain" China. Thus China's military assistance, with only a few exceptions, no longer conflicts with U.S. or Western arms aid.

In addition to its global ideological perspective, China's policies since 1949 have been conditioned by military and political realities.[5] In the 1950s the United States surrounded China with military bases and sought to "contain" Chinese expansion. China needed both military and economic aid, and there was no place to go other than to the Soviet Union. China also needed an ally to cope with the U.S. nuclear threat; again, only the Soviet Union could provide such help. Thus a Sino-Soviet alliance was signed and sealed in 1950. For a decade it played a central role in the formulation of China's foreign policy, and, of course, its decisions on military assistance.

Thus during the Korean War China provided military aid to North Korea in response to what Chinese leaders perceived to be a direct U.S. threat. Beijing, at the same time, also provided some arms to North Vietnam and to communist guerrillas in Indochina. In both regions, although Mao later boasted that Soviet aid had been repaid, China saw its efforts as working in tandem with the Soviet Union's against the West. Generally throughout the 1950s China viewed its security as augmented by its ties with Moscow, and threatened by the West. Krushchev's announcement of peaceful coexistence in 1956, Moscow's subsequent flirting with the West, the Soviet Union's weak stand toward the United States in 1958 during the second offshore island crisis, and the USSR's unwillingness in 1959 to supply China with nuclear weapons (except those the Soviet Union controlled), all eventually led to a change in China's reliance on Moscow.

In response to growing hostility toward the Kremlin, China sought to upgrade its relations with Third World countries and try to compete with the Soviet Union for influence in the poor countries of Africa, Asia, the Middle East, and Latin America. By taking a more radical stance toward colonialism and imperialism and by providing small amounts of less sophisticated arms aid, particularly to guerrilla or insurgency groups, China was able to win support among Third World leaders, especially the more radical ones. In so doing China was also able to make a bid for leadership of the Third World nations and to challenge both the United States and the Soviet Union for a leadership role in world affairs.

During the Cultural Revolution (1965 to 1969), China's stance toward the two superpowers became even more hostile and its support of Third World radical regimes even stronger. However, due to turmoil within China and a preoccupation with domestic problems, this did not translate into increased military assistance. Moreover, as relations with the Soviet Union continued to deteriorate; as conflict with the United States escalated as the Vietnam War entered a new phase in 1965; and as few tangible gains were seen from its policies of supporting insurgency groups and wars of national liberation in the Third World, Chinese leaders perceived a need for a general foreign policy shift.

Thus, after 1969, when the Chinese army fought Soviet forces over a small, uninhabited island in the Ussuri River and when the Nixon Doctrine made official the United States' policy of withdrawing militarily from Asia and no longer trying to contain China, Chinese leaders designated the Soviet Union China's primary enemy. Also influencing China to alter its foreign policy was the fact that Moscow was steadily increasing its military power -- with the purpose, in the Chinese view, of "containing China." By the late 1960s the Soviet Union had placed 20 percent of its forces and firepower on the Sino-Soviet border. And the Soviet Union was building an impressive navy which could be used to "contain" China.

Moscow also aligned militarily with China's enemies or competitors, most importantly India and later Vietnam. In Beijing's eyes, Soviet military assistance was increasingly given to China's enemies, or nations where Moscow sought to obtain bases to complete its plan to "surround and contain China," and to Third World countries and revolutionary movements where the USSR could undermine Chinese influence. In response, China established a policy of arming the enemies of the Soviet Union's allies, in addition to governments and insurgency groups in Third World countries that China perceived to be anti-Soviet. Little or no military assistance was rendered to nations or insurgency groups opposed to the United States.

The question must now be asked: What capacity does China have to render military assistance? An assessment of China's military aid strategy necessitates an examination of its military capabilities.[6] In terms of manpower China ranks first in the world, with a total of 4,750,000 in its regular forces in 1981.[7] Military manpower figures have shown a fairly steady increase in recent years -- the figures for 1975 and 1980 were 3,250,000 and 4,450,000 respectively -- until 1982, when China's military manpower was cut.[8] China's defense budget gives China the rank of third in the world, with expenditures estmated at $56.9 billion in 1980.[9] However, in contrast to manpower figures, China's military expenditures do not rank it with the superpowers. Moreover, in 1981 China cut its defense budget somewhere in the range of 12 to 20 percent.[10] And another cut was ordered in 1982.

China's nuclear weapons program is an important ingredient in its defense strategy and absorbs an estimated 10 percent of its military budget. Thus, by the mid-1970s China had become the world's third-ranking nuclear power. It now possesses two to three hundred nuclear weapons, with various kinds of missile delivery systems, including intercontinental missiles.[11] However, even though China has acquired a certain level of deterrence vis-a-vis the Soviet Union, it has shown no evidence of making its nuclear status relevant to its military aid program.

Because of unevenness in its military capabilities, China suffers from an inability to meet a wide range of contingencies between simple ground warfare and nuclear warfare. This has two immediate implications for China's military assistance program. First, as its own forces lack the equipment to make them effective fighting forces in many situations, China's military leaders understandably want the Party and government to refrain from providing large quantities of arms assistance to other countries. Second, China's lack of power projection capabilities resulting from overemphasizing guerrilla and nuclear warfare means that when Beijing provides arms assistance to other nations or revolutionary groups abroad it must do so with the knowledge that it can provide little or no direct support for its use. Even the pressure it can bring to bear because of its nuclear power status is generally limited by its vast inferiority compared at the strategic level to the United States and the Soviet Union.

The main reason for this situation, and an underlying limitation on China's ability to provide arms assistance, is the absence of a large and balanced munition industry. Prior to 1949 Mao relied primarily upon captured weapons as a source of supply. At the close of World War II the Chinese Communists obtained additional weapons from disarmed Japanese soldiers and from the Soviet Union. Similarly, the Nationalists relied upon the United States as their source of weapons and did little to start a weapons industry. Thus when Mao conquered mainland China he had almost no arms factories.[12]

After 1950 the Soviet Union helped China produce weapons. As a result, within the decade China had developed a military-industrial complex that produced arms in almost all categories, including jet fighter planes. However, when deteriorating Sino-Soviet relations reached a point of no return in 1960 and the Kremlin cut its aid to China, Beijing could not maintain its arms industries. In fact, the production of conventional weapons other than small arms was drastically curtailed. It is noteworthy that the Soviet withdrawal retarded China's fledgling arms industries more than other industries, a factor the Kremlin no doubt calculated.

During the 1964-1965 and 1969-1971 periods China's defense industries made some progress, but in both cases progress was followed by sharp declines. After the 1964-1965 period of growth, a period of decline ensued as a result of the Cultural Revolution; after the 1969-1971 growth period, priorities changed because of Defense Minister Lin Biao's demise after an alleged attempt on Mao's life.[13] The onset of the 1980s saw China's weapons industries being given a low priority due to the emphasis on economic development and consumer- and trade-oriented industries.

China's leaders now seem to be favoring importing weapons from the United States and other Western countries to offset as quickly as possible deficiencies in China's military capabilities. By doing so, however, China will forego any future hope of building a comprehensive arms industry.

As a consequence China is faced with rather serious constraints in providing sophisticated arms aid or weapons assistance in large volumes. And China has so far obtained little help from Western countries in its efforts to upgrade its weapons factories. Thus production remains based in large part upon Soviet designs transferred more than two decades ago. China has tried to improve Soviet-designed weapons, but has experienced serious problems in that effort. For example, plans to produce its own advanced jet fighter, the F-9, encountered serious difficulties in the 1960s and early 1970s, and Beijing ended up buying engines for the plane from Britain. That arrangement, however, did not prove entirely satisfactory. Thus China does not build a competitive high-performance jet fighter plane; here it even lags behind India.[14]

The basic obstacle to future progress in weapons production is China's serious weaknesses in advanced technology. Importing foreign technology may help rectify the situation, but imports cannot be expected to constitute a real solution. Moreover, there is considerable reluctance on the part of the United States and other Western countries to provide any nation, other than a formal ally, with advanced military technology. And China probably cannot allocate a greater portion of its sophisticated industrial sector to defense production; it already devotes a larger percentage of its advanced industrial production to defense than do other countries.[15]

On the other hand, compared to Third World countries and other communist countries except the Soviet Union, China possesses a network of defense industries that produce a broad spectrum of weapons. And China has on numerous occasions demonstrated the willpower to make the necessary sacrifices in order to provide even sophisticated weapons, including jet aircraft, missiles, and ships, to friendly countries, and smaller arms to many liberation movements. Thus, while China's military assistance program has limits, it is also an instrument of its foreign policy that must be reckoned with.

ARMS AID TO BORDER NATIONS FOR SECURITY REASONS

China has purveyed more military assistance to nations on or near its borders than to nations or groups in any other category. These nations include North Korea, North Vietnam, Cambodia, and Laos. Pakistan and Afghanistan might also be put in this category, but for reasons that will be evident later they are included in another grouping. Cambodia (Kampuchea) and Laos are also discussed again in the next section inasmuch as Beijing has and is now supporting anti-government guerrilla movements in these countries. In the case of arms assistance to this group of countries, especially North Korea and North Vietnam, China's motivation can be directly related to a threat or a perceived threat to China's security.

North Korea was the first nation to receive military assistance from China. The North Korean government received some arms help from Beijing prior to the Korean War, though most of China's arms aid was given during the war years. This aid was both valuable and extensive and saved North Korea from defeat by UN forces; yet it is very difficult to estimate its total cost.

China initiated a full-scale effort to help North Korea militarily in October 1950 after UN forces crossed the 38th parallel and began to march toward the Chinese border. Prior to this event China had apparently considered the Korean conflict a "national liberation struggle." The decision to enter the Korean conflict was a difficult one because of economic conditions in China and Beijing's concern to capture Taiwan, which it ultimately sacrificed due to its involvement in Korea. However, when Chinese leaders perceived a direct threat to Chinese territory China immediately sent "volunteers" -- eventually numbering two and one-half million. These volunteers were equipped in the early stages of the war (approximately the first six months) with Japanese weapons that the Chinese Communists had acquired at the end of World War II and U.S.-made weapons captured from the Nationalists.[16]

China subsequently obtained large quantities of weapons and military equipment from the Soviet Union, which it used in Korea or provided to the North Korean military. Although neither the Soviet Union nor China has provided any figures on the value of this aid, it was obviously considerable. Moreover, the conditions under which the Soviet Union provided the weapons and equipment to China are uncertain, as are the understandings between China and North Korea -- although it is generally assumed that China's arms assistance to North Korea was provided free of charge. Later Chinese publications suggest that a portion of Beijing's debt service for a number of years included payments for Soviet weapons delivered at this time and used during the Korean War.[17] Soviet writers, on the other hand, have argued that only 20 percent of the credits the USSR granted to China for military purchases were repaid and that half the arms provided to China at this time were not used in the war.[18]

If one accepts the thesis that the North Korean invasion of the South was provoked by the Kremlin, with little or no Chinese input and perhaps without Chinese knowledge, the Soviet Union does not appear very generous. On the other hand, while some have opined that Stalin may have asked or even ordered the Chinese to enter the war, it seems just as likely that the Chinese decision to make a large commitment of forces to the war effort was China's own and may even have been opposed by the Soviet Union. Thus different conclusions regarding Chinese generosity and motives are possible.[19]

In any event, the costs of involvement were extremely high for China. China suffered casualties totaling possibly one million.[20] Its losses were significant enough to raise questions about Chinese military tactics, about the need for better weapons, and even about Mao's wisdom in entering the war.[21] Chinese losses were also something the North Korean government referred to frequently in subsequent years, perhaps explaining the fact that North Korea has never sided unequivocally against China in the Sino-Soviet dispute even though it has at times become quite dependent upon the Kremlin for military and economic assistance.

Some bits of information on the value of Chinese arms aid are available. In October 1951, General Chen Yi proclaimed that the people of East China had pledged 897 planes, 33 pieces of artillery, 17 anti-aircraft guns, and two tanks to the "Resist America, Aid Korea" campaign.[22] This, he said, constituted one-third of the total donation of the nation up to that time. It is also reported that China provided the North Korean government during the war with direct financial grants worth $75 million.[23] At the end of the war China, in addition, canceled a trade debt of $56.9 million and promised $338 million in the form of a grant to be used during the period 1954-1957 to help North Korea repair its war damage.[24]

In subsequent years North Korea recovered economically while China's economic growth faltered. Thus, neither country provided documentation for Chinese military assistance beyond the middle- to late-1950s. Although there is other evidence to confirm such aid the value of this is difficult to judge.

In 1961, in the wake of a military takeover in South Korea, North Korea concluded treaties of mutual defense and assistance with the Soviet Union and with China. These treaties stipulated that each party would "immediately render military and other assistance with all the means at its disposal." This, however, did not translate into new Chinese promises of arms assistance or more deliveries of military hardware. However, in mid-1970 military representatives from North Korea visited China and were promised assistance in the form of ships, fuel, and technical help.[25] During the 1970s and early 1980s North Korea received more military assistance from China, though neither side has provided any details on the kind of weapons China provided or their value. According to a Western source, in the spring of 1982 China gave or sold North Korea forty MiG 21s -- constituting the most meaningful recent arms aid package.[26]

However, the most important recipient of Chinese military assistance in terms of total value was North Vietnam. China provided North Vietnam with small arms even before 1949, when Mao won control over China from the Nationalists. In early 1950, after the communist victory, Ho Chi Minh visited China and requested more assistance. China responded by sending military advisers to Indochina and by inviting Vietnamese officers to China for training.[27]

China, in fact, established a center at Nanning in south China specifically to transport weapons and supplies to Hanoi. During the next few months the French army reported that the Vietnamese were using heavier arms and that they had switched from guerrilla operations to conventional war.[28] By late 1951 the French admitted that victory was now beyond the grasp of the French Expeditionary Corps.[29]

In the fall of 1951 Chinese worker-soldiers completed a rail line into Vietnam from south China. By the end of the year four to six thousand Chinese troops and advisers had entered Vietnam on the line.[30] By 1953 Chinese trucks, cannons, and heavy equipment were in North Vietnam -- military assistance that clearly contributed to the defeat of the French forces at Dien Bien Phu in 1954.[31]

However, it should be noted that China did not provide arms assistance to the Vietnamese equivalent to that which the United States gave France. Thus a final victory was beyond Ho Chi Minh's grasp. The result was a negotiated settlement at Geneva in 1954. Chinese leaders may have preferred this to a final victory for Ho, wanting to preserve their own direct influence in Southeast Asia.

After the truce China provided significant quantites of economic assistance to North Vietnam and more arms. During the 1950s and 60s, many of the weapons in use in the South by the National Liberation Front of South Vietnam (Viet Cong) were of Chinese origin delivered through North Vietnam. In late 1964, in reaction to U.S. air raids against North Vietnam after the Gulf of Tonkin incident, China stepped up its arms assistance to Hanoi. Beijing forthwith sent fifteen MiG-15 and MiG-17 subsonic jet fighters to Hanoi and agreed to train Vietnamese pilots in China.[32] China also began construction of airfields in south China to provide sanctuary and repair facilities for the North Vietnamese Air Force.[33] In the ensuing months, however, Chinese arms assistance did not increase, and Mao stated publicly that Chinese forces would not fight beyond the Chinese frontier.

In February 1965, when U.S. air strikes were resumed and Washington announced a continuous air campaign against North Vietnam, China again responded. Beijing sent various kinds of weapons to North Vietnam, including large quantities of anti-aircraft artillery. China also provided help in rebuilding roads, railroads, and airfields, and offered the use of airfields in China that were safe from U.S. air attacks.[34] By September China had sent 35,000 soldiers to North

106

Vietnam; by the following spring the number had increased to 50,000.[35] According to one source, Chinese anti-aircraft artillery divisions fired on U.S. planes and were bombed in return, while Chinese construction battalions worked to keep transportation and communications links open despite repeated U.S. air strikes.[36]

Again, however, Beijing's military assistance to North Vietnam was in certain critical ways limited. The use of bases in China was restricted to the "safe-basing" of aircraft used by North Vietnam; they were not to be used for missions. Mao also refused to allow the Soviet Union to use bases in China to supply North Vietnam, to garrison troops in China for use in Vietnam, or to establish an air corridor through China to Hanoi. Such would have increased the risk of China directly confronting the United States. It would also have given the Kremlin special rights in China that Beijing could reasonably deny on the basis of preserving its sovereignty. Two other factors also influenced China to limit its military assistance to North Vietnam. First, Mao launched the Great Proletarian Cultural Revolution in 1965, engendering turmoil in China and strife between China and other countries. The Cultural Revolution also disrupted arms shipments. Second, due to the U.S. escalation of the war, Hanoi needed more sophisticated weapons than China could provide. Thus North Vietnam had to call more on the Soviet Union for weapons.

During the following years of the war, China continued to supply Hanoi with assistance of various kinds. Between 1965 and 1973, China provided North Vietnam with aid in the range of $75 million to $250 million annually.[37] However, the portion of arms in this figure probably decreased in comparison with earlier periods because North Vietnam received more and more weapons and equipment from the Soviet Union.[38] Nevertheless, Hanoi continued to get most of its small arms, uniforms, food and supplies, and help in building roads and railroads from China. Chinese worker-soldiers also continued to man anti-aircraft artillery in Vietnam.

However, in the early 1970s because of its new policy of rapprochement with the United States and its apparent desire to have Indochina remain fragmented rather than united under Hanoi's control, China's military assistance to Vietnam declined significantly. Consequently, it was Soviet rather than Chinese arms that made possible Hanoi's final victory in 1975 possible.

Until 1978 China continued to provide aid to Hanoi, including military assistance and help in repairing war damage -- though in markedly reduced amounts. Chinese aid was then severed -- according to one source, causing the termination of seventy-two projects valued at $1 billion.[39] Vietnamese officials at the time admitted that the suspension of Chinese aid would cause "immediate difficulties."[40] Beijing's stated reason for terminating its aid to Vietnam was that China felt the government was persecuting Chinese residents in Vietnam: Hanoi had expelled more than 100,000, many of whom were eventually relocated in China. Also Hanoi openly tilted toward the Soviet Union, as indicated by its willingness to give Moscow basing rights in Vietnam.

At this time China provided some official figures on its aid to Hanoi. Deng Xiaoping stated that China had given Vietnam a total of $14 billion in aid.[41] Another source put the total at $18 billion.[42] Later People's Daily referred to the "more than $10 billion" of assistance rendered to Vietnam "most of which was in grants." The remainder was, it said, in interest-free loans.[43] People's Daily also mentioned that $6 billion had been given the form of in complete plants, one hundred locomotives, thousands of railroad cars, seven hundred ships, and tens of thousands of motor vehicles. It also said that China had provided Vietnam with better weapons than China had at home and that "many Chinese had shed their blood and laid down their lives" in Vietnam.[44]

Although these figures are considerably higher than Western estimates, China's overall military assistance to Vietnam over a period of three decades may, in fact, have exceeded or even exceed $10 billion. Clearly it was large in terms of what China could afford. It was also generous when considering China's weapons production capabilities. Finally, it generally matched or exceeded Soviet arms aid until the early 1970s. In terms of effects it may be said to have matched at least half of U.S. efforts, whose costs exceeded $160 billion.[45]

In addition to its arms assistance to Hanoi, China rendered military assistance to Cambodia and Laos during the Vietnam conflict. Some of this assistance can be categorized as arms aid connected to the Vietnam War and therefore related to China's security concerns there. (Military assistance to Cambodia and Laos was also given for other reasons, and therefore, will be discussed again later.)

In December 1960, China and Cambodia signed an agreement that included undefined Chinese assistance to Cambodia. Aid was apparently tied to a treaty of friendship between the two countries that specified that neither could join an alliance against the other -- thereby preventing Cambodia from joining the Southeast Asia Treaty Organization (SEATO). There is some evidence to suggest that this agreement was later expanded to include military assistance (if, in fact, such assistance was not included in the original pact).[46] China apparently sought to compensate Cambodia for Hanoi's use of its territory as an infiltration route and as a sanctuary; or Beijing wanted to gain some direct influence with the Cambodian government, seeing the war situation as a means to accomplish this. Thus, in 1967 and 1968 after the war in Vietnam escalated, China made specific promises military assistance to Cambodia.[47] Chinese military equipment, including aircraft and anti-aircraft guns, was subsequently seen in Cambodia.

In early 1970 Prince Sihanouk was overthrown, and the United States immediately stepped in to aid the new regime. In response, China announced that it would support Sihanouk's government-in-exile with arms as well as other equipment.[48] At the same time China increased its support to communist guerrilla forces in Cambodia that opposed the new Lon Nol government. In fact, China was the primary supplier of military assistance to the Khmer Rouge until its victory in 1975. After 1975 China provided arms aid to the Pol Pot government; and since the 1978 Vietnamese invasion and occupation of Cambodia, China has again provided weapons to Khmer Rouge guerrillas. This will be discussed in a subsequent section of this chapter.

China also extended both military and economic assistance to the government of Laos, although it must be noted that this assistance was actually intended to benefit the Pathet Lao and not the Laotian government. In 1961, in the context of the Geneva Conference that established the neutrality of Laos, China negotiated an agreement with the government to build a road in the northern part of the country. Work on several roads proceeded intermittently, and by 1968 China reportedly had 3,000 worker-soldiers in Laos.[49] By 1971 this figure had reached 20,000.[50] At the same time China supplied weapons, ammunition, and equipment to the Pathet Lao. The formal aid agreement with the Laotian government was thus used as a means of legitimating China's presence in Laos, which made supplying arms aid to the Pathet Lao easier.

In addition to its construction assistance, which was provided to give Beijing easy access to Laos in the event of a crisis there, China also protected the roads with anti-aircraft guns, thereby defending some of Laos against U.S. air strikes. According to one source, one-third to one-half of China's worker-soldiers in Laos were positioning or manning anti-aircraft artillery.[51] By 1971 China reportedly had in place 395 radar-directed guns that were effective to an altitude of 68,000 feet.[52]

After the victory of the communist forces in Laos in 1975, the Soviet Union and Vietnam moved to undermine and reduce Chinese influence there. Since then, China has provided military assistance to anticommunist forces in Laos. Ironically, some of the forces that have received Chinese military assistance since 1975 are the very forces China opposed before that date.

CHINA'S MILITARY ASSISTANCE TO CLIENT OR FRIENDLY NATIONS

In many instances, China has extended military assistance to increase its diplomatic influence, thereby affecting a regional balance of power, or because Chinese leaders have perceived particular nations to be geopolitically important. In the 1950s China's aid to this category of client or friendly nations was generally anti-West in its tenor; after 1960 it was both anti-West and anti-Soviet. During the 1970s and 1980s it became primarily anti-Soviet. The most important nations in terms of China's efforts to influence regional power relations have been Pakistan, Tanzania, Egypt, and Albania. But a large number of other recipients fit into this category in other ways. Some of China's military aid to friendly nations has also been given to win diplomatic recognition or to influence voting in a regional organization or the United Nations.

In terms of the value of military assistance, Pakistan is the largest recipient in this category. In July 1964 China granted an interest-free loan to Pakistan totaling $60 million. Although this transaction was not labeled military assistance and was not formally announced until the next year, Chinese deliveries of weapons clearly suggest that it was a military assistance agreement. During 1965 Chinese-made T-34 and T-59 tanks and MiG-19 aircraft were seen in Pakistan.[53] China also sent military advisers, provided training for Pakistani pilots in China, and helped establish guerrilla training centers in Kashmir.[54] In late 1965 China stepped up its arms deliveries when the United States cut its military assistance to Pakistan thereby leaving Pakistan in a weak position vis-a-vis India. Chinese leaders hoped to strengthen Pakistan militarily in order to offset Indian dominance on the subcontinent and to keep the India-Pakistan conflict alive so as to undermine India's leadership of the nonaligned nations movement.

After 1965, Beijing continued to give Pakistan both economic and military assistance, competing with the Soviet Union and the Aid Pakistan Consortium in this effort. China was, however, the only nation willing to provide significant military assistance. In 1970 China extended a $200 million interest-free loan to Pakistan, after which more Chinese weapons began to arrive in Pakistan. That year, in addition to the kinds of weapons cited above, China provided Pakistan with two or three submarines and some fast patrol boats fitted with 37 mm. guns and torpedo tubes.[55]

In 1971, when the Pakistan government faced an escalation of hostilities in the eastern section of the country, where an independence movement was threatening, China accelerated work on an all-weather road connecting China with Pakistan. At the same time Beijing warned that it would open hostilities with India if New Delhi got involved in the conflict. Despite this warning, India entered the conflict late in the year. The Pakistani army was defeated, and East Pakistan became the nation of Bangladesh. China did not open a second front against India.

In February 1972, in order to regain its influence with Pakistan, China wrote off a $110 million loan and deferred payment of the 1970 $200 million loan for twenty years. Beijing also promised additional military assistance, and in June delivered sixty MiG-19 fighter planes, 100 tanks, and an unspecified number of small arms.[56] China was obviously committed to maintaining its ties with Pakistan and preventing India from assuming a position of dominance on the subcontinent.

Since 1972, China has continued to provide military assistance to Pakistan. In 1976 China agreed to help Pakistan build a munition factory. Also that year it was reported that China had agreed to provide Pakistan with sixty more Shenyang F-6 fighter planes.[57] In 1977 China sent three fast patrol boats to Pakistan.[58] In 1978 the second segment of the all-weather Karakoram Highway was finished, thereby linking China with Pakistan's capital city. This road had military as well as commercial purposes.[59] The same year China responded to growing tensions in Afghanistan by building a string of small military bases along the road and adjacent to the border with Afghanistan to protect the road against sabotage.[60] It was also reported that China had 3,000 soldiers in Pakistan at the time.[61]

Two months after the Soviet invasion of Afghanistan in December 1979, China promised more military assistance to Pakistan. Foreign Minister Huang Hua visited Islamabad and pledged to aid Pakistan "in various ways" -- taken by foreign observers to mean more military assistance.[62] Later in the year an Indian source reported that China had delivered 65 Fantan jet fighters (an improved version of the MiG-19), a sizable number of SAM-2 missiles, and other arms in accordance with an agreement signed earlier in the year.[63] Both Pakistan and China, however, denied this report as well as charges concerning the presence of Chinese troops and nuclear rockets in Pakistan.

During 1979 and 1980, China provided additional arms assistance to Pakistan designed primarily to strengthen Pakistan in the face of the Soviet threat from Afghanistan, and to encourage Pakistan to build staging areas to aid Afghan rebels. (This will be discussed again in the next section.) Interestingly, there is some evidence that China placed conditions on this assistance to force the Pakistani government to change its attitude toward the United States and to accept U.S. military aid.[64] In any event, in late 1980 and early 1981, observers noted that China was still sending large amounts of military assistance to Pakistan. In November a repair facility for Chinese-built MiG-19 aircraft was completed.[65] In early 1981 India again claimed to have evidence that China was helping to build airfields in Pakistan for military use.[66]

Neither China nor Pakistan has given any indication of the amount of military assistance Beijing has provided to Islamabad. Obviously it is considerable, and apparently most has been given either free or on very favorable terms. One source put the total value at $2 billion through the beginning of 1980.[67] Clearly Chinese leaders have been committed to seeing that Pakistan continues to resist India's efforts to dominate the region militarily. Also, Beijing wants to keep Pakistan from falling into the Soviet orbit. In view of the Afghanistan and Iran situations Pakistan is now more important than ever, suggesting that Chinese military assistance will continue.

The second most important recipient (in terms of impact, though not in terms of value) of Chinese military assistance in this category is Tanzania. Even before Tanzania was formed by the union of Tanganyika and Zanzibar in 1964, some Chinese arms had been seen in Zanzibar. At the time of the union, China signed an agreement that included a $2.8 million gift and a $42 million interest-free loan.[68] Although most of this assistance would be defined as economic, the agreement specifically mentioned weapons and military training and in so doing set a precedent for China in entering the arms business in sub-Saharan Africa.[69] Within a few months Chinese arms and advisers arrived in Tanzania.

Chinese leaders probably had several purposes in this first important delivery of arms assistance to an African country. First, China had tested its first nuclear weapon in October 1964 and was preparing to test missile delivery systems. Tanzania provided an ideal location for tracking facilities for tests conducted over the Indian Ocean. Second, Mao may have perceived that military assistance would complement economic assistance and help China gain a foothold in Africa. Finally, Beijing continued to support wars of national liberation elsewhere in Africa and needed a permanent base of operations. China apparently stipulated in the agreement, or had an expression of willingness by Tanzanian authorities, that some of the military assistance would go elsewhere to support guerrilla or insurgency operations. In any event, Tanzania became a transshipment point for Chinese weapons en route to insurgents in the Congo (now Zaire) and for guerrillas operating against neighboring Mozambique.[70]

In 1965 Chinese negotiators held talks with the Tanzanian government on a major railroad project. A final agreement was made in 1967, and the project became China's largest aid project anywhere. In fact, the Tanzam Railroad surpassed in cost the Soviet Union's largest overseas aid project, the Aswan Dam. Such a commitment entailed further military assistance to Tanzania to protect China's investment and keep out Soviet and Western influence. Therefore, in June 1966 China delivered four patrol boats to the Tanzanian navy and provided some other kinds of weapons aid.[71]

In 1970 Tanzanian military representatives visited China and probably asked for additional military assistance. In any event, within months Chinese engineers were working on a naval base in Tanzania. A military hospital built with Chinese aid was also opened. In early 1971 China delivered more arms to Tanzania, including: two 100-ton patrol boats, sixteen tanks, twenty-four field guns, one hundred trucks, and an unspecified number of jeeps, mortars, and small arms.[72] Three to four hundred Chinese advisers were also sent to help train the Tanzanian army. During 1972 an airbase was reportedly under construction in Tanzania with Chinese help, in anticipation of a squadron of Chinese-built MiG fighter planes, which arrived in 1973.[73] In addition, 300 Tanzanian pilots were sent to China for training, and China agreed to build a radar station in Tanzania capable of tracking missiles and planes.[74]

Chinese motives can be assessed as follows: Chinese leaders probably sought to stave off Tanzanian acceptance of offers of military aid by the Soviet Union, protect the Tanzam railroad project, preserve close relations with the Tanzanian government, and continue to use Tanzania as a base of operations in East Africa. Beijing may also have been motivated by a desire to protect Tanzania from threats from militarily superior South Africa and Rhodesia, and from potential challenges to Tanzanian security from nearby Somalia and Uganda, both having received large quantities of Soviet aid.

Since 1975, China has given very little arms assistance to Tanzania, with the exception of a military academy built in 1976 and parts and repair for weapons already supplied.[75] It can be argued that China had already provided so much arms aid that Tanzania's needs were filled. Nonetheless, an arms race continues in the area, and Tanzania is a participant. Thus Tanzania has gone to the West for additional military assistance, a fact which apparently has not bothered Chinese leaders.

Albania is the third most important recipient of Chinese arms aid in this category of nations and is the only country besides Tanzania to ever become dependent solely upon China for military assistance. During the mid-1950s China extended some economic aid to Albania in an effort to promote bloc unity, and in 1959 gave assistance designed to keep Albania on China's side in the growing ideological dispute with the Soviet Union. In 1960, when Moscow simultaneously cut its aid to China and Albania, Beijing became Albania's provider. In fact, in the following years the Albanian economy became utterly dependent upon China's economic assistance.

However, until the Soviet invasion of Czechslovakia in 1968, most of China's support for Albania consisted of economic rather than arms assistance. At that juncture China announced that it would assist Albania in the event of a military threat, and signed an agreement that included arms assistance (though no details were released). Almost simultaneously China leased four naval bases from Albania for sixty-six years and stationed a number of naval vessels there. It was also reported that China built missile bases in Albania and equipped the Albanian military with jet fighter planes and submarines.[76] In early 1970 the two nations signed another agreement which included military assistance.[77] A Western source noted at the time that China had agreed to provide Albania with thirty-two hydrofoil patrol boats, four Shanghai-II patrol boats, and an unknown number of MiG-21 fighters and armored personnel carriers.[78]

Beijing's motivation in giving such extensive economic and military assistance to Albania was its antipathy toward the Soviet Union. Chinese leaders seemed particularly anxious to demonstrate to the world that Soviet assistance was neither generous nor indispensable. Mao may also have perceived that Albania could serve as a base of operations if Sino-Soviet differences escalated and China wanted to establish a second front in Europe -- even though this was probably not very realistic. Finally, even before 1969 Beijing had found Albania a useful staging area for assisting revolutionary forces in Algeria and elsewhere and may have wanted to maintain this base of operations.

In any event, the improvement in United States-China relations in the early 1970s alienated Albania, which criticized China for its changed policies. Eventually, relations between the two countries deteriorated to the point where, in 1978, China terminated its assistance to Albania. At that time Beijing announced that it had given Albania more than $5 billion in economic and military assistance since 1954 -- though it did not specify how much of each.[79] Subsequently China noted that it had trained 2,000 Albanian economic and military cadres in China, that it had provided the Albanian government with new tanks and fighter aircraft before China's own military was outfitted, and that its military support for Albania had all been free.[80]

Relations between the two countries have remained strained in ensuing years. As China's relations with the United States continued to improve, Albania seemed less important to China. And although it seems unlikely that China will again become the provider of vast quantities of economic and military aid to Albania, as of late 1982 Albania had not found a substitute for China's arms aid.

China's military assistance to Egypt was also motivated by its anti-Soviet stance. China during the Suez crisis promised to send "volunteers" to Egypt, though the offer was not accepted. And during the 1950s and 1960s China provided Egypt with some economic aid. However, it was 1977, when Moscow presented Cairo with an ultimatum to abandon its anti-Soviet policies -- i.e., Egypt's efforts to draw Somalia out of the Soviet camp and its support for the Eritrean independence movement in Ethiopia -- that China stepped in with meaningful offers of military assistance. One month after Moscow cut its aid to Egypt, China promised Cairo spare parts for its Soviet-built MiG-17 and MiG-21 aircraft and other military assistance.[81]

Little was said at this time in Egypt about Chinese arms assistance, probably to avoid causing alarm in the United States regarding Israel's military assistance needs. However, in June 1979 President Sadat announced publicly that China had given Egypt forty F-6 jet fighters and that four were already in service.[82] Sadat also noted that negotiations were under way for forty or fifty more of these planes and that Egypt in return had given China a Soviet MiG-23 that would provide China with new technology to facilitate its aircraft production. Another source states that China gave Egypt sixty F-6 aircraft in June 1979, 30 F-7 fighters in August, and an undisclosed number of SAM missiles in early 1980.[83]

In any event China's military assistance to Egypt at this time was quite extensive and was apparently given for the most part free or on the basis of no-interest loans. This assistance clearly helped to prevent Egypt from returning to the Soviet orbit. It also enhanced China's reputation and influence in the region. Finally, it may have been intended to bring China and the United States into closer cooperation against the Soviet Union; in any case, it did have that result.

In addition to Pakistan, Tanzania, Albania, and Egypt, a number of other countries have also been important beneficiaries of China's military assistance in this category. Indonesia was the first country in this category to receive substantial Chinese arms support. In early 1965, Indonesia dropped its membership in the United Nations and swore to establish a "revolutionary" world organization. Simultaneously, it engaged in conflict with Malaysia. In response to these events, China reportedly delivered 100,000 small weapons, mostly rifles, to Indonesia.[84] China also allegedly promised Indonesia help in becoming a nuclear power and discussed conducting a nuclear test in or for Indonesia.[85] But the Indonesian government was overthrown in the fall of 1965, and relations with China were broken and have remained so since then. (Some of China's arms aid to Indonesia both at this time and after 1965 consisted of aid to revolutionary groups and will be mentioned in the next section.)

In the early 1970s China's relations with Romania improved as Romania became alienated from the Soviet Union. As a result, China reportedly provided the Romanian government with arms, including eighteen Shanghai patrol boats, thirteen torpedo boats, and twelve hydrofoil patrol boats -- weapons some of which were subsequently produced in Romania (the only instance, with the possible exception of production in North Korea, of Chinese-designed weapons being produced by another country).[86]

In 1972 China delivered five gunboats to Sri Lanka for coastal defense.[87] These were intended for protection against India, which had recently defeated Pakistan and had expressed anger at Sri Lanka over its "tilt" during the war. That same year China promised Sudan eight MiG-17 aircraft and enough tanks for an armored division.[88] China's good relations with the Sudan and fear of Soviet influence in the area allegedly justified this assistance. Also in 1972, China promised four gunboats to the government of Guinea, which it delivered the next year.[89] The gunboats were to strengthen the government of Guinea, to help China gain a foothold in West Africa, and to protect the Chinese interests there in view of its considerable economic aid. In 1973 China donated two Shanghai-class gunboats to the government of Sierra Leone, after having provided some small arms and military training in previous years.[90] This assistance was given by Chinese leaders to strengthen China's influence in West Africa. In 1975 China delivered two patrol boats to the government of Cameroon, and the next year Beijing sent two more patrol boats to Tunisia and Guinea.[91]

During 1977 and 1978 China extended military assistance to several more Third World countries, including Zaire, Zambia, Bangladesh, Botswana, and Somalia. During the invasion of Shaba province of Zaire in 1977 it was reported that Zaire's only tanks were provided by Beijing -- enough Chinese-made T-62 tanks to form an armored battalion.[92] Another source reported that Zaire received 30 tons of military equipment from China that year.[93] In 1978 China's foreign minister promised Zaire "full support" against "new aggression by Soviet social imperialism." Subsequently the Zaire government asked China for two patrol boats and twenty tanks, all of which were delivered within a few months.[94] China wanted to support the Zaire government in view of the increasing influence and presence of the Soviet Union and Cuba in nearby Angola.

In 1977 Western sources reported that China had sent a squadron of MiG-21 jet fighters to Bangladesh and was providing training for Bangladeshi pilots in China[95] Another source cited a September 1978 Chinese donation to Bangladesh of thirty-six MiG-19 aircraft, which arrived in 1979. The same source also recorded that China had agreed to give Bangladesh an undisclosed number of training aircraft in 1979 and made delivery that year.[96] In December 1980 it was reported that China had signed an agreement with the government of Bangladesh to provide thirty-six tanks, to be delivered in 1981.[97] Chinese leaders ostensibly wanted to cement close ties with Bangladesh because of India's friendship with the Soviet Union. And Bangladesh was a willing recipient because of deteriorating relations with India.

In 1978 China agreed to provide Zambia with twelve MiG-19's.[98] This aid was apparently motivated by Zambia's difficulties with

Rhodesia and South Africa, its proximity to the continuing conflict in Angola, and Soviet efforts to establish a presence in Angola.

Beginning in 1978, however, China's military assistance began to diminish because of Beijing's new stress on economic development and consumer goods. Chinese leaders apparently perceived that China could no longer afford a large military assistance program. During 1980, however, China made another promise of arms assistance to Sudan in the form of twelve F-6's and pledged military assistance to Sri Lanka in the form of two Shanghai II ships.[99] With these two exceptions and the aid to Pakistan and Bangladesh cited above, China's military assistance to nations in this category has been much lower since 1978-1979.

CHINA'S ARMS ASSISTANCE TO SUPPORT WARS OF NATIONAL LIBERATION

The third category of China's military assistance is to groups fighting what Beijing has termed "wars of national liberation." (This term includes what other observers might call competing regimes, guerrilla or insurgency groups, and even terrorist groups.) The amount of China's assistance in this category is much less than in either of the two categories already discussed, yet in many ways it is as important, both to China and in terms of its impact on world politics. This type of assistance is cheaper for China, but more expensive for other nations, such as the United States or the Soviet Union, to counteract. And it has also helped win for China a leadership position among Third World countries. To China's disadvantage, however, is the fact that Beijing has not been able to control most national liberation groups, especially after they have gained political power. In other words, China has been able to threaten the status quo but not to take advantage of the changes it has fostered.

China rendered aid to North Korea after the outbreak of the Korean War, entitling that conflict a "war of national liberation." The same rubric was used when China extended support to communist guerrilla forces in South Vietnam, Laos, and Cambodia prior to the communist victories in these countries. In the case of Korea this assistance was very small, and the conflict soon turned into a conventional war. In Indochina, most of China's assistance was delivered through North Vietnam, which acted as the go-between in China's arms support effort to the guerrilla groups. Thus, although both at times belong in the category of liberation struggles, for reasons already discussed, China's aid to North Korea and that to North Vietnam are classified differently.

The most important recipient in this category is the Khmer Rouge, although it is difficult to separate military assistance given to Pol Pot when he was in power (between the spring of 1975 and late 1978) from that which was given later, after Vietnamese forces invaded the country and established the Heng Samrin government in Phnom Penh. In September 1975 China reportedly promised Pol Pot $1 billion in economic and military assistance to be used over a period of five to six years.[100] Assuming that much of this promised support was not used by 1978, that China anticipated the Vietnamese invasion, and that little of the support took the form of economic assistance (confirmed by the modicum of emphasis on economic development, with the exception of rice production) much -- in fact, most -- of this assistance probably fits into the category discussed here. On the other hand, China provided rather substantial amounts of sophisticated military hardware to Pol Pot prior to the Vietnamese invasion, including MiG-19s, naval weapons, artillery, and tanks.[101] It was even reported that China sent military advisers to help Pol Pot and trained his pilots in China.[102]

In any event since 1978 Pol Pot has been fighting an insurgency against superior Vietnamese forces, and much of China's arms assistance anticipated or was suited to that type of conflict. In fact, prior to the Vietnamese invasion China delivered large quantities of small arms that were hidden in the countryside for use in a subsequent guerrilla war.[103]

During 1979, after the Vietnamese invasion, it was reported that China had established supply lines to Poi Pot's forces from several islands off the coast of Cambodia, from ships offloaded in coastal waters to smaller boats, and through Thailand.[104] Both Western and Vietnamese sources confirmed that China's supply of weapons to Pol Pot was very substantial and included small arms for 30,000 guerrillas plus other equipment, including field radios to keep the command structures intact.[105] Vietnamese sources called China's military assistance "huge" and noted that it included military advisers.[106] Simultaneously, China provided food and other assistance to several international organizations that helped sustain Pol Pot's guerrillas.[107]

During 1980 and 1981 Beijing continued to provide Pol Pot's forces with arms and supplies, guaranteeing that they did not lack weapons to do battle against the Vietnamese occupiers. China's invasion of the northern part of Vietnam in the spring of 1979 may also be seen as a form of arms aid to Pol Pot, as it made it impossible for Hanoi to send more troops to Kampuchea and considerably damaged the Vietnamese economy. However, it should be noted that China did not provide sophisticated arms to Pol Pot. China has also been reluctant to make too much of its aid in view of the Pol Pot regime's human rights record and China's efforts to improve relations with the United States and other Western nations.

In 1981 China delivered assistance for the first time to Son Sann, a noncommunist leader of anti-Vietnamese guerrillas in Kampuchea. According to various reorts, early in the year, Beijing provided weapons, including 82 mm mortars, AK-47 rifles, and "tons of supplies," to Son Sann's forces.[108] This aid may have been intended to persuade Son Sann and his 3,000 to 5,000 soldiers to join with Pol Pot or to undertake joint efforts against Vietnamese occupation forces; or it may have been sent at the request of the United States. Washington wanted to take some action, but felt restrained because of the "Vietnam syndrome" in the United States and because of legal limitations on the war-making authority of the president contained in legislation written after the Vietnam War.[109]

In any event, China has been successful in sustaining an insurgency war against the Vietnamese-supported Heng Samrin government, costing Vietnam and the Soviet Union a great deal to counteract it. China's assistance has also been responsible for the international condemnation of Vietnam because of its military presence in Kampuchea. To many observers of China's activities in the past it is ironic that China is now devoting arms assistance to support an insurgency movement struggling against a communist regime. However, given Sino-Soviet relations and the course China's military assistance has taken elsewhere, this phenomenon is not so difficult to understand.

A similar situation prevails in Laos. After the communist victory in 1975, Vietnamese and Soviet influence increased and Chinese influence declined. Beginning in 1978, Western sources reported that China was giving arms aid to Meo tribes in northern Laos that were engaged in insurgency warfare against the Laotian government.[110] During 1979 China armed and trained a large number of Meo and other soldiers in northern Laos, even paying them salaries.[111] China also brought Meo and Lao guerrillas into China for training and reportedly during the year sent a division of 4,000 guerrillas it had organized and equipped into northern Laos. In addition, Chinese representatives visited refugee camps in Thailand at this time and accepted many -- but only young men -- for resettlement in China.[112] During 1981 the Laotian government continued to charge that China was training guerrillas in China to send to Laos.[113]

Chinese leaders evidently held the same views and goals vis-a-vis Laos as Kampuchea: that China could support a national liberation movement fighting against the Laotian government, which, as in the case of Kampuchea, was propped up by the Vietnamese army (in this case 40,000 Vietnamese troops) and Vietnamese and Soviet aid. Again China's efforts cost the opposition many times more than China was spending. However, as in Kampuchea, there was little evidence China was winning. Outside observers predicted a protracted struggle. China's purpose again seemed to be to prevent Vietnamese hegemony over Laos, and, by extension over Indochina, and to reduce Soviet influence in the area.

It is also worth noting that China over the past three decades has provided some arms assistance and aid to communist guerrilla or insurgency groups in several other countries in Southeast Asia, including Burma, Thailand, Malaya (now Malaysia), Indonesia, and the Philippines. China also provided arms aid and assistance to communist insurgency groups in India. Most of this support has consisted of small arms. With two or three exceptions, this weapons assistance has not been very substantial and has not had much impact upon the political or military situation in the region. Moreover, in the case of all of the noncommunist Southeast Asian nations, Chinese leaders have recently given hints or pledges that arms assistance to insurgency movements will cease -- in order to win support from these nations against Hanoi's and Moscow's activities in the region. On the other hand, Beijing has hedged on these promises and has stated that it cannot drop completely its support of communist parties or organizations in the region, as they would then be forced to turn to the Kremlin for help.

In Indonesia, evidence was found after the 1965 coup instigated by the Indonesian Communist party that China had provided the Indonesian communists with military assistance in the form of small arms at the same time that it delivered military aid to the government.[114] There was no proof, however, that this aid was extensive. In any event, the Indonesian communist movement was decimated by the army, and Chinese aid did not achieve its purpose.

China has provided military assistance to the Burmese (White Flag) Communist Party periodically since the early 1950s in the form of primarily small arms and equipment in addition to food and medicine.[115] China's support for the Burmese Communists, in fact, has been sustained over a longer period of time than its aid to other communist or insurgency groups in the region, though it has been offset by both military and economic assistance to the Burmese government. In this unique case China has aided one or the other, or both, depending upon its perception of the situation in Burma, as a means of exerting influence over both.

According to reports emanating from a variety of sources, several communist groups or movements in Thailand, communist insurgents in Malaysia, and both communist and Muslim rebels in the Philippines have received military assistance from China. In no case, however, has China's aid proved significant, or critical to these groups or to the political or military situations in these countries.[116] As mentioned above, China has generally reduced or suspended its arms assistance to this category of recipients in Southeast Asia to win support for the nations of the region against the Soviet Union and Vietnam. In the case of Thailand, China has promised the government arms aid in the event of an attack by Vietnam.

While its aid to guerrilla movements has generally been given a lower priority China has developed a new interest in Afghanistan. One month after the December 1979 Soviet invasion, U.S. officials stated publicly that China was supplying small arms to Muslim rebels there.[117] Subsequently it was reported that China had provided arms aid to Afghan refugees in Pakistan. However, other sources concluded that while China had extended military assistance to the Afghan guerrillas it was quantitatively insignificant.[118] This situation remained through 1982.

There are several reasons for Beijing's inhibitions in arming Afghan rebels. First, Beijing has been unable to send arms to Afghan insurgents directly because of the narrowness of their common border and because of Soviet forces in the area. Second, Chinese leaders have been reluctant to get too involved without a commitment by the United States. Thus, China has directed most of its arms aid efforts to Pakistan and to the Afghan guerrillas through Pakistan. Third, Beijing may perceive that the Afghanistan situation has been so detrimental to the Kremlin's image that China should not get involved directly for fear of making the situation appear something other than a Soviet invasion and occupation and a Soviet war against local anti-Soviet guerrillas.

In the Middle East, China's first military support to a revolutionary movement went to the Algerian National Liberation Front in 1958 after leaders of that group asked Beijing for arms.[119] In the spring of 1959 an Algerian delegation went to Beijing and was promised weapons worth about $10 million.[120] In 1960, Chinese leaders offered to send "volunteers" trained in guerrilla warfare, together with twenty to twenty-five fighter-bomber aircraft and other weapons. One source maintained that China's offers of arms forced de Gaulle to negotiate.[121] In ensuing years China continued to provide military assistance to help the Algerians win their independence from France, though Chinese weapons constituted only a portion of the arms aid Algerian rebels received.[122] And Algerian rebel leaders were cautious about receiving too much arms aid from China for fear of evoking a counterresponse from the United States.

After independence China continued to provide arms assistance to Algeria to establish guerrilla centers where revolutionaries from Angola, Mozambique, Portuguese Guinea, and South Africa could be trained and equipped.[123] In 1964, guerrillas reportedly trained by Chinese advisers in Algeria tried to overthrow the government of Morocco.[124] Algeria at this time also served as a transshipment point for Chinese weapons going to rebels for use in the Congo.

However, after 1962, Algeria as a new nation needed economic assistance in amounts that China could not provide. Thus, Algeria had to seek other sources, and as a result Chinese influence in Algeria started to diminish. Then in June 1965 the Algerian government was overthrown. The new government was considerably less pro-China, and Chinese influence waned further. Thereafter Algeria ceased to serve as an important training site for guerrillas or a transshipment point for Chinese arms.

China provided weapons and other assistance to leftist forces in both North and South Yemen during the late 1960s and early 1970s. In North Yemen in 1969, Chinese technical assistance personnel directly participated in the civil war, there repairing bridges and roads for use by leftist forces.[125] After the conflict ended, China continued friendly relations with the government of North Yemen, providing both economic and military assistance. Although Chinese assistance was soon overshadowed by support from a number of other countries, Beijing seemed concerned only about Soviet influence in the area, especially the presence of Soviet bases. Thus China continued its aid contacts with North Yemen, South Yemen and several other nations near the Horn of Africa.

China has also given arms assistance to some opposition groups in the Middle East. In 1969 the Syrian army overthrew the Ba'ath Socialist party. It was reported later that the Syrian army had been given $15 million in weapons as a gift by China, which proved instrumental in its victory.[126] However, this was the only report of Chinese arms aid to any group or faction in Syria. There have been similar reports of Chinese arms aid to leftist groups in Iraq and several other Middle East nations, but this has not been very consequential.

China has also extended military assistance to al-Fatah and the Palestine Liberation Organization (PLO). Beijing established good relations with both early on, unlike the Soviet Union which was distrusted because of its support for the creation of Israel. Yet there is little evidence that China rendered meaningful arms assistance to either of these groups before the mid-1960s. At that juncture, Beijing began to give strong verbal support to the "Arab-Palestinian nation" in the struggle against Israel, and promised "political and other aid." Subsequently, China sent both small arms and provided military training.[127] In the late 1960s it was reported that "many" Palestinians were receiving six months of guerrilla training from Chinese personnel and that small arms had been given to the PLO by China.[128]

However, China did not provide tanks or heavy weapons to the PLO, claiming that guerrillas must rely more upon spirit and morale. The reality was that China experienced difficulties sending weapons to the PLO via Iraq or Syria, through which most of the arms aid the PLO received was transshipped. Thus the PLO became dependent upon Soviet weapons. China, however, has since continued to supply small arms and other forms of assistance and seems to be waiting to take advantage of Soviet difficulties.[129]

China's first military support for a liberation struggle in Sub-Saharan Africa went to rebels in the Democratic Republic of the Congo (formerly the Belgian Congo and now Zaire). In 1964 China provided the neighboring Congo Republic (Congo-Brazzaville) with a $20 million interest-free loan, much of which was reportedly used to furnish arms to rebels in the Congo.[130] It is uncertain, however, how much of this loan was used for arms or how much was intended for use by rebel forces. In any event, China also sent arms to the liberation movement in the Congo through Algeria, and Kenya, and perhaps Cameroon, Ghana, and Guinea as well.[131] In 1964 it was reported that 75 tons of Chinese military supplies had been intercepted in Kenya en route to the Congo.[132] Chinese arms provided to Tanzania and Zambia also were transshipped to the Congo at this time.

As a result of China's purveying weapons to the Congolese guerrillas through Kenya, the Kenyan government accused China of providing military training and aid to groups there without the permission of the government. Later, Kenyan officials charged that China had attempted to overthrow the government of Kenya and had spent as much as $1 million in that effort.[133]

Quantities of Chinese arms aid to rebels in the Congo may also have been transshipped through Uganda. In any event, China provided arms to the government of Uganda in 1964. According to one report, these arms were given primarily to Tutsi refugees who were sent back to Rwanda and Burundi to start guerrilla campaigns there.[134] China at this time was also supporting revolutionary movements in Burundi and Mozambique; however, few details are available on the scope, value, or importance of this military assistance.[135]

In the mid-1960s China sent some military assistance to Somalia to support a guerrilla campaign against neighboring French Somaliland. The amount was no doubt small, and as Soviet influence increased, China's economic support, which provided the framework for its arms assistance, was terminated.[136]   Also in 1966 Ghana's President Nkrumah visited China and while there his governmnt was ousted from power. He subsequently lived in exile in Guinea and from there tried to regain power in Ghana.   At the time China promised him $1 million in help, presumably arms, to accomplish this goal.[137]

During the late 1960s and early 1970s China began to funnel most of its arms assistance to liberation movements in sub-Saharan Africa through Tanzania and, to a lesser extent, Zambia.   Even before the union of Zanaibar and Tanganyika to form Tanzania, China operated a training school for guerrillas on Pemba Island in Zanzibar.[138] Guerrillas trained there were sent to the Congo and other countries in the region.   Later, Tanzania established a policy of financing guerrilla training camps and bases of operation against the Portuguese colonial government in Angola, Rhodesia, and South Africa.   Tanzania thus welcomed Chinese help to support wars of national liberation in these areas.[139]

In 1968 Chinese arms were sent through Tanzania to support the Biafran struggle in Nigeria, though the amount was not substantial. A much larger number of Chinese arms went to guerrillas fighting against the governments of Rhodesia, South Africa, Angola, and Mozambique.   China placed the greatest emphasis on Rhodesia, and this aid ultimately brought results.[140]

Beijing also used the Congo Republic as a base of operations and supported liberation struggles elsewhere through Brazzaville.   In 1968 Chinese personnel built a radio station in Brazzaville that subsequently identified itself as the "Voice of the Congolese Revolution" and broadcast to liberation forces in the nearby Congo-Kinshasa.[141] China likewise supplied arms directly to groups in the neighboring Congo as well as the Central African Republic, Chad, and Cameroon from Congo-Brazzaville.   In the fall of 1968, China reportedly also sent significant quantities of arms to Angolan revolutionaries through Congo-Brazzaville.[142]

During the late 1960s and 1970s China continued to seek bases of operations in Africa to assist wars of national liberation, even though China's overall military and economic assistance declined as a result of the Cultural Revolution.   China's arms assistance during this period also remained consistent in terms of tactics and objectives, although it became much more anti-Soviet in terms of the groups China supported.   With the possible exceptions of SWAPO and FRELIMO, China consistently supported different liberation or guerrilla groups than did the Soviet Union.[143] In some cases this cost China influence; in other cases it gave China special opportunities.   Clearly China's independent position gave Beijing a chance to vent its anger toward the Kremlin and establish its own special reputation as a supporter of change.

China's more extreme policies, in the sense of supporting anti-status quo or anti-Soviet groups, however, were balanced by Chinese economic and military support for established governments (for example, the Tanzam railroad) during the 1960s and through most of the 1970s. Likewise its policy of detente with the United States made China somewhat more status quo oriented.

At least one case in which China aligned itself with the United States and other Western nations is worth citing -- Angola. In 1975 China rendered some arms assistance to Jonas Savimbi's UNITA in concert with the United States and South Africa. The Soviet Union and Cuba supported the MPLA and provided much more extensive military support, thus helping the MPLA emerge victorious. Although China's arms assistance to UNITA was not large, Beijing lost considerable prestige both by helping the faction supported by South Africa and by supporting the losers in the struggle.[144]

In Zimbabwe-Rhodesia, in 1979 and 1980, Beijing granted significant assistance, including arms and advisers, to Robert Mugabe's ZANU.[145] This assistance helped repair China's repuation in southern Africa, and it gave China a special relationship with the Zimbabwe government when Mugabe subsequently came to power. China has also extended what appears to be considerable assistance to SWAPO since about 1979 to help liberate Southwest Africa and create another similar situation on South Africa's border.[146] It has also given weapons and other aid to opposition groups in South Africa, especially the Pan Africanist Congress.[147]

Clearly China remains committed to supporting wars of national liberation in Africa and elsewhere. On the other hand, its policies have reflected and continue to reflect a realization on its part of its inability to compete in quantitative or qualitative terms with U.S. or Soviet military assistance. China's preoccupation with domestic economic development, its continuing hostilities with the Soviet Union, and its efforts to improve relations with the United States also present problems or obstacles in terms of its policies regarding supporting wars of national liberation with military aid.

CONCLUSIONS

The preceding assessment of China's military assistance program is revealing in a number of ways. It clearly proves that China has been a larger purveyor of arms than has been assumed. However, placing a value on China's arms assistance, however, is difficult for a variety of reasons. China does not want to advertise its assistance. Recipients also generally do not, for fear of a negative U.S. or Soviet reaction. And even when a list of weapons is provided, it is difficult to put a price tag on these weapons given because prices of Chinese weapons have not been agreed upon. Equipment, training, and personnel are even more difficult to price.

If the cost of comparable Western weapons, technical help and manpower is used to put a value on Chinese military assistance (though the author is not suggesting this is necessarily accurate) and military aid is defined broadly to include supplies, road building, rehabilitation aid, etc. (without, however, including insurance payments to soldiers killed, hospitalization or pensions as is included in Western countries' military budgets), China's aid to Korea would no doubt exceed $2 billion and its aid to Vietnam $10 billion. High estimates could double these figures. China's aid to the friendly countries category totals in the range of $5 to 10 billion. Its aid to guerrilla and insurgency movements tallies around $2 to 4 billion.

China's military assistance to support wars of national liberation has generally been exaggerated. The value of this category of China's arms aid does not compare to that of the other two categories. China has been more cautious than is generally presumed in aiding guerrilla and insurgency groups. Numerous guerrilla movements in Africa and the Middle East have received no Chinese support. In other words China - despite its reputation - has been quite selective in aiding revolutionary groups. Chinese arms assistance to Latin American revolutionary groups is almost nonexistent. By being daring and seemingly indiscriminate in a few cases, China during the 1960s built a reputation as an unequivocal supporter of liberation struggles, a reputation that was supported by the reactions of the United States and later the Soviet Union. The fact that a number of revolutionary groups have practiced Mao's theories of guerrilla war also focused attention on Chinese activities, as did the fact that in recent years Chinese weapons and military advisers have been seen in places where there has been no Chinese presence in the past. It is also worthy of note that China is the only Asian country providing arms and advisers to a large number of liberation groups. It is similarly necessary to point out that China has been more willing to extend military assistance to nations over which it has little political or economic control, and has been quick to provide arms to liberation groups simply because they are anti-imperialist or anti-status quo.

The fact that China has given much more military assistance to nations on its borders and more to specially selected friendly governments than to insurgency movements probably reflects accurately Beijing's global perspective. Chinese leaders during the 1950s and 1960s were fearfully anti-U.S. Since then they have been as strongly anti-Soviet. Chinese leaders perceive that Southeast Asia should be a Chinese sphere of interest and that South Asia should not be dominated by India, and they have been willing to channel arms and other forms of military assistance to nations in those regions in accordance with these perceptions. The Middle East and Africa constituted more distant battlegrounds where China first competed with the West and now with the Soviet Union. In the 1960s, China also made a bid for leadership of the communist world, but since the early 1970s has ceased to perceive this as important or has written it off as a lost cause.

Still other conclusions can be drawn from China's military assistance: The scope of its assistance suggests that China, more than other nonsuperpower nations, aspires to be a global power. (Two or three Western European nations are larger purveyors of arms than China, but most of their arms transfers are for profit rather than to exert influence abroad.) This is indicative of a large amount of ambition and willpower on China's part. On the other hand, China's military aid program may also be seen as a way of offsetting China's limited ability to project its military power. Thus arms assistance can be seen as a means to establish bases of operation abroad and to project influence through friendly governments or liberation groups when no other instruments of foreign policy are available.

However, it should be stressed that these efforts are not without limits. As already noted, China has not extended military assistance to liberation movements in Latin America, with only one or two exceptions. In the 1950s and 1960s Chinese leaders apparently perceived that Latin America was in the U.S. sphere of influence and that there was little hope of making inroads there, especially considering its lack of proximity. China early expressed an interest in Castro's revolution and gave him some support, but only for a brief time. As Cuba was drawn into the Soviet sphere, China became unfriendly and ignored or opposed Cuban efforts to spread revolution in the regime. China also expressed some interest in the Allende government and delivered some assistance, both economic and military; but when Allende was overthrown and the successor government proved to be anti-Soviet, China was quick to establish formal ties with the new region.

Last but not least, changes in China's military assistance programs have reflected and have even anticipated its relations with the United States and the Soviet Union. As relations between Moscow and Beijing began to change in the late 1950s, China's military assistance reflected an independent foreign policy, and, in some instances, anti-Soviet aims. This was even more clear after 1960. It was particularly obvious in the realm of Chinese support for new, and especially leftist, African regimes and liberation groups. By the late 1960s China's military assistance was lucidly no longer very anti-U.S. or anti-Western. And by the 1970s there were few cases -- the exceptions being China's support for guerrillas fighting South Africa and Israel -- where China's objectives, as measured by its military assistance, were different from Washington's. This suggests that United States-China relations had progressed further than other evidence might indicate. It is especially noteworthy that in the Angolan civil war, the struggle in Kampuchea, and the fighting in Afghanistan, China and the United States were and remain on the same side. And in these cases their military assistance seemed to be complementary.

In conclusion, it is evident that China's arms assistance has been an important implement of its foreign policy. It has reflected China's global and strategic objectives, and it has fairly accurately mirrored China's stance toward the two superpowers. Both superpowers, first the United States and now the Soviet Union, have spent many times what the Chinese have spent on military aid to counteract that assistance.

Since about 1970 China's military assistance has declined, largely because of the end of its military assistance to Vietnam and Albania and cutbacks in its support for Tanzania. This decline is no doubt a product of China's greater concern in recent years for its own economic development. It also reflects changes in China's foreign policy, especially its improved relations with the United

States. Another factor is also relevant: increased demands by the Chinese military for more and better weapons and equipment. However, the decline in China's military assistance probably does not indicate a termination of its arms aid; Chinese military assistance has been and no doubt will remain a useful tool of Chinese diplomacy, especially in its relations with the superpowers.

NOTES

1.   World Military Expenditures and Arms Transfers, 1967-1976 (Washington, D.C.:   Arms Control and Disarmament Agency, 1978), p. 26.

2.   World Military Expenditures and Arms Transfers, 1969-1978 (Washington, D.C.:   Arms Control and Disarmament Agency, 1980) p. 159.

3.   Handbook of Economics Statistics, 1980 (Washington, D.C.:   National Foreign Assessment Center, 1980), p. 111.

4.   For an excellent summary of China's world view, see Samuel Kim, China, The United Nations and World Order (Princeton, N.J.: Princeton University Press, 1979), Chapter 2.   Also see John F. Copper, "China's Global Strategy," Current History, Vol. 80, No. 467 (September, 1981), pp.241-244.

5.   See Jonathan D. Pollack, "China as a Military Power," in Onkar Marwah and Jonathan D. Pollack (eds.), Military Power and Policy in Asian States: China, India, Japan (Boulder, Colo.: Westview Press, 1980), pp. 58-74.

6.   See John F. Copper, China's Global Role (Stanford, Calif.: Hoover Institution Press, 1980), Chapter 5, for further details on this point.

7.   Asia 1982 Yearbook (Hong Kong: Far Eastern Economic Review, Inc., 1981), p. 30.

8.   Ibid.

9.   Ibid.

10.   Ibid. p. 32.   Also see June T. Dreyer, "China's Military Power in the 1980's," (monograph published by the China Council of the Asia Society), August 1982.

11.   Harry G. Gelber, Technology, Defense, and External Relations in China, 1975-1978 (Boulder, Colo.: Westview Press, 1979), p. 56.

12.   Vividly reflecting this situation is the fact that the Chinese Red Army never used tanks until 1946 or aircraft until 1949. See Robert C. North, The Foreign Relations of China (North Scituate, Mass.: Duxbury Press, 1978), p. 79.

127

13.   Ibid, p. 85.

14.   See Pollack, "China as a Military Power," p. 78, for further details on this point.

15.   See statement of George Bush (then director of the Central Intelligence Agency) on May 27, 1976, before the Joint Economic Committee of the U.S. Congress in Allocation of Resources in the Soviet Union and China—1976 (hearings), cited in ibid, p. 96.

16.   Melvin Gurtov and Byong-Moo Hwang, China Under Threat: The Politics of Strategy And Diplomacy (Baltimore: Johns Hopkins University Press, 1980), p. 54.

17.   Chou-ming Li, "China's Industrial Development, 1958-63," in Roderick Macfarquhar (ed.), China Under Mao: Politics Takes Command (Cambridge, Mass.: M.I.T. Press, 1966), p. 202.

18.   See O. Ivanov, "Peking's Falsifiers of the History of Soviet-Chinese Relations," Mirovaya Ekonomika Mezhdunarodmyye Otnosheniya, November 19, 1975, cited in Pollack, "China as a Military Power," p. 81.

19.   See Gurtov and Hwang, China Under Threat, p. 53, for a detailed discussion on this point.

20.   Werni Levi, Modern China's Foreign Policy (Minneapolis: University of Minnesota Press, 1953), p. 294.

21.   Gurtov noted that many in the top leadership hierarchy were opposed to the war from the start and openly challenged Mao's decision. See Gurtov and Hwang, China Under Threat, pp. 47-48. It is also relevant that a leadership crisis in 1959, during which the defense minister was purged and Mao gave up his position as head of state, was in part an outgrowth of China's experience during the Korean War.

22.   People's Daily, November 27, 1951.

23.   Alexander Eckstein, Communist China's Growth and Foreign Trade: Implications for U.S. Policy (New York: McGraw-Hill, 1966), p. 161.

24.   New China News Agency, November 23, 1953.

25.   People's Daily, October 18, 1970; also see New China News Agency, September 9, 1971 regarding another promise of aid.

26.   Mike Tharp, "The North, The South and the Superpower Glacier," Far Eastern Economic Review, November 12, 1982. Also see Melinda Lin and Larry Rohter, "China Shuffles the Cards,"

128

Newsweek, October 4, 1982. The letter says "at least twenty Mig-21 jets."

27.   Chih-ying Wu, Biography of Ho Chi Minh (Shanghai: Pacific Press, 1961), p. 49.

28.   Bernard B. Fall, Street Without Joy (New York: Schocken, 1972), p. 29.

29.   Joseph B. Buttinger, Vietnam: A Dragon Embattled (New York: Praeger Publishers, 1967), p. 767.

30.   New York Times, June 29, 1951.

31.   See Melvin Gurtov, The First Vietnam Crisis: Chinese Communist Strategy and United States Involvement (New York: Columbia University Press, 1968), p. 15.

32.   Richard M. Bueschel, Communist Chinese Air Power (New York: Praeger Publishers, 1968), p. 83.

33.   Allen S. Whiting, "How We Almost Went to War with China," Look, April 29, 1969, p. 76.

34.   Gurtov, First Vietnam Crisis, p. 166. The author cites a number of sources.

35.   Allen S. Whiting, The Chinese Calculus of Deterrence (Ann Arbor: University of Michigan Press, 1975), pp. 186-187.

36.   Ibid.; New York Times, January 8, 1968.

37.   The New York Times, July 28, 1968, put the figure at $150-250 million. The same source estimated China's aid in 1972 at $75 million; (New York Times, November 19, 1972). The Central Intelligence Agency and the Department of State estimated Soviet and Chinese aid together to North Vietnam during the period 1970-1974 at $2 billion. The New York Times, April 7, 1973, reported that the United States had an understanding that China and the Soviet Union would limit their aid to between $600 million and $700 million annually, suggesting that less than half was provided by China.

38.   According to one source the Soviet Union was providing 75 percent of North Vietnam's arms needs during the late 1960s. See U.S. News and World Report, April 3, 1968.

39.   Nayan Chanda, "Southeast Asia Comes into Focus," Far Eastern Economic Review, July 7, 1978.

40. Kyodo News Service, July 9, 1978.

41. China News (Taipei), June 6, 1978, citing an interview with Tomokazu Sakamot, chairman of the Japan Broadcasting Company.

42. Asian Recorder, July 23-29, 1978, p. 14427.

43. See Frank Ching, "China's Cutoff of Aid to Old Allies Creates Doubts Among Its Friends," Asian Wall Street Journal, July 27, 1978. The author cited a People's Daily article of the previous week.

44. Ibid.

45. Joseph Buttinger, Vietnam: The Unforgettable Tragedy (New York: Horizon Press, 1977), p. 93.

46. See Alain-Gerard Marsot, "China's Aid to Cambodia," Pacific Affairs, Vol. 43, No. 2 (Summer 1969), pp. 189-198.

47. New York Times, January 5, 1969.

48. People's Daily, August 10, 1970.

49. Far Eastern Economic Review 1970 Yearbook, p. 180.

50. Far Eastern Economic Review, September 11, 1971.

51. Donald P. Whitaker et al., Area Handbook for Laos (Washington, D.C.: Government Printing Office, 1972), p. 38.

52. Ibid., p. 283.

53. New York Times, March 24 and 27, 1966.

54. S. K. Ghosh, "China's Military Assistance Programme," unpublished paper, Institute for Defense Study and Analysis (India), February 1969.

55. International Institute for Strategic Studies (IISS), The Military Balance, 1970-71 (London: International Institute for Strategic Studies, 1971), p. 102.

56. New York Times, June 3, 1972; The Chinese War Machine (New York: Crescent Books, 1979), p. 50. The latter source states that the number of MiG aircraft delivered was 100.

57. See Far Eastern Economic Review, July 30 and December 17, 1956; and Foreign Broadcasting Information Service, November 9, 1976.

58.   Chinese War Machine, p. 50.

59.   See John F. Copper, "China's Foreign Aid in 1976," Current Scene, June-July 1977, for further details.

60.   Daily Telegraph (London), June 4, 1979.

61.   Kyodo News Service (Tokyo), January 22, 1980.

62.   Asian Wall Street Journal, November 1, 1980.

63.   Ta Kung Pao (Hong Kong), January 14, 1980; China Times (Taipei), January 17, 1980.

64.   "North Korea, The Kim Dynasty," Far Eastern Economic Review, November 14, 1980.

65.   Asian Wall Street Journal, February 27, 1981.

66.   Mohemmed Aftab, "China Confirms Aid to Pakistan in Face of Threat by Soviet Union," ibid, January 22, 1980.

67.   Ibid. Author cites an Indian "source."

68.   John K. Cooley, East Wind over Africa (New York: Walker and Company, 1965), p. 52.

69.   The immediate reason for China's arms aid was to replace weapons lost after Tanzanian troops mutinied against British officers. For details on China's use of Tanzania as a transshipment point, see Alaba Ogunsanwo, China's Policy in Africa, 1958-71 (London: Cambridge University Press, 1974), p. 172.

70.   Chiang Tao, "Economic Aid to Asiatic-African Countries by Communist China," Studies on Chinese Communism, February 28, 1967.

71.   George T. Yu, China and Tanzania: A Study on Comparative Interaction (Berkeley: University of California Press, 1970), p. 66.

72.   Sunday Telegraph (London), June 20, 1971.

73.   Times (London), April 30, 1972.

74.   Mainichi Daily News (Tokyo), January 15, 1973.

75.   New York Times, June 21, 1976.

76.   David Bligh, "Red China in Europe," America, March 8, 1969.

77.   People's Daily, January 21, 1970.

78.   Chinese War Machine, p. 50.

79.   New China News Agency, July 3, 1978.

80.   Peking Review, July 21, 1978.

81.   New York Times, June 26, 1977.

82.   Keesings Contemporary Archives, May 25, 1979.

83.   IISS, The Military Balance 1980-1981 (London: IISS, 1980), p. 102.

84.   Justus M. von der Kroef, "Soviet and Chinese Influence in Indonesia," in Albin Z. Rubinstein (ed.), Soviet and Chinese Influence in the Third World (New York: Praeger Publishers, 1975), p. 69.

85.   Antonie C. A. Dake, In the Spirit of the Red Banteng: Indonesian Communism Between Moscow and Peking, 1959-1965 (The Hague: Mouton Co., 1964), p. 327.

86.   See The Chinese War Machine, p. 50, for details on the weapons originally given.   See also Bradley Hahn, "The People's Republic of China — Recent Naval Developments and Trends," Proceedings of the Second International Symposium on Asian Studies, 1980 (Hong Kong: Asian Research Service, 1980), p. 90.

87.   Nation (Sri Lanka), February 25, 1972.

88.   New York Times, July 18, 1972.

89.   IISS, The Military Balance, 1973/74, (London: IISS, 1974), p. 66.

90.   Irvin Kaplan et al., Area Handbook for Sierra Leone (Washington, D.C.: U.S. Government Printing Office, 1976), p. 339.

91.   Chinese War Machine, p. 50.

92.   Irvin Kaplan (ed.), Zaire: A Country Study (Washington, D.C.: U.S. Government Printing Office, 1978), p. 251.

93.   New York Times, April 8, 1977.

94.   Facts on File, August 25, 1977.

95.   Far Eastern Economic Review, April 22, 1977; The Chinese War Machine, p. 50.   The latter source does not give an exact date, but puts the number of planes at fifty.

132

96.   IISS, The Military Balance, 1979-1980, (London: IISS,
1980), pp. 104, 102.

97.   Asia 1982 Yearbook, p. 25.

98.   IISS, The Military Balance, 1979-1980, p. 104.

99.   Asia 1982 Yearbook, p. 25.

100.   Le Monde (Paris), September 13, 1975.

101.   Asian Recorder, September 10-16, 1978.

102.   "Intelligence," Far Eastern Economic Review, November
17, 1978.

103.   Nayan Chanda, "Cambodia's Cry for Help," ibid.,August
11, 1978.

104.   "Quarterly   Chronicle   and   Documentation,"   China
Quarterly, No. 77 (March 1979), pp. 157-216; Keesings Contemporary
Archives, May 25, 1979.

105.   Michael Leifer, "Kampuchea in 1980:   The Politics of
Attrition," Asian Survey, January 1981.

106.   Keesings Contemporary Archives, May 25, 1979.

107.   Leifer, "Kampuchea in 1980."

108.   Japan Times, May 2, 1981; Far Eastern Economic Review,
August 28, 1981.

109.   Nayan Chanda, "Haig Turns the Screw," Far Eastern
Economic Review, June 26, 1981.

110.   Nayan Chanda, "A New Threat from Mountain Tribes,"
ibid., September 1, 1978.

111.   Nayan   Chanda,   "A   Nonchalant   Revolution,"   ibid.,
December 28, 1979.

112.   Asia 1980 Yearbook, (Hong Kong: Far East Economic
Review, 1979) p. 222.

113.   Asia 1982 Yearbook, p. 188.

114.   J. D. Armstrong, Revolutionary Diplomacy: Chinese
Foreign Policy and the United Front Doctrine (Berkeley: University
of California Press, 1977), p. 147.

115. See Copper, China's Foreign Aid, pp. 55-58.

116. See ibid, passim, for further details.

117. Facts on File, January 18, 1980.

118. See, for example, K. Wafadar, "Afghanistan in 1980: The Struggle Continues," Asian Survey, Vol. 21 (January 1981), pp. 172-180.

119. China offered aid to Egypt in 1956 in the form of "volunteers" to help Cairo during the Suez crisis, but the aid did not materialize.

120. Harold C. Hinton, Communist China in World Politics (Boston: Houghton Mifflin Co., 1966), p. 185.

121. Ogunsanwo, China's Policy in Africa, p. 101.

122. Ibid.

123. Newsweek, January 13, 1964.

124. New York Times, February 12, 1965.

125. Ibid., February 11, 1969.

126. Facts on File, January 10, 1969.

127. Noshe Ma'oz, "Soviet and Chinese Influence on the Palestinian Guerrilla Movement," in Rubinstein (ed.), Soviet and Chinese Influence in the Third World p. 114.

128. Al-Hawadith (Beirut), November 5, 1971 and Daily Telegraph (London), August 26, 1970, cited in ibid.

129. See Far Eastern Economic Review, October 9, 1981.

130. See Gordon C. McDonald, Area Handbook for the People's Republic of the Congo (Washington, D.C.: U.S. Government Printing Office, 1971), p. 116.

131. In July 1963 the government of Cameroon accused China of supporting terrorism there. Apparently this accusation was connected to events in the Congo. Chinese military instructors were also in Ghana at this time. For further details, see Ogunsanwo, China's Policy in Africa, pp. 171 and 173.

132. East Wind Over Africa, p. 57.

134

133.   New York Times, March 11, 1966.

134.   Christian Science Monitor, June 5, 1964.

135.   Armstrong, Revolutionary Diplomacy, p. 218. According to another source, five delegations from Mozambique visited China in 1963; the next year armed struggle began there. See Ogunsanwo, China's Policy in Africa, p. 172.

136.   Marshall I. Goldman, Soviet Foreign Aid (New York: Praeger Publishers, 1967), p. 180.

137.   New York Times, October 26, 1960.

138.   Armstrong, Revolutionary Diplomacy, p. 222.

139.   Ogunsanwo, China's Policy in Africa, p. 172.

140.   Ibid.

141.   Area Handbook for the People's Republic of the Congo, p. 206.

142.   Sreedhar and Ghosh, "China's Foreign Aid Programme," p. 11.

143.   Hendrik J. Reitsma, "China in Africa," Focus, Vol. 26, No. 1 (Sept.-Oct., 1975) pp. 9-14.

144.   For background on China's involvement in the Angolan situation, see Alan Hutchinson, China's African Revolution (Boulder, Colo.: Westview Press, 1975), pp. 235-240.

145.   "Quarterly Chronicle and Documentation," China Quarterly, No. 78 (June 1979), pp. 400-443.

146.   Ibid.

147.   Roland Tyrvell, "China's African Cards," Far Eastern Economic Review, December 10, 1982.

6
Cuban Military Assistance to the Third World

W. Raymond Duncan

Cuba's greatly expanded program of military aid to Third World countries since 1975 commands attention for at least three reasons. First, Havana's military aid reflects its revolutionary ideology, which stresses an international duty to aid other people in their struggles for socialism and national liberation. As much applied in practice as advocated in theory, this ideology led the Fidel Castro regime toward a remarkable record of military assistance to Africa, Asia, the Middle East, and Latin America during the latter half of the 1970s.

Second, Cuban military aid abroad is linked closely to a high allocation of economic and human resources for homeland defense and to the general militarization of Cuban society. These features became pronounced at the outset of the 1980s as Cuba faced the Reagan administration in Washington, which escalated Cold War tensions and responded sharply to Havana's new military activities in the Caribbean and Central America.

Third, Cuba's advanced military aid programs coincide neatly with Soviet foreign policy objectives in the Third World as well as with Cuba's dependence on the USSR for economic and military assistance. In fact, this relationship complicates the analysis of Cuba's foreign military assistance program, blurring the lines between independent decisions made in Havana and those made in or influenced by Moscow. In light of these points, one simply cannot understand the Cuban Revolution and its foreign policy without taking cognizance of its military aid to Third World countries.

PRELIMINARY OBSERVATIONS

The early 1980s witnessed a high profile of Cuban military activity at home and abroad. In his main report to the Second Congress of the Cuban Communist Party on December 17, 1980, for example, Fidel Castro stressed the need to increase Cuba's own defense capacity to insure that all the island's people were "ready for action" against the "Yankee imperialist threats" represented by the new administration soon to take office in Washington.[1] This

objective would be met by the continued development of the new
Territorial Troop Militia, a voluntary organization of men and women,
peasants, workers, and students who were not members of the
reserves, the regular forces, or the Civil Defense forces.[2]   In
reviewing the 1975-1980 period in international perspective, Castro
especially praised the work of Cuba's Revolutionary Armed Forces
(FAR) in its internationalist aid to Angola and Ethiopia, noting that
"more than 100,000 Cubans -- the initial troops and their successive
replacements -- have been sent to Angola and Ethiopia as members
of our Revolutionary Armed Forces."[3]   Castro particularly focused
on the Caribbean and Central America in his speech, emphasizing
that, given the revolutionary political and military struggles in that
arena, the Cuban government considered it "necessary to promote
and support all the actions and attitudes of the governments and
political forces of the region that constitute an expression of
sovereignty and defense of legitimate national interests.[4]   This view
may well have been behind the increased military assistance to the
Salvadoran leftist guerrillas during 1980, a policy that evoked direct
opposition from the Reagan administration in early 1981.

By the early 1980s, then, observers of Cuban affairs saw a
combined emphasis on extraordinary defense efforts at home, a
continued military presence in Africa, Asia, and the Middle East,
and expanded military aid in the Caribbean and Central America.
This picture of the situation as it relates to Cuban military assistance
was perhaps best described by Castro himself in April 1981:

> Today we have tens of thousands of regular and reserve officers
> in our Revolutionary Armed Forces; today we have a degree
> of knowledge, experience, organization and technical know-how
> we didn't have then (twenty years previously when the socialist
> nature of the Cuban Revolution was proclaimed). At that time
> we didn't have, as we have now, the hundreds of thousands of
> reservists who have served in our Revolutionary Armed Forces
> or the tens of thousands -- no, more than that -- the tens upon
> tens of thousands of internationalist fighters who have been
> through the experience of combat, war and sacrifice. . . .
> This means that we're not fooling around; the Revolution doesn't
> fool around. It knows how to do things seriously and it is doing
> things seriously.[5]

The purpose of this chapter is to probe the experience of Cuba's
military assistance to Third World countries, with special attention
to the period since 1975, when its weapons aid increased in scale
and became more closely associated with activities of the Cuban
Revolutionary Armed Forces. This chapter is less concerned with
the FAR's domestic posture, although some attention is required to
that matter to place the foreign setting in more distinct focus.[6]

BACKGROUND

Origins of Cuba's Military Aid Programs

Cuba's sense of an international duty to support wars of national liberation is high -- indeed, it is one of the more remarkable attributes of that country's foreign policy. Students of Cuba's external relations are struck by its commitment to military intervention abroad, a commitment that often appears to be motivated more by altruism than by realist concepts of national interest (territorial security, defending political sovereignty, promoting economic development).[7] This is not to say that national interest is not at work in Cuba's military activities abroad. The government, and certainly Fidel Castro, are concerned with affirming Cuba's own identity and its role within the global political community as well as with helping to expand Cuban physical security. In fact, this line of reasoning supports the thesis that Cuba's numerous foreign involvements -- approximately 50,000 Cuban military and economic advisers in the Third World, from Angola to El Salvador -- are in many ways self-serving, inasmuch as they provide international prestige to the Cuban government, training opportunities for its military and paramilitary forces, and eventually even increased security, as the world "correlation of forces" between capitalism/imperialism and socialism/communism allegedly moves toward the latter.

Yet there remains that unique Cuban desire to shed blood for others who now share with Cuba some of the same types of problems formerly experienced by the Castro government. The origins of this aspect of Cuban foreign policy lie in history - a history of nationalist revolutionary struggles against colonialism dating back to 1868, continued efforts to gain economic and political independence from the United States after 1898, and a successful revolution waged by Fidel Castro against Fulgencio Batista that culminated in the revolution of 1959. Since then, the Castro regime has sought both to enhance its own security and to apply Cuba's revolutionary ideals abroad through support for other national liberation struggles. Cuba's own nationalist legacy, then, is one major driving force behind its willingness to send its people into battle for other countries.[8]

Marxism-Leninism under the stewardship of Fidel Castro forms a second motivating force underlying Cuba's military assistance policies. Grafted onto Cuban radical nationalism, it contains its own interpretation of class struggle, competition between the capitalist/imperialist camp and the socialist/communist camp, and the requisite urging of support for national liberation struggles. With worldwide imperialism led by the United States cast in the role of the main adversary, Marxism-Leninism reinforces Cuba's nationalist past and Castro's revolutionary movement, considering its affinity with Third World struggles against capitalism and imperialism.

Cuba's dependence on the Soviet Union for substantial economic and military aid and its increasingly close political links with Moscow form a third motivating force behind Cuba's own extensive military assistance programs. This dependence, examined in greater detail below, stems from Cuba's need for external support during the early 1960s and the resultant turn toward Marxism-Leninism and association with the USSR. The Moscow-Havana arrangement has provided tangible benefits for both the Soviet Union and Cuba since that time. For Moscow, Cuba's performance as an ideological and political ally provided the Soviet Union with its first significant leverage in the Caribbean and Latin America -- a geographic arena of increasing strategic importance to the Kremlin during the late 1970s. Cuba also became a means to promote Soviet interests in other areas of the Third World, which Cuban involvement in Africa and the Middle East so vividly illustrates from the mid-1970s onward. For these reasons, Moscow has continued its vast economic and military assistance to the island despite Cuba's poor economic performance and growing indebtedness to the USSR.[9]

Havana, in turn, derived a number of benefits from its links with the Soviet Union. It acquired a partner without whose economic and military help Cuba could not have survived the 1960s and 1970s. Even more, the Soviet connection greatly enhanced Cuba's economic and military ability to play the role of a major regional actor in distant areas as well as within its own region. And finally, the Soviet partnership helped to propel Cuba into a highly visible leadership role within the Third World movement, albeit not without some disadvantages.

Past and Present Support of Client States

Cuba's active support of revolutionary movements in the Third World dates back to the 1960s. During this early period the Castro government initiated a variety of types of aid to Third World countries, including the training of internal security forces in Guinea and Congo-Brazzaville, political ties with the MPLA in Angola, and subsequent educational agreements with that country and Mozambique. It publicly encouraged revolutionary struggles in Latin America, one of which had been joined by Ernesto "Che" Guevara in Bolivia. By late 1968, however, Castro was forced to modify his very public yet clandestine activities in Latin America, e.g., Bolivia and Venezuela. He did so for several reasons: (1) They were not working well; (2) they ran directly counter to Moscow's efforts to strengthen its government-to-government ties in the region; (3) Soviet economic pressure on Cuba to change its armed struggle thesis in Latin America was mounting; and (4) Havana found itself largely ostracized by the Latin American family of nations for advocating armed struggle against established governments.[10]

Given this situation in Latin America, Cuba gradually increased its military assistance in Africa and the Middle East as the decade of the 1970s began. Syria is a case in point; Cuban military aid there rose during and after the 1973 Arab-Israeli war.[11] These Cuban forces, however, were not used for front-line combat. Their general role was to provide logistical support or training, and as a result casualties were limited.[12]

The Angolan war of late 1975 changed this earlier pattern of military aid dramatically. It marked a turn toward much larger commitments of forces abroad, especially in Africa. Thenceforth a large military establishment became justified not only for the defense of the homeland but also for the projection of power abroad in support of national revolutionary movements.[13]

Cuban military assistance policy appears to have undergone still another transformation in the late 1970s. In Central America, where politically unstable conditions had produced a number of left-wing guerrilla movements, e.g., in Nicaragua with the Sandinistas and in El Salvador and Guatemala, Cuban weapons aid increased sharply, although Cuban troops were not sent into combat, as was the case in Africa. Cuba had supported the Sandinistas with low-level assistance prior to their victory and increased that amount substantially in 1978.[14] After Somoza's fall, Cuban military assistance to the Sandinistas continued with approximately 200 military advisers, who were officially invited by the new government (in addition to about 1,700 Cuban teachers, physicians, agricultural advisers, and construction workers in Nicaragua in 1980). Cuba meanwhile continued to increase its cooperation with guerrilla groups in El Salvador and Guatemala, as well as with the Communist Party of Honduras. This activity was undoubtedly stimulated by the Sandinista victory and perhaps also by disenchantment among Cuba's population regarding military involvement elsewhere.[15]

El Salvador's case underscores Cuba's return to increased military support of guerrilla movements in Latin America at the outset of the 1980s. A key report released by the U.S. Department of State in February 1981, for example, described Cuban involvement with the guerrilla operations in El Salvador. It documented the following types of Cuban activity: unifying the Salvadoran leftist forces, helping leftist guerrillas plan their military operations, providing aid in transshipping nearly 200 tons of arms through Cuba and Nicaragua to El Salvador in preparation for the guerrillas' failed January 1981 "general offensive," and sending weapons (largely of Western manufacture to cover its involvement).[16]

The late 1970s also found Cuba highly active in the Caribbean, which had become by then an area of growing Soviet interest. Havana began to send aid to Jamaica, a country led by Prime Minister Michael Manley, a leftist-leaning radical nationalist but not a Marxist-Leninist. By 1980, during the last year of Manley's leadership, approximately 350 Cuban construction workers were in Jamaica. Jamaica's new prime minister, conservative Edward Seaga, who was elected in late 1980, promised to curtail these Cuban activities. He began by requesting the departure of the Cuban ambassador.[17]

In Grenada, soon after the overthrow of Sir Eric Gairy's government in March 1979 by Maurice Bishop, Cuban military equipment and military personnel began to arrive to train Grenada's army. Accompanying these military advisers were civilian workers, some of whom would help build an international airport.[18] Still another country of interest to Cuba was Guyana, although through the 1970s Cuba extended more economic assistance than military aid. And the 1980s began Cuban-Guyanan relations deteriorated.

Arms Transfer and Military Assistance Capabilities

Cuba's ability to engage in arms transfers and military assistance of other types is extraordinarily high for so small a country. This capability has several bases. To begin with, the Castro government allocates a large amount of economic resources to military expenditures. If free Soviet military deliveries are added to Cuba's expenditures, Cuba's military wherewithal far exceeds that of its neighbors. During the late 1970s Cuba's annual military expenditures were estimated at $949 million, or about 11.9 percent of its gross national product.[19] By 1980 this figure had reached approximately $1.1 billion.[20] Given the growing problems with the Cuban economy, however, the government may find it increasingly difficult in the future to allocate so large a proportion of its annual budgetary expenditures to the military sector.

Havana's capabilities are also founded upon the highly militarized nature of Cuban society. Military service for three years is obligatory and universal. Cuba seeks to establish a very large standing army, as well as to provide ample personnel for the navy, air force, paramilitary groups and for the reserves. The FAR historically evolved from a period of large growth in the 1960s toward a slight decline in the late 1960s and early 1970s, followed by renewed growth in the middle to late 1970s. Reliable estimates place the size of the FAR at about 300,000 in the early 1960s, when it was at its peak.[21] In the early 1970s the FAR was in a period of decline, undoubtedly reflecting the government's turn toward more peaceful state-to-state relations, although it retained low-profile military assistance programs in parts of Africa and the Middle East. The FAR was estimated at 250,000 in 1970 and at 100,000 in 1974.[22] By 1975, however, the rebuilding of the FAR was reflected in a force structure of 117,000 and a ready reserve of approximately 90,000[23] Five years later, after a period of extraordinary troop commitment and other military assistance to Angola and Ethiopia, the FAR totaled 206,000 with 90,000 reserves.[24]

The militarization process is extremely entrenched in Cuba; in fact it is so pervasive that when individuals are sent abroad as part of Cuba's civilian programs, e.g., in health, construction work, or education, they also may be trained to engage in military activities. Castro's emphasis on the role of Cuba's overseas forces as "workers and soldiers at the same time" suggests that Cuba's overseas military influence may be greater than the number of military personnel stationed abroad implies. What exists here, in the words of one scholar, is the "civic soldier."[25]

The Soviet Role

On the question of technical training and equipment of the Cuban armed forces, the role of the USSR is paramount. Outside of some small arms ammunition, Cuba does not manufacture its own hardware, depending instead on the Soviet Union. Moscow provided Cuba with all the equipment it received during the first fifteen years of the revolution (1960-1975) free of charge, although some reimbursement is believed to have become part of their arrangement since 1975.[26] The decade of the 1970s witnessed an increase in the level of Soviet military deliveries and technical assistance to Cuba, especially since 1975, in the wake of Cuba's willingness to become heavily involved in Angola and Ethiopia, a policy indispensable to Moscow's own African adventures. Soviet arms deliveries to Cuba between 1960 and 1970 were valued at approximately $1.5 billion, but that amount doubled by 1975.[27]

After the Cubans intervened in Angola, the monetary value of Soviet arms delivered to Cuba again escalated sharply. This was probably due to the need to replace older weapons transferred to Angola, to Cuba's demonstrated ability to use modern equipment in that country, and to the Castro government's willingness to engage in support of Third World national liberation movements.[28] The number of Cubans studying in the Soviet Union also increased during the 1970s, as did the number of Soviet specialists coming to Cuba.[29] About 1,000 Soviet specialists were on the island in the early 1970s, compared to approximately 5,000 by 1980.[30] Soviet soldiers and technicians play various roles in Cuba. They help guard sophisticated communications facilities on the island and train Cuban armed forces for overseas assignments and for joint Cuban-Soviet activities. Soviet aircraft (TU-95s) also perform reconnaissance missions that monitor U.S. naval operations in the Atlantic region.[31]

The Soviet Union has greatly strengthened and modernized the Cuban armed forces over the years, with the general emphasis being on defense. As part of this continuous modernization process, Moscow provided Cuba with twenty MiG-23 fighter-bombers in 1977-1978. In 1979 the USSR gave Cuba its first submarine (a Foxtrot-class attack vessel), together with two new Tura-class high-speed torpedo boats and twenty new AN-26 transport aircraft all under terms of an agreement concluded in 1977.[32] The operational range of the MiG-23 allows it to reach the southeastern United States, Mexico, Central America, and the western islands of the Caribbean. These planes give Cuba a limited offensive capability in the Caribbean, although the aircraft is believed to be essentially defensive. However, neither the MiG-23's capabilities nor those provided by the AN-26 transport aircraft give Cuba long-range military power outside the Caribbean. Hence Cuba's reliance upon the Soviets for transportation, arms, and other logistical support remains great.[33] Yet given Soviet supply of the MiG-23s, Cuba has the best-equipped air force in Latin America.

By 1982 the Cuban Armed Forces structure was, according to the International Institute for Strategic Studies in London, fully reorganized and modernized. All its weapons are Soviet-produced. (see Table 6.1.)

What has given Cuba mobility in its more prominent military assistance efforts is Soviet transport and logistical support. Cuban military involvement in Angola and Ethiopia since 1975, to illustrate

TABLE 6.1 Cuban Armed Forces Structure, 1982

ARMY: 100,000

9 infantry divisions (brigades), some mechanized
Some artillery brigades
More than 600 tanks, including 60 IS-2 heavy, T-34/-54/-55/-62
PT-76 light; BRDM-1 armored cars; BMP mechanized infantry
combat vehicles; 400 BTR-40/-60/-152 armored personnel
carriers; M-116, 75mm pack, 122mm, 130mm, 152mm
guns/howitzers; 100 SU-100 SP guns; 50 FROG-4 surface-to-
surface missiles; 57mm, ATK guns; 57mm recoilless launcher;
Snapper, Sagger antitank guided weapons; ZU-23, 37mm, 57mm,
85 mm, 100 mm towed, ZSU-23-4 SP AA guns; SA-7 surface-
to-air missiles

NAVY: 11,500

3 ex-Soviet submarines; 2 F-, 1 W-class.
1 ex-Soviet frigate; 10 ex-Soviet large patrol craft: 9 SO-1,
1 Kronshtadt
26 ex-Soviet fast attack-class (missile) with Styx
    surface-to-surface missile; 5 OSA-I, 13 Osa-II, 8 Komar
    (under 100 tons)
24 ex-Soviet fast attack-class (torpedo): 6 Turya,
    6 P-6 (under 100 tons), 12-P-4 (under 100 tons)
16 ex-Soviet Zhuk fast attack-class (patrol)
    9 minesweepers
7 T-4 medium landing craft
Some 50 Samlet coast-defense surface-to-surface missiles

AIR FORCE: 16,000, including Air Defense Forces

189 combat aircraft, 12 armed helicopters
4 Fighter (ground attack) squadrons: 2 with 30 MiG-17; 2 with
20 MiG23
14 Interceptor squadrons: 2 with 30 MiG 21; 3 with 34 -21PFM;
2 with 20 -21 PFMA; 6 with 70 -2lbis; 1 with 15 MiG 23
4 Transport squadrons
7 Helicopter squadrons
Air-to-air Missiles: AA-1; AA-2; AA-8
30 SAM battalions with 200 SA -2/-3/-6.

Source: IISS, The Military Balance 1982-1983 (London: IISS, 1982),
pp. 103.

the point, could not have been undertaken without Soviet air and sea transport facilities or without additional Soviet-provided equipment, logistical support, and financing supplied during the fighting. In the case of Ethiopia, the Soviets provided superior aircraft, artillery, and tanks and the bulk of the foreign-supplied manpower in both Angola and Ethiopia was Cuban.[34] By December 1979 Cuban combat troops numbered about 13,000 in Ethiopia and approximately 19,000-21,000 in Angola,[35] backed by Soviet logistical support, weapons, and an estimated $7 million per day to subsidize the Cuban economy.

This emphasis on Soviet logistical support should not lead one to assume that the Cubans were coerced into going to Angola in 1975 or to Ethiopia in 1978. Cuban commitments to African countries long preceded these dates, and when the time came, Cubans demonstrated a popular and energetic desire to go to Africa in large numbers. They did so for a variety of reasons — their perceived African heritage, national pride, perhaps even the need for a new campaign abroad to reignite sagging revolutionary elan at home. Thus, if Soviet logistical support was one major variable, Cuban independent initiatives to go abroad were another regarding Cuban military assistance capabilities.[36]

As to other effects of Cuban military aid abroad on the economy at home, some discontent has been reported as a product of Havana's overseas involvement. This is due in part to the redeployment of manpower from domestic economic activity to foreign projects and to the establishment of a privileged class of high communist officials, bureaucrats, and military officers who have guided high-priority missions. As one observer put it, "many Cubans feel that a major contributing factor to economic problems is overseas military involvement."[37] However, this opposition does not appear potent enough to prompt any major cutback in Cuban military operations abroad in the near future. Nor does the Soviet Union indicate a desire to reduce significantly its enormous subsidizing of the Cuban economy, which makes Havana's overseas ventures possible.[38]

THE SCOPE AND STYLE OF CUBAN MILITARY ASSISTANCE POLICIES

The scope of Cuban military assistance policies now varies considerably from country to country. On a regional basis, the following major trends can be identified. The presence of Cubans in Africa, as noted above, dates back to 1963 when Castro first sent weapons (and reportedly troops) to Algeria during its border war with Morocco.[39] In the mid-1970s, however, Cuba became directly engaged in combat in Africa on a major scale when it entered the Angolan civil war. Approximately 20,000-25,000 Cubans, supplemented by another 4,000 civilian technicians, were estimated to have been sent. Later, in 1977, when Ethiopia and Somalia went to war over the Ogaden, Havana deployed an estimated 16,000-17,000 troops to support the Ethiopian Marxist regime, a deployment that peaked at 17,000 troops in 1978.[40] Cuba's troops were not used in Ethiopia's battle with the Eritreans for very practical reasons. Cuba had important economic and ideological links with radical Arab states, particularly Iraq, which supported the Eritrean rebels.[41] Cuba also supported ZAPU in Zimbabwe-Rhodesia, and ZANU. Havana also had an estimated 1,000 personnel in eleven other African countries. These personnel served as advisers, guerrilla trainers, and bodyguards.[42]

TABLE 6.2   Cuban Military Personnel in Africa, 1980

Country	Cuban Military Personnel
Algeria	15
Angola	19,000
Equatorial Guinea	200
Ethiopia	13,000
Guinea	50
Guinea-Bissau	50
Mozambique	215
Other	530
TOTAL:	33,060

Source: Central Intelligence Agency, National Foreign Assessment Center, Communist Aid Activities in Non-Communist Less Developed Countries, 1979 and 1954-79 (Washington, D.C., October 1980), p. 15.

In the Middle East an estimated 1,000 Cuban military personnel were in Marxist South Yemen in late 1979. Approximately 150 additional personnel were in Iraq.

Havana's foreign military interests in the Caribbean and Central America expanded sharply at the close of the 1970s. These regions offered a variety of opportunities to project a Cuban presence.[43] The emergence of leftist groups and movements offered points of contact and influence-seeking for Havana through the Caribbean.[44] Indeed, a number of leftist-leaning governments came to power during the 1970s, some with direct Cuban military support, as in the case of Nicaragua's Sandinistas, who then invited both Cuban military and civilian personnel to provide assistance.

Havana's assistance programs, military and otherwise, are widespread in the Caribbean. By January 1980, more than 1,200 Cuban teachers had arrived in Nicaragua, joining more than 300 medical personnel and 200 construction and other advisers, who worked on agriculture and fisheries projects.[45] Meanwhile, there were 50 military advisers or other personnel in Nicaragua by 1979 and 200 by 1980. By 1980, 1,000 Cuban construction workers had begun to arrive in Grenada to build a new international airport, for which Cuba supplied the materials; other Cubans participated in education, agriculture, medical care, and political indoctrination in that country.[46]   Military advisers went along or followed; an estimated 100 military advisers were in Grenada by 1980. In Jamaica, Cuba became very active during the era of Michael Manley (1972-1980), by helping that country improve its water supply and build houses and schools, by modernizing Jamaica's agriculture and fisheries techniques, and by aiding in medical services.[47]   An estimated 600 Cuban civilians were in Jamaica when the conservative Edward Seaga defeated Manley in the 1980 presidential election. These events are summarized in Table 6.3.

TABLE 6.3   Cuban Economic and Technical
Personnel (E & T) Compared to Military Personnel
(M) in the Caribbean and Central America, 1978-1980

Country	1978		1979		1980	
	E & T	M	E & T	M	E & T	M
Grenada			350	50	1,000	100
Guyana		10	65			
Jamaica	100		450		600	
Nicaragua			1,600	50	1,700	200
Total:	100	10	2,465	100	3,300	300

Sources: Central Intelligence Agency, National Foreign Assessment Center, Communist Aid Activities in Non-Communist Less Developed Countries, by year; Tad Szulc, "Confronting the Cuban Nemesis," New York Times Magazine, April 5, 1981, pp. 36ff.; and Impact of Cuban-Soviet Ties in the Western Hemisphere, Spring 1980, Hearings before the Subcommittee on Inter-American Affairs of the House Committee on Foreign Affairs, March, April, and May 1980 (Washington, D.C.: Government Printing Office, 1980).

This pattern of essentially peaceful diplomacy in the Caribbean and Central America shifted toward a greater emphasis on military aid in the late 1970s (see Table 6.3).   The shift found expression through a number of activities.   After having provided low-level assistance to the Sandinistas in Nicaragua for the two decades before their 1979 victory over Somoza, the Cuban government began to increase its aid to the Sandinistas in that year to help them achieve victory.   Support was extended by financing training, arms, and advice.[48]   The Sandinista victory stimulated leftist guerrillas to renewed activity and vigor in El Salvador.   Cuba in turn increased its training for members of these groups and increased its arms shipments to them.[49]

146

It is the Sandinista victory, then, that seems to have pressed Havana toward increased military influence-seeking in the Caribbean and Central America, coupled, of course, with its previous experience in Africa since the mid-1970s. By 1980, Cuba, in association with the USSR, had emerged as a major weapons supplier to the Salvadoran guerrilla factions and was the overall "driving organizational force," in the words of one analyst, behind the broad insurgency movement in Central America.[50] The role of Cuba in Central American armed struggles is documented by the U.S. Department of State White Paper entitled Communist Interference in El Salvador, dated February 1981. It cites positive evidence of Cuban military involvement in El Salvador, a point with which other Latin American governments subsequently were to agree.[51]

The White Paper reported that before September 1980 the various guerrilla groups in El Salvador did not possess modern weapons. Their arsenal consisted essentially of pistols, hunting rifles, and shotguns. But by January 1981, when they launched their "general offensive" against the centrist government of Jose Napoleon Duarte, Cuban efforts had helped them acquire about 200 tons of modern weapons.[52] These weapons, transshipped through Cuba and Nicaragua, are identified in Table 6.4

TABLE 6.4   Modern Weapons in Guerrilla Inventory,
El Salvador, 1981

Belgian FAL semi-automatic rifles
German G-3 rifles
U.S. M-1, M-16, and AR-15 semi-automatic and
    automatic rifles
Israeli UZI submachine gun and Galil assault rifles
30- and 50-caliber machine guns
U.S. M-60 machine guns
U.S. and Soviet hand grenades
U.S. and Chinese grenade launchers
U.S. M-72 light antitank weapons
U.S. 81mm mortars

Source: U.S. Department of State, Bureau of Public Affairs, Communist Interference in El Salvador, Special Report No. 80, February 23, 1981, p. 3.

Several explanations for Havana's renewed emphasis on military activity in the Caribbean and Central America are possible.[53] First, Soviet interest in the Caribbean and Central America grew from the mid-1970s onward in line with the tides of leftism then in motion. Moreover, Moscow's own proclivity to opt for military intervention, as in Angola and Ethiopia, emerged during this period and was sealed in place with the Afghanistan intervention of late 1979. This apparently new Soviet policy orientation placed Moscow more in line with Havana's older doctrines, developed in the days of Fidel Castro's guerrilla struggles with Fulgencio Batista, than had previously been the case.[54] Second, Cuba's experiences in Africa enhanced not only its Soviet-supported military capabilities but also its own military prowess to work in Third World setttings. Thus, Africa in many ways set the scene for the Caribbean and Central American versions of Cuban military assistance. Third, Cuba could reason that its leadership role in the Third World movement would be enhanced by aiding national liberation movements close to home in the Caribbean and Central America as well as those in more distant Africa and the Middle East.

CUBA'S MILITARY ASSISTANCE PROGRAMS: A CRITIQUE

Cuba's military actions in Africa since 1975 and in the Caribbean and Central America since the late 1970s led to diverse reactions from other actors in the international system. These responses are examined in an effort to analyze the successes and failures of Cuban foreign policy, especially since 1975.

U.S. Reactions

A key obstacle to normal relations between the United States and Cuba since the mid-1970s quite naturally has been Havana's military policies in Africa, the Caribbean, and Central America. Before the Reagan administration entered office in January 1981, the government of Jimmy Carter espoused a policy of improving relations with Cuba that dated back to the period of the U.S.-Soviet detente launched in 1972-1973. This trend included signing an antihijacking agreement in 1973, removing the U.S. ban on travel to and spending of U.S. currency in Cuba, and Havana's releasing a number of political prisoners. Yet obstacles to full normalized relations continued to block the road -- the Soviet military and economic presence in Cuba, Soviet aid of more than $3 billion for Cuba's military modernization, Soviet air deployments in Cuba that gave the USSR the capacity to observe U.S. forces in the Atlantic, and perhaps most important, Cuban military activity in Angola and Ethiopia.

The last months of the Carter administration coincided with Cuba's stepped-up military presence in Africa and with Castro's new high-risk military policy in Nicaragua and subsequently in El Salvador. President Carter became concerned with Cuban-supported Sandinista activity against the Somoza regime in Nicaragua, although his concern was not as vociferous as that of the U.S. Congress.[55] Even more difficult for the Carter administration during its last year in office were events in El Salvador. With Cuban military advisers in Nicaragua and Grenada, the Carter administration began secretly to train Salvadoran officers and helicopter pilots in the United States and at U.S. installations in Panama.[56] Simultaneously, it began to send in military equipment to the centrist Salvadoran junta, but it suspended these when three U.S. nuns and a lay leader were murdered in late 1980.

The Reagan administration, coming to power in a period of renewed Cold War tensions with the USSR, soon determined to draw the line on Cuban, and by implication Soviet, power projection to Third World countries throughout the world by making El Salvador a test case. Viewing Cuba essentially as a surrogate for the Soviet Union, Secretary of State Alexander M. Haig, Jr., testified before the House Foreign Affairs Committee in March 1981 that Moscow was responsible for "international terrorism," that it had a "hit list" for the domination of Central America, and that Nicaragua had already been lost.[57] This type of language followed a period of greatly intensified concern in Washington during February about the Cuban-Soviet involvement in El Salvador, leading to publication of the White Paper discussed above. In addition, the United States issued clear warnings to Cuba on possible direct U.S. action against Cuba if arms deliveries to the Salvadoran leftists did not cease. The United States also increased its commitment of military aid and advisers to El Salvador and cut off its development aid to Nicaragua, which had been implicated in the Cuban transshipment of weapons to El Salvador.[58] It must also be said that after considerable Western European and Mexican opposition to this sharp U.S. reaction to the Cuban involvement in El Salvador, the U.S. government began to put increased pressure on the Salvadoran junta to restrain its tacit and actual support of right-wing terrorism. At the same time, Washington began to move toward more long-range planning for economic aid to the region in an effort to get at the roots of the economic and political instability.[59]

Soviet Reactions

The Soviet reaction to Cuban military policy in Third World countries since the mid-1970s is one of pronounced support for Cuba in Africa and a new willingness to support Cuban risk-taking in the Caribbean and Central America. Yet Moscow, at times at least, manifested a sensitivity to becoming too closely identified with military support for leftist guerrillas in the Western Hemisphere, for in this region it has worked hard over the years to establish a reputation of dealing strictly with governments in peaceful state-to-state arrangements. This was true even during the 1960s when Cuba openly advocated support of armed struggle as the only path to change.

On the African continent, large-scale Cuban military intervention in Angola and Ethiopia could not have occurred without Soviet logistical and economic support. Indeed, Cuban willingness to "go to Africa" fits neatly with Soviet great-power aspirations in that region and greatly facilitated attainment of Soviet as well as Cuban policy objectives. Cuban combat readiness and performance made possible the projection of Soviet power because the Cubans— as Third World comrades — were more acceptable in African host countries as combat allies. The Cubans, moreover, had prior guerrilla training, if not conventional war experience, and Cuban troops undoubtedly possessed a greater sense of motivation and morale in this type of engagement than their Soviet counterparts. One might even go so far as to argue that Cuban forces were better organized and prepared for the type of fighting in Angola and Ethiopia than were Soviet forces, whose multilingual and multiethnic composition later raised serious problems in Afghanistan.

What is striking about the Caribbean and Central America is the new element of Soviet willingness to become, at minimum, involved clandestinely in Western Hemisphere armed struggles, perhaps at Castro's urging, in light of the newly emerging opportunities in that region. To be sure, Soviet interest in the region escalated perceptibly during the late 1970s.[60] Moscow continued to demonstrate its sensitivity about this region, however, by attempting to distance itself from the Cubans as the shock waves about the latter's interference reverberated from Washington.[61] A remaining question is to what extent Moscow's reputation with other Latin Amrican governments was tarnished by the El Salvador case. The Cuban involvement raised the specter of older Cuban postures of the 1960s, which led to Havana's isolation in the hemisphere; the Soviet involvement, coming in the aftermath of Afghanistan, may have reduced Soviet leverage within the region.

Third World Reactions

Third World reactions to Cuban military policy abroad must be divided into two regional groups: those of African countries, on the one hand, and those of Caribbean, Central America, and the remaining Latin American countries on the other. In both these regions, views of Havana since the mid-1970s, as one might guess, have been mixed.[62] Reactions from this Third World arena especially merit our attention, for it is in these regions that Cuba most loudly proclaims its version of internationalist morality and that its civilian and military personnel have been so active in promoting national liberation movements.

In part for his impressive support of left-wing movements and regimes in Africa, the Caribbean, and Central America, Castro was rewarded by receiving the chairmanship of the nonaligned movement for a three-year term beginning in 1979. With approximately 50,000 Cuban military and civilian personnel spread throughout the Third World at this time, much of the developing countries' response to Cuban internationalism was favorable. Indeed, this generally favorable reaction was underscored by the selection of Havana as the site for the Sixth Summit Meeting of the Nonaligned Movement. Cuban prestige had been built not only upon its willingness to shed blood for Third World brethren but also on developmental assistance — Cuban medical teams, teachers, construction workers, and agricultural technicians were in countries from Nicaragua to Ethiopia.

The beginning of the 1980s, however, witnessed a period of increasingly negative Third World responses toward Cuba. Moscow's

December 1979 invasion of Afghanistan, a member of the nonaligned movement, did not help Havana's position, especially in light of its insistence that Moscow was the "natural ally" of Third World countries. When nonaligned members voted 56 to 9 (26 abstaining or absent) in favor of a UN General Assembly resolution condemning the Soviet invasion, Cuba voted against that resolution and found itself isolated.[63] Havana eventually lost its bid for a Security Council seat in the UN, and the lingering question is to what extent Cuba's popularity among Third World countries was and will be eroded by its continued close association with the Soviet Union.

Soviet-Cuban activities in Africa are a case in point. As numerous reports, books, and comments in the recent past stress, Moscow is not "winning" in Africa.[64] This is so for a variety of reasons, including the low level of Soviet economic aid measured against African expectations, Moscow's patently clear pursuit of self-interest in most African states, the disenchantment of many African leftists with the USSR, and indeed, a rather impressive list of Soviet policy failures in Africa. As Soviet power is found wanting in this region in terms of its ability to influence local governments and events, so too the Cubans may find themselves less welcome than during the early days of their presence, although, to be certain, the Cubans are perceived as different from the Soviets. And in Cuba itself, a substantial amount of graffiti in Havana seems to indicate discontent with the African involvement. Other signs of discontent also exist.[65]

Caribbean, Central American, and South American responses to Cuba's increased military activity have been different but also mixed. From one perspective, Havana can take pride in its greatly expanded presence in the region, a process that dates back to the early 1970s. Compared to its virtual isolation in the 1960s, Havana's ties reach out to eleven Caribbean and Central American countries and include military roles in Grenada and Nicaragua and civilian help in Guyana, Jamaica, and Panama.[66] This pattern of widening activities in the region, based on government-to-government contacts, matches those of the Soviet Union and Eastern Europe. On the other hand, as of 1981, Cuban contacts and general acceptance in the Western Hemisphere had begun to decline perceptibly.

The events leading to lessened Cuban influence are easy enough to document, but their long-run impact is more difficult to evaluate. Guyana experienced difficulties with Cuba and became disillusioned with Cuban political interference and economic assistance.[67] Cuban-Venezuelan relations turned sour over an airline incident, and parties friendly to Cuba lost elections in Antigua, St. Vincent, Dominica, and St. Kitts-Nevis.[68] Colombia has broken diplomatic relations with Cuba over Havana's training of guerrillas on Colombian territory. Mexico, long a supporter of Cuba's revolutionary model, supplied El Salvador's ruling junta with oil and food despite its public stand favoring the left-wing guerrilla cause supported and armed by Cuba.[70] No less significant is Cuba's waning image as a revolutionary model to be emulated elsewhere. Havana's continued dependence on Moscow, its unspectacular economic performance, its past economic and political mistakes, and its rigid society all contribute to this more tarnished image. These events, combined with new U.S. government plans for substantially increased economic aid to the Caribbean and Central America, suggest that Cuba's image among Caribbean and Central American countries may be less favorable in the 1980s than it was in the late 1970s, and will further deteriorate should Havana continue its military activities there. Havana's medical teams, educators, agricultural specialists, and construction workers, on the other hand, are likely to continue to be welcome.

SUCCESSES AND FAILURES

In the 1970s Cuban foreign policy, with its military and civilian components, produced a distinctly positive set of outcomes from the Cuban perspective compared to events of the early 1960s. The government demonstrated a remarkable adaptability in its relations with the Soviet Union, moving from the strains of the late 1960s into a much closer relationship during the 1970s. This transition resulted in substantially increased military aid and modernization of Cuban defense and foreign-engaged forces, increased technical assistance, and a heightened level of economic support flowing from the USSR to Cuba. The Castro government, moreover, moved from virtual isolation, particularly in the Western Hemisphere, toward greatly expanded power projection in Africa, a new level of prestige and leadership in the Third World movement, and remarkably widened contacts in the Caribbean, Central America, and South America -- all consistent with Havana's claims of an internationalist morality and support of national liberation movements. In each of these regions, the Castro government demonstrated a unique ability to modify policies to fit evolving opportunities, to combine state-to-state relations with military assistance to national liberation movements, and to use both military aid and civilian brigades of teachers, medical people, construction workers, and agricultural technicians. For a country that previously had been the object of colonial and imperial pressures, the accomplishments of this island state in international affairs constitute no mean set of achievements.

Castro's capacity to adapt policy to fit evolving opportunities is offset by several negative factors. These features began to appear after the Sixth Summit Meeting of Nonaligned Countries in September 1979, the Soviet invasion of Afghanistan late that year, and the heightened Cuban willingness to support left-wing guerrilla movements during the same period. At the Nonaligned Conference, for example, Castro faced growing resistance from Third World governments over his efforts to move the organization closer to the USSR -- a resistance again demonstrated when Cuba lost its bid for a Security Council seat. The lengthy stay of Cubans in Africa, meanwhile, has increased the concern of some governments there about Soviet and Cuban intentions.[71] Meanwhile, by 1980, Caribbean, Central American, and South American governments began to react negatively to the Cuban's military posture an indication that the Havana government's return to its 1960 thesis of armed struggle, now with Soviet support, may produce the same results it did then.

Perhaps Cuba's greatest failure is its inability to develop economically. Here the existence of so large a military establishment and the pursuit of military goals abroad raises the issue of guns versus butter. Cuba's military programs at home and abroad, to be sure, help guarantee high levels of Soviet economic and military support, and the militarization of Cuban society is translated into psychological motivation toward work and struggle, both at home and abroad, in the face of "imperialist" threats. These are clear benefits. Yet such a great concentration of resources and manpower in the military sector may have contributed directly and indirectly to low economic growth.

Opportunities for Cuban military involvement in the Third World will exist as long as national liberation struggles continue to flourish. This is not only because of the left-wing political movements and the stagnating economic conditions that produce these struggles, as in El Salvador, Guatemala, or Honduras, but also because the Soviet Union became increasingly willing to project its own power to the Third World by the late 1970s. This willingness brought Soviet and Cuban diplomacy more into alignment, which was not the case during the 1960s. Soviet involvement in arms transshipments to El Salvador in 1980 illustrated this trend, as did the alleged Soviet military involvement in Nicaragua in June 1981 -- undoubtedly inspired by the Cuban military presence in that country.[72]

Yet the Cuban military profile should not be overestimated. Limits clearly exist. Cuba's close association with the USSR and the long-term effects of the Soviet occupation of Afghanistan on Havana's image among Third World countries are two cases in point. Consider also the limited Cuban economic and technical capabilities, measured against the developing world's staggering economic poverty and development needs. Additionally, internal political characteristics of the African, Middle Eastern, and Latin American settings affect Havana's influence. Finally, the waning image of Cuba as a revolutionary model and the international constraints on Cuban power in all these regions help to limit Havana's power.[73] The Cuban presence, then, does not guarantee increased Cuban influence, and it does entail costs as well as potential gains. Those who make Cuba's military assistance policies in Havana -- as well as those who influence them or respond to them elsewhere -- would do well to remember that.

NOTES

1.   Granma Weekly Review, December 28, 1980. Granma is the official organ of the Central Committee of the Cuban Communist party.

2.   Ibid. See also Castro's speech at the ceremony to set up the Territorial Troop Militia units of Granma province, Granma, Year 16, No. 5 (February 1, 1981); 2-3.

3.   Granma Weekly Review, December 28, 1980.

4.   Ibid., p. 15. Increased Cuban activity in the Caribbean and Central America during the late 1970s and early 1980s is reflected in testimony before the House Subcommittee on Inter-American Affairs. See Impact of Cuban-Soviet Ties in the Western Hemisphere, Spring 1980, Hearings before the Subcommittee on Inter-American Affairs of the House Committee on Foreign Affairs, March, April and May 1980 (Washington, D.C.: Government Printing Office, 1980). Also note that at the closing rally of the Second Party Congress in Cuba, Humberto Ortega, Commander-in-Chief of Nicaragua's Sandinista People's Army, and Maurice Bishop, chairman of the New Jewel Movement and Prime Minister of Grenada, appeared.   These individuals represented movements that had received substantial amounts of Cuban military aid, which in the case of Nicaragua may have played a key role in the Sandanista victory over Anastasio Somoza in 1979. See Impact of Cuban-Soviet Ties in the Western Hemisphere, p. 12. Other speakers that day included representatives from the Soviet Union, Angola, North Korea, Czechoslovakia, Ethiopia, Hungary, East Germany, Laos, Mongolia, Bulgaria, Mozambique, Poland, and Vietnam.   Many of these countries had received or were given Cuba military assistance, the more prominent recipients of Cuban support being Angola, Ethiopia, Mozambique, and Vietnam.

5.   Speech given at the military ceremony to commemorate the twentieth anniversay of the proclamation of the socialist nature of the revolution and Militia Day, April 16, 1981 (Granma Weekly Review, April 26, 1981).

6.   The most comprehensive overview of Cuba's armed forces and foreign relations through the latter part of the 1970s is Jorge I. Dominguez, "The Armed Forces and Foreign Relations," in Cole Blasier and Carmelo Mesa-Lago (eds.), Cuba in the World (Pittsburgh: University of Pittsburgh Press, 1979), pp. 53-88.

7.   Ibid., pp. 53-54.

8.   See W. Raymond Duncan, "Nationalism in Cuban Politics," in Jaime Schlicki (ed.), Cuba, Castro and Revolution (Coral Gables, Fla.: University of Miami Press, 1972), pp. 22-43.

9.   Moscow extended many types of economic help to Cuba
after 1960, including direct subsidies for Havana's trade deficits with
Moscow, payment for Cuban sugar above the prevailing world market
price, lowered prices for Soviet petroleum products, supplies of
military equipment, and direct credit for economic development. See
Jorge I. Dominguez, "Cuban Foreign Policy," Foreign Affairs, Vol.
57 (Fall 1978); 90. During the 1981-1986 period, the USSR planned
to double its scientific and technical aid to Cuba (Latin American
Report, 1 May 1981).

10.   On these and other aspects of the Soviet-Cuban
relationship during the 1960s, see D. Bruce Jackson, Castro, the
Kremlin, and Communism in Latin America (Baltimore: Johns Hopkins
University Press, 1969); Andres Suarez, Cuba: Castroism and
Communism, 1959-1966 (Cambridge, Mass.:   M.I.T. Press, 1969);
Edward Gonzalez, Cuba Under Castro: The Limits of Charisma
(Boston: Houghton Mifflin Co., 1974); and Jorge I. Dominguez, Cuba:
Order and Revolution (Cambridge, Mass.:   Harvard University Press,
1978).

11.   Dominguez, "Armed Forces and Foreign Relations," p. 61.

12.   Ibid., pp. 60-61. On early Cuban and Soviet ties in
Angola during the 1960s, see Jiri Valenta, "The Soviet-Cuban
Intervention in Angola, 1975," Studies in Comparative Communism,
Vol 2 (1978); 4-6.

13.   Dominguez, "Armed Forces and Foreign Relations," p. 61.

14.   Testimony by Martin J. Scheina, analyst for Cuban
Affairs, Defense Intelligence Agency, in Impact of Cuban-Soviet Ties
in the Western Hemisphere, p. 12.

15.   Ibid.

16.   U.S. Department of State, Communist Interference in El
Salvador, Special Report No. 80, (Washington: Department of State,
1981), pp. 1-8.

17.   See "First Month of JLP Government," Caribbean
Contact, Vol. 8, No. 8 (December 1980); 9.

18.   Jorge Luna, "Internationalist Cooperation with Grenada,"
Bohemia, February 15, 1980, pp. 80ff.; Scheina testimony, p. 12.

19.   Trevor N. Dupuy, et al., The Almanac of World Military
Power (San Rafael, Calif.: Presidio Press, 1980), p. 116.

20.   International Institute for Strategic Studies (IISS) The
Military Balance 1980-1981 (London: IISS, 1980), p. 81.

21. Dominguez, "Armed Forces and Foreign Relations," p. 55.

22. Ibid.

23. Ibid.

24. IISS, Military Balance 1980-1981, p. 81.

25. See Jorge Dominguez, "The Civic Soldier in Cuba," in Catherine Kelleher (ed.), Political-Military Systems: A Comparative Analysis, (Beverly Hills, Calif.: Sage Publications, 1974), pp. 219-236. See also Tad Szulc, "Confronting the Cuban Nemesis," New York Times Magazine, April 5, 1981, pp. 36ff.

26. El Dia (Mexico City), December 1, 1980.

27. Dominguez, "Armed Forces and Foreign Relations," p. 54.

28. Scheina, testimony, pp. 5-6. See Jiri Valenta, "The Soviet-Cuban Alliance in Africa and the Caribbean," The World Today, Vol. 37, No. 2 (February 1981); 45-53.

29. Ibid.

30. Dupuy et al, Almanac of World Military Power, p. 118.

31. Valenta, "Soviet-Cuban Alliance," p. 47.

32. Keesings Contemporary Archives, February 15, 1980, p. 30085.

33. Scheina testimony, p. 24.

34. See David D. Newsom, "Communism in Africa," Africa Report, Vol. 24, No. 1 (January-February 1980); 44-48. Also A. M. Kapcia, "Cuba's African Involvement: A New Perspective," Survey (London), Vol. 24, Nos. 106-109 (1979), 142-159.

35. Central Intelligence Agency, National Foreign Assessment Center, Communist Aid Activities in Non-Communist Less Developed Countries, 1979 and 1954-79; A Research Paper, ER-10318U (Washington, D.C., October 1980), p. 15.

36. On the independent aspects of Cuban military policies abroad, see Kapcia, "Cuba's African Involvement"; and Edward Gonzalez, "Complexities of Cuban Foreign Policy," Problems of Communism, Vol. 26 (November-December 1977), 1-32.

37.   Scheina testimony, p. 9.

38.   See Latin America Weekly Report, May 1, 1981, p. 3, which reports that the USSR plans to double its economic aid to Cuba in the 1981-1986 period.

39.   Congressional Research Service, Library of Congress, Soviet Policy and United States Responses in the Third World, A Report for the House Committee on Foreign Affairs, (Washington, D.C., March 1981), p. 61.

40.   Scheina testimony, pp. 9-10; and Szulc, "Confronting the Cuban Nemesis."

41.   Soviet Policy and the United States Response in the Third World, p. 61.

42.   Ibid.

43.   See W. Raymond Duncan, "Caribbean Leftism," Problems of Communism, Vol. 27 (May-June 1978); 35ff; also Scheina testimony, p. 13.

44.   Scheina testimony, p. 13.

45.   Testimony of Randolph Pherson, analyst, Office of Political Analysis, National Foreign Assessment Center, Central Intelligence Agency, in Impact of Cuban-Soviet Ties in the Western Hemisphere, p. 46. Cuban teachers began to return home in July 1980, but new groups went to Nicaragua in September 1980. (Managua Radio Broadcast, July 1, 1980, and Havana Radio Broadcast, September 18, 1980).

46.   Testimony by Myles R. R. Frechette, director of Cuban affairs, U.S. Department of State, in Impact of Cuban-Soviet Ties in the Western Hemisphere, pp. 58ff.

47.   Duncan, "Caribbean Leftism," p. 55.; Scheina testimony, p 13.

48.   Scheina testimony, p. 12; see also testimony by Lt. Col. Rafael E. Martinez-Boucher, chief, Latin American Branch, Defense Intelligence Agency, in Impact of Cuban-Soviet Ties in the Western Hemisphere, p. 28.

49.   Martinez-Boucher testimony, p. 29.

50.   Ibid.

157

51.   Communist Interference in El Salvador, pp. 1-8.

52.   Ibid.   As to agreement by other Latin American governments, this conclusion is based upon the observations of James Nelson Goodsell, Latin American editor, Christian Science Monitor, conversation, March 18, 1981.

53.   See W. Raymond Duncan, "Cuba in the Caribbean and Central America: Limits to Influence," paper presented to the 1981 meeting of the Caribbean Studies Association, St. Thomas, U.S. Virgin Islands, May 26-30, 1981.

54.   On the earlier period of Cuban-Soviet reations, see Jackson, Castro, the Kremlin, and Communism in Latin America, passim.

55.   See the full-page appeal in the New York Times by U.S. Congressmen to President Carter, urging him not to allow "another Cuba" in Nicaragua.   The appeal, with 125 signatures, depicts a Soviet arm (bearing the hammer and sickle) drawn across the island of Cuba, thrusting a large sickle into Nicaragua (New York Times, June 18, 1979).

56.   Szulc, "Confronting the Cuban Nemesis," p. 39.

57.   New York Times, March 19, 1981, p. 1.

58.   Ibid., February 18, 1981; February 23, 1981, p. 1.

59.   See Daniel Southerland, "New U.S. Aid-Caribbean Plan Would Find Room for Economic Solutions," Christian Science Monitor, May 26, 1981, p. 3.

60.   See W. Raymond Duncan, "Soviet Power in Latin America: Success or Failure," in Robert H. Donaldson (ed.), The Soviet Union in the Third World: Successes and Failures, (Boulder, Colo.: Westview Press, 1981), pp. 1-25; also W. Raymond Duncan, "Moscow and Havana in the Third World," in W. Raymond Duncan (ed.), Soviet Policy in Developing Countries, (Huntington, N.Y.: Robert E. Krieger Publishing Co., 1981), pp. 115-144.

61.   See, for example, the observations by Leonid M. Zamyatin, a senior Soviet official, who stated in February 1981, that "the Soviet Union does not provide El Salvador with arms. It never has. It never will. The President (of the United States) is absolutely incorrect. When the State Department invents White Papers that repeat lies many times, the lies do not then become the truth." (New York Times, February 26, 1981)

62.   See Michael Erisman, "Cuban Internationalism: The Impact of Nonaligned Leadership and Afghanistan," a paper prepared

for presentation at the 1980 conference of the Latin American Studies Association.

63.   The total Third World vote was 78 for censure, 9 against, and 28 abstentions/absences. Grenada joined Cuba in voting against. See New York Times, January 12, 1980, p. 4.

64.   See Alvin Z. Rubinstein (ed.), Soviet and Chinese Influence in the Third World (New York: Praeger Publishers, 1975); Arthur J. Klinghoffer, "Soviet Policy Toward Africa," in W. Raymond Duncan (ed.), Soviet Policy in the Third World, (New York: Pergamon Press, 1980), pp. 196-211; Robert Legvold, "The USSR and the World Economy; The Political Dimension," in The Soviet Union and the World Economy, (New York: Council on Foreign Relations, 1979), pp. 5-16; Elizabeth Valkenier, "Moscow Is Not Winning Africa," Christian Science Monitor, May 20, 1981, p. 22; and Tom Gilroy, "Red Star Dims in Africa," Christian Science Monitor, May 27, 1981, p. 1.

65.   Scheina testimony, pp. 8-9; 21, 22.

66.   Cuba found itself cut off from all of Latin America except Mexico in the early 1960s. By 1980 fourteen Latin American countries had embassies in Havana.

67.   Robert S. Leiken, "Eastern Winds in Latin America," Foreign Policy, No. 42 (Spring 1981), p. 101.

68.   See Joseph C. Harsch, "U.S., U.S.S.R. Agitated About Tiny, Troublesome Neighbors," Christian Science Monitor, February 20, 1981. On the Cuban-Venezuelan rift over the airline incident, in which the Venezuelan government acquitted four people accused of dynamiting a Cuban plane over the Caribbean, killing seventy-three, see Paris Radio Broadcast, October 1, 1980, Federal Broadcast Information Service (FBIS). When the Venezuelan foreign minister, Alberto Zembrano Velasco, returned from the UN after receiving chairmanship of the Group of 77 Third World countries at the UN he attacked Castro on public television for his conduct with the nonaligned movement, e.g., trying to align it with the Soviet position (Paris Radio Broadcast, October 1, 1980, FBIS).

69.   Seaga, moreover, resolved to wage a struggle against communism in the Caribbean to try to prevent the Caribbean Sea from becoming a zone of "Soviet influence" (Caribbean Contract, Vol. 8, No. 8 (December 1980), 809.

70.   Conversation with Goodsell.

71.   In a meeting of the Organization of African Unity in July 1978, Sudan President Gaafar el-Nimeiry urged African nations to reject foreign troops, and Nigerian leader Lt. Col. Olusegun

Obasanjo stated that the USSR and Cuba should not overstay their
welcome (Facts on File, Vol. 38, No. 1978, p. 561).

72.   See Communist Interference in El Salvador, pp. 1-2. The
June 6, 1981 edition of the Providence (R.I.) Journal-Bulletin quoted
Nicaraguan sources as saying that twelve Soviet advisers were in
Nicaragua to teach pilots and technicians how to fly and maintain
two Soviet helicopters (cited in Democrat and Chronicle (Rochester,
N.Y.), June 7, 1981, p. 6A).

73.   On these constraints on Cuban power, see Duncan, "Cuba
in the Caribbean and Central America."

7
Vietnam's Military Assistance

Douglas Pike

The Socialist Republic of Vietnam's (SRV) military assistance programs can be divided into two distinct categories by recipient. The first category comprises aid to the other two countries of Indochina, Laos and Kampuchea (formerly Cambodia), which to Hanoi are not "external" countries but are rather linked with the SRV in a confederated "special relationship." The second category of recipient is the rest of the world, in practice principally in other Southeast Asian nations. This natural division provides the format for this chapter, which begins with a discussion of military aid provided by the SRV within Indochina, then considers similar efforts in the rest of the world, and concludes with an estimate of how great an arms merchant Hanoi is likely to become in the mid-1980s.

In the way of a general summary, it can be said that Hanoi's military assistance to its two Indochinese allies in Laos and Kampuchea now and in the past has been maximal: all that the two could absorb. Conversely, military assistance outside Indochina, to date, has been minimal. Thus there is much to be said about the former and a limited amount about the latter. In terms of philosophy, the Vietnamese leaders remain in the grip of a messianic zeal to spread the fire of revolution against capitalism and to convert Southeast Asia into a string of "people's republics." The Vietnamese may not be the Cubans of Asia, as the Chinese charge; but they do represent a continually dangerous potential for intrusion wherever they sense vulnerability.

VIETNAMESE ARMS AID TO LAOS AND KAMPUCHEA

Vietnamese military assistance to Laos and Kampuchea is, of course, part of a broader assistance effort that includes food, petroleum, foreign policy advice, and a long list of other forms of aid. The extent and nature of these programs are the result of the Vietnamese Politburo's perception of a "special relationship" with Laos and Kampuchea originating in the earlier relations among the three revolutionary movements of those countries, that is, the

Vietnamese Communist (formerly Worker's) Party, the Pathet Lao, and the Khmer Rouge. At one time, about 1930, Vietnamese Marxists regarded the Indochinese revolutionary effort as a single entity and assumed that monolithism would remain after victory over colonialism. Hence Ho Chi Minh and others concluded that a single Indochina was the proper ultimate political configuration for the peninsula.

There were, in those early days, no Vietnamese, Laotian, or Cambodian communist parties, only a single Indochinese Communist Party (ICP).[1] National allegiance was dismissed as "bourgeois sentimentality," and good Indochinese revolutionaries were expected to overcome the pull of ethnolinguistic and other parochial ties. During World War II, for tactical reasons and later as a concession to burgeoning Lao and Khmer nationalism, the idea of a unified or federated Indochina was replaced by the "special relationship" concept. This term was never precisely defined, but it generally implied close mutual relations built around Vietnamese paternalistic preeminence. The basic notion was that what was good for Vietnamese communism was good for Laotian and Cambodian communism. It is on the basis of this set of perceptions that the SRV emphasizes its military and other assistance programs to Laos and Kampuchea. Obviously, geographical proximity plays a major role as well, as does the desire to eliminate Chinese influence from Indochina.

The Vietnamese have their work cut out for them, to put it mildly, if they hope to create a Federation of Indochina. But they are in no hurry. They see this strategy as a long-term and protracted struggle. Support for federation is still found in Laos, perhaps due mostly to Laotian resignation to Vietnamese dominance and to the creation of the People's Republic of Kampuchea (PRK) propounded by Hanoi's cadres in Phnom Penh. Thus since 1975 the probability of eventual integration of the SRV and the PRK has been enhanced. The point to be made here in terms of our interest is that the ruling Politburo in Hanoi does not think of relations with Laos and Kampuchea as being "external." Rather military assistance is extended within what is considered a single system.

In a military sense, the SRV probably views Laos and Kampuchea as areas of potential strategic weakness where hostile forces, either internal or external, could develop, first challenging local control and then posing a threat to Vietnam itself. Thus Hanoi's security is a constant in this relationship. In a certain sense, Vietnam seeks to maintain and expand its influence in Laos and Kampuchea for the same reasons the USSR seeks to maintain and expand its influence in Eastern Europe: national chauvinism and the maintenance of security beyond one's own borders. In both cases, military presence and assistance constitute a useful tool.

In Laos, the Lao People's Liberation Armed Force's strength in 1981 was about 50,000 in militia and security forces. This force is augmented by some 45,000 members of the People's Army of Vietnam (PAVN) on duty in Laos. For practical purposes the two can be considered a combined force. Logistically, Laotian forces are supported entirely by Hanoi, either directly or acting as agents for war materiel supplied by the USSR. This cost is conservatively estimated at about $75 million a year. In addition, the PAVN forces in Laos cost Hanoi an additional estimated $55 million a year.

In Kampuchea, the Kampuchean People's Liberation Armed Force is still being built. At the time of the Vietnamese invasion, in December 1979, there was no Kampuchean armed force in the full meaning of the term. Such military forces as did exist were part of the Democratic Kampuchea government of Pol Pot, that is, what was left of the original Khmer Rouge. It was not a national army in the true sense, having been transformed by Pol Pot in the 1975-1978 period into "people's forces," that is, local elements of more or less self-contained quasi-military security and guerrilla units. This transformation was in keeping with Pol Pot's drive to eliminate virtually all modern transnational social and governmental institutions in Kampuchea.

The Vietnamese entered Kampuchea with some 300 Khmer cadres who became the nucleus of the government of the PRK. They claimed to be accompanied also by 40,000 "liberation volunteers" — Khmers who had been recruited in Khmer refugee camps in Vietnam and Laos and then organized into military units. The 40,000 figure is obviously too large an estimate, and the Khmer whom the Vietnamese have recruited are at best only the base on which an army may someday be fashioned. The Vietnamese now are faced with the formidable task of creating an entirely new Kampuchean army from the ground up. This they must accomplish in the face of sturdy opposition from guerrillas and in a psychological climate in which both the fledgling Kampuchean military and the PRK government are elsewhere regarded as "lackey tools" of the Vietnamese. One of the reasons is that the PRK is totally dependent on Vietnam for its military wherewithal. It is unknown how much of the arms and equipment that Vietnam forwards to Kampuchea originate outside Vietnam, but virtually all Kampuchean arms and equipment have been sent to Kampuchea from Vietnam.

VIETNAMESE ARMS AID TO THE REST OF THE WORLD

Hanoi inherited a vast amount of exportable armaments and war supplies when it took over Army of the Republic of Vietnam (ARVN) stocks. Most of these armaments and supplies originated in the United States, and in early 1975 they had an estimated value of about $5 billion. Not all of this was available for export, however, as the $5 billion figure included fixed installation costs such as the Cam Ranh Bay facilities.[2]

In the days immediately following the fall of South Vietnam, the SRV's windfall of weapons left by Washington then excited a fear that the victorious Hanoi regime, moved by ideological impulses and financial needs, would launch an aggressive weapons sales campaign that would flood Southeast Asia, the Middle East, and elsewhere with captured ARVN equipment. The Ford administration even went so far as to develop contingency plans for direct action, such as intercepting Vietnamese arms shipments on the high seas. However, nothing ever came of these plans. In the 1975-1976 period, the shadowy world of international gun running was awash with rumors and reports of vast amounts of captured U.S. weapons about to be put on the world market. At the same time, there were official inquiries to Hanoi by several governments, including some Association of Southeast Asian Nations (ASEAN) countries, regarding purchases of certain items, such as spare parts for planes and helicopters.[3] Some of these inquiries may have had the tacit blessing of the United States which would not have minded seeing Hanoi sell this material if it went to responsible governments. Nothing, however, came of these inquiries.

The reasons for Hanoi's reluctance to export its new-found military wealth appear to be twofold. First, apparently Hanoi had a genuine fear of retaliatory reactions by the United States, ASEAN nations, Israel, or other countries that might have been attacked by recipients of Hanoi's sales or aid. Also, Hanoi would have paid a high price in loss of international goodwill for a relatively small financial gain if it had become a major supplier of arms to insurgency and terrorist groups. Second, the items sought by legitimate governments were critical items in the SRV defense inventory and therefore had to be retained by the PAVN. Vietnam had been the recipient of billions of dollars worth of militaryy aid and assistance during its war with the South and the United States, but arms imports fell rather rapidly after 1975. With no arms industry of its own capable of producing major military weapons and with its external sources of supply drying up, Vietnam was understandably reluctant to part with any of its military hardware. Vietnam's military leaders anticipated that the post-Vietnam War years would be lean as far as military stocks were concerned and were fairly determined to keep everything on hand. Hence they were able to block the efforts of those advocating sale, chiefly subcabinet officials in the economic sector.

The possibility that Vietnam would engage in large-scale sales of weapons and military supplies existed only in the first few years after victory, when it was generally assumed that peace was at hand in Indochina. However, as early as 1977 and certainly by 1978, Hanoi's leaders once again heard the drums of war coming from Kampuchea and then from China. By this time, the PAVN high command could convincingly argue that no war material should be sent abroad because it might be needed at home. At the same time, Hanoi's military planners began requesting new weapons and supplies from the USSR. It would be reasonable to assume that the Vietnamese Politburo felt it could hardly send Moscow a long list of needed military stocks while it was shipping weapons out of Vietnam.

Despite Hanoi's no-export policy, weapons from Vietnam have on occasion appeared abroad. For the most part, these have been small arms and infantry weapons, such as M-16 rifles, 81mm mortars and M-60 50-caliber machine guns, almost all of which are traceable, as they bear serial numbers or other identifiable markings. Such weapons appeared in Lebanon in 1978, in Singapore in 1979, and in

El Salvador in 1981. In each instance there was no doubt that the weapons had come from Vietnam. What was unclear, however, was whether the arms had been exported on Politburo orders or had been smuggled out with the connivance of, perhaps, a PAVN field-grade officer working with Chinese businessmen in Bangkok. The Indochinese peninsula is saturated with weapons and military hardware, some of it dating back to the Russo-Japanese war. Corrupt officials in Hanoi, Phnom Penh, and Vientiane are always ready to do business. Hence any enterprising foreigner in Indochina can purchase just about any arms he wants.

As far as can be determined from the few known instances of arms transfers, Hanoi does not extract any agreement in return for, or attach any strings to, its assistance; rather it is satisfied with making token gestures of fraternal support. Information on prices charged, if any, is virtually nonexistent. However, as any aid effort would be closely coordinated with Moscow, and as the SRV is not known for its altruism, it is probable that ultimately all costs are borne by the USSR.

The El Salvador case is probably the most persuasive instance of official SRV government involvement in arms export. The weapons that turned up in the war there in early 1981 -- rifles, pistols, light machine guns, and mortars — came from Vietnam. Although it is clear that these weapons left Vietnam with some degree of collusion by Vietnamese officials, the question remains how high in the hierarchy official support for weapons export went. The best clue is volume. Small numbers of weapons could easily seep out of the SRV through the entrepreneurial efforts of PAVN field-grade officers. Major quantities of weapons, however, probably could not be exported without authorization from the top. Currently, the volume of Vietnamese arms captured by the El Salvador government forces does not support the latter conclusion. Furthermore, some Hanoi watchers have suggested that the arms for El Salvador were solicited by Cuba. Havana propagated the theme of international socialist fraternity, and Hanoi acceded to the request with a token gesture of some U.S.-made arms so as to maintain good relations with Cuba.[4]

One imponderable is the size of the stockpile of U.S. captured arms still in existence from which the SRV can draw. The $5 billion "book price" of U.S. arms lost in South Vietnam as discussed earlier is misleading. Further, there is considerable evidence from departing refugees and even from the PAVN newspaper Quan Doi Nhan Dan, that much of the captured material was not properly cared for after its capture in 1975. Much was left in open storage yards at the mercy of torrential tropical rainstorms. Weapons packed in cosmolene can withstand such treatment, but other war materials, such as ammunition, cannot. Thus the total amount of captured U.S. arms available for sale abroad is probably less than is generally believed. And what surplus Soviet weapons the SRV has are being moved into Laos and Kampuchea to arm the Vietnamese-sponsored forces there. Quantities are unknown, but they are apparently limited.

THE PHILOSOPHICAL BASIS OF FUTURE
VIETNAMESE ARMS EXPORTS

With past being prologue, it is appropriate to conclude with an analysis of the philosophical basis for future Vietnamese external military assistance. Specific policy, of course, will stem from the dominant Politburo world view, which is fundamentalist and hard-line Marxism. To Vietnamese leaders, three major forces now dominate the world scene and will largely determine the future. The first force is the ever-growing economic strength and the ever-expanding military capability of the socialist world, emanating from the superiority of the socialist system over the "bankrupt" capitalist system. The second force is the rise of new national attitudes of independence, an outgrowth of the previous generation's anticolonial sentiment. This sentiment, the Vietnamese believe, has metamorphosed into a kind of xenophobic, nihilistic, anti-interdependence hostility to all outside influences. Events in the Middle East, especially in Iran, and elsewhere in the world, are viewed in these terms. The third dominating force is the solidarity perceived among the so-called Third or Fourth World nations (i.e., nations both small and poor), which are bound together by grievances against the established West and by the determination to redress existing economic imbalances. These three forces, Hanoi theoreticians assert, combine to create a fertile climate in which progressive forces will flourish. Vietnamese leaders tell Third and Fourth World visitors that they should press for immediate revolution in their respective countries, arguing that never have revolutionary forces been stronger nor imperialists weaker. Significantly, however, the SRV's own limited military resources, dependency on the USSR for new military equipment, and the threatening regional situation preclude significant Vietnamese extensions of military aid and assistance to nations other than Laos and Kampuchea.

Added to this world view is an abiding faith in and commitment to the doctrine of protracted conflict, i.e., revolutionary war as practiced and perfected in the Vietnam War. The chief meaning of that war, Hanoi theoreticians believe, is vindication of the Vietnamese communist strategy. The doctrine of "offensive strategy for revolution" proved itself superior, say the Hanoi leaders, to the two other anticapitalist strategies, the "compromise strategy" of coexistence or detente advocated by the USSR and the "negative strategy" of playing for time while awaiting communism's eventual victory advocated by the People's Republic of China. The essence of the successful doctrine developed by Hanoi was the proper combination of armed struggle and political struggle.[5]

This reasoning inevitably influences Hanoi's evaluation of requests for weapons from abroad. It means that potential arms recipients must pass a doctrinal litmus test. They must subscribe to the Vietnamese dogma that what is required is a kind of elemental and primitive attack on the citadels of capitalism, an assault that is head-on and full-scale. Also, recipients must accept fully Hanoi's strategic package of revolutionary guerrilla war divided into pincers of armed struggle and political struggle and deliberately fought as a protracted conflict. Only if the applicant is judged to be pure doctrinally and right-thinking strategically will his request for assistance be treated sympathetically. These are severe strictures. When they are combined with Vietnam's own needs and capabilities, it is understandable that Vietnamese arms exports outside Indochina are infrequent.

Vietnam's present leaders, moved by a messianic ideological impulse, see themselves as leaders of the world's masses marching to an ideological Armageddon. But for those who would change the history of the world, great is the gulf between dream and eventuality. For the moment, and for the foreseeable future, Hanoi faces enormous constraints. The society suffers from severe economic malaise and great social disarray. Its army is bogged down in a war in Kampuchea, unable to win or withdraw. China looms as a continual threat. Discontent with the present leadership grows where it counts in Vietnam, in the upper cadre structure of the Vietnam Communist Party. These and other constraints serve to inhibit Hanoi's impulse to export revolution through arms transfers. However, by all indications, the determination of the Politburo to keep alive the stark, although now somewhat fading, confrontation between communism and capitalism in Southeast Asia remains. If that proves impossible, however, Hanoi's Politburo appears ready to transfer the cold war arena from political ideology to economic ideology. There is a great desire in Hanoi to maintain a high ideological cast to whatever Vietnam does abroad. Eventually, this desire may burn out. Barring a change of guard in Hanoi, such a hope appears a long-term process.

The bottom line, then, is that Hanoi's role in the political/armed struggles in Southeast Asia in the foreseeeable future probably will be, at most, as a supplier of a limited quantity of arms, training, and how-to-do-it manuals. This role would at all times be minimal, following the principle that revolutionary guerrilla war must be the product of indigenous forces and not something done for indigenous forces by outsiders. A more complicated set of conclusions may be reached with respect to Hanoi's activities beyond Southeast Asia.

First, it appears that there are few if any ideological constraints on such activities. Practical arguments that such activity might be counterproductive or "adventuristic" might exist at senior Hanoi decision-making levels, but moral arguments would not be persuasive there. Indeed, to the contrary, Hanoi's present leaders believe that they have at least a moral responsibility to support organized efforts to topple existing noncommunist governments through the use of force.

The second conclusion is that Vietnam by itself can never become a significant arms merchant. Because there are no arms factories in Vietnam, everything it has to offer for export must come from elsewhere. Its Vietnam War cache is now being depleted, much of it having been expended in Kampuchea or lost because of poor storage or lack of maintenance. With only a few exceptions, the PAVN high command appears determined to retain for its own use what remains of these stocks. Token arms shipments, as to El Salvador, are possible, but truly sizable shipments are highly unlikely. If massive arms shipments out of Vietnam occur, these will have to be replaced by the USSR.

The third conclusion is that Vietnam could act as surrogate arms broker for the USSR. Undoubtedly, this would happen only in the event of great pressure from Moscow or because Hanoi perceived it to be clearly and immediately in its interest to do so.[6] The leadership is, in effect, cautious in linking itself to armed struggle as it sees another approach -- political struggle -- as better, safer, and cheaper. Resolute opposition by the United States, ASEAN nations, Japan, and others to SRV exports of arms could have, in some instances, a decisive deterrent effect. All of these conclusions apply only to the present leadership, which is anachronistic and aging. We do not know what position the next generation of Hanoi leaders will take on arms transfers or, for that matter, on other major issues.

168

NOTES

1.   For a brief history of these Indochinese communist movements, see Douglas Pike, History of Vietnamese Communism (Stanford, Calif.: Hoover Institution Press, 1979).

2.   Inventory in early 1975 included 500 tanks, 1,100 armored personnel carriers, 40,000 trucks, 800,000 M-16 rifles, 100,000 45-caliber pistols, 15,000 M-60 machine guns, 50,000 M-79 grenade launchers, 12,000 60mm and 81mm mortars, and 50,000 hand-held rockets (LAWS). Much of this inventory was expended in the last weeks of the war. For a detailed list of material see Douglas Pike's Documentary History of the Vietnam War on Microfilm, now in preparation.

3.   Nigeria in 1975 expressed interest in fighter planes, 105mm artillery and M-16 rifles. Pakistan and Libya expressed interest in C-130 transport planes. ASEAN nations also made inquiries.

4.   The flow of arms into El Salvador from Vietnam continued into May 1981 and gave little indication of tapering off. Also appearing at the same time were larger (crew-served) weapons. The total number of weapons captured by the El Salvador government traceable to Vietnam by mid-May 1981 was about 8,100.

5.   Another reason for Hanoi's reluctance to fund insurgencies in Southeast Asia may have been the low esteem in which Hanoi officials held the various insurgent movements in terms of sheer competency. This is particularly true of the three separate insurgent movements in Thailand.

6.   The Vietnamese at this writing are deeply dependent on the USSR for food and security and hence are subject to greater pressure from Moscow than would normally be the case.

8
North Korean Military Assistance

Nack An and Rose An

Until fairly recently, North Korea, or the Democratic People's Republic of Korea (DPRK), was more a recipient than a donor of military aid. In fact, the DPRK's very existence was owed to a foreign power, the Soviet Union, and it was spared certain extinction during the Korean War by yet another neighboring power, the People's Republic of China. Following the Korean War, North Korea took a considerable amount of economic and military aid from the Soviet Union, the People's Republic of China, and other fraternal communist nations to rehabilitate its war-torn economy and to refurbish its badly battered armed forces. In the post-Korean War decade alone the Soviet Union provided at least 2 billion rubles in grants and credits, the services of 1,500 technicians, advice, and technical equipment for some forty industrial enterprises. Chinese contributions of grants and credits to North Korea were no less significant, estimated at 1.8 billion rubles by 1961. The combined total aid to 1961 from East Germany, Poland, Czechoslovakia, Romania, Bulgaria, and Hungary amounted to 620.1 million rubles, which proved to be critical in rebuilding the economic infrastructure and the industrial edifice needed to reorganize and refurbish North Korea's armed forces.[1] Without this external aid, the North Korean economy would have lain prostrate for a much longer period.

The task of reconstruction was truly formidable, given the magnitude of the destruction and the loss of human resources during the three years of war. By the end of the 1950s and throughout the 1960s, North Korea was totally absorbed in domestic economic rehabilitation efforts which would eventually provide the basis for its military programs.

In the early 1970s North Korea began to bolster its international standing and to refurbish its badly tarnished image abroad. With the passage of time, it had become obvious to North Korea that confining its diplomatic contacts solely to fraternal communist nations hampered the pursuit of diplomatic and political objectives abroad, particularly in the Third World. Its membership in international agencies and its participation in the United Nations as an observer sharpened the DPRK's perception that it needed more trading partners and more support among nations of Africa, Asia, the Middle East, and Latin America. To win their support and to be able to exert influence in these nations, Pyongyang decided to employ military assistance programs as an instrument of its foreign policy.[2] First, however, the DPRK was faced with the problem of rationalizing its ideological emphasis on revolutionary self-sufficiency.

IDEOLOGICAL UNDERPINNINGS OF MILITARY ASSISTANCE

Throughout its history, North Korean foreign policy had been based upon a concept called "Juche," a rather ambiguous term that could be translated as "self-identity," "autonomy," or "self-reliance."[3] Kim Il-sung in 1955 explained Juche as follows:

> What is Juche in our Party's ideological work? What are we doing? We are not engaged in any other counrty's revolution, but solely in the Korean revolution. Devotion to the Korean revolution is Juche in the ideological work of our Party. Therefore, all ideological work must be subordinated to the interests of the Korean revolution. When we study the history of the Communist Party of the Soviet Union, the history of the Chinese revolution, or the universal truth of Marxism-Leninism, it is entirely for the purpose of correctly carrying out our own revolution.[4]

This narrow construction of the concept was consistent with the DPRK's immediate desire to be free from the domineering hands of the Soviet Union and China yet consistent with North Korea's need for external economic support. With Pyongyang's decision to play a more independent role in the global community, Juche had to be either discarded or redefined. The latter option was chosen. To that end, Kim Il-sung has disavowed on numerous occasions the alleged incongruence of Juche with internationalism:

> The Juche idea is fully in accord with proletarian internationalism. The Juche idea is not an idea counterpoised to proletarian internationalism; it rather strengthens proletarian internationalism and promotes the advancement of the world revolution.[5]

On another occasion, he said:

> The independence we advocate does not by any means conflict with proletarian internationalism. It is, on the contrary, aimed to strengthen proletarian internationalism and should never weaken it. There can be no internationalism apart from independence, and vice versa. If one turns his back on Marxism-Leninism and proletarian internationalism and takes to national egoism, under the pretext of maintaining independence, he is making a grave mistake. What is more, the renunciation of

the principle of class solidarity and the rejection of joint action and joint struggle by class brothers, using "independence" as a rationale, is not an attitude befitting a Communist. Such acts will do enormous harm to the development of the world revolution and, moreover, result in undermining the revolution in one's own country.[6]

The rhetoric represented in the above statements is repeated in the DPRK's 1972 Constitution. Article 16 provides that:

. . . the state, in accordance with the principles of Marxism-Leninism and proletarian internationalism, unites with the socialist countries,unites with all the people of the world opposed to imperialism and actively supports and encourages their struggles for national liberation and their revolutionary struggles.

Thus, by the early 1970s, the DPRK had recognized a need for its involvement in the field of external military assistance and therefore rationalized in ideological terms its entry to the field. Its small economic base limited the scale of its potential involvement, but the DPRK soon was actively rendering military assistance.

TYPES OF NORTH KOREAN MILITARY ASSISTANCE

Acting on the principle cited above embodied in its Constitution, North Korea has extended financial and military aid to revolutionary forces waging wars of national liberation. During the Vietnam War, for instance, of all the countries in the communist bloc, no nation verbally supported the "struggle of the Vietnamese people against imperialism and for their liberty and independence" more than did North Korea. Whether Pyongyang was generous with material aid to Hanoi and the National Liberation front of South Vietnam can only be speculated on. At least a modest amount of North Korean economic, technical, and military aid was channeled to Hanoi. North Korea even repeatedly expressed its willingness to send "volunteers" to help repel "the American imperialist aggressors," although Hanoi did not accept the offers.[7]

The extent of DPRK military aid is difficult to document accurately, for much of the information is classified. Nevertheless, a composite picture emerges from fragmented information gleaned from diverse sources. It shows that North Korean military aid has been extended both to revolutionary forces seeking to overthrow existing governments and to established regimes. In the former case, military assistance includes outright financial grants, small arms, and training of insurgents both at training facilities in North Korea and at guerrilla bases in various countries. In the latter case, military assistance includes sharing military expertise in some instances and selling that expertise in others. All in all, it is clear that North Korean military assistance consists primarily of providing military training and small arms in modest quantities to groups throughout the Third World, supplemented occasionally by modest cash donations.

During the 1970s, North Korea stepped up its foreign military activities by providing $50,000 to the Forces for National Liberation (FALN) in Venezuela for the purpose of overthrowing the Caracas government. It also expanded its activities into other Latin American countries, as well as to the Asian and African continents.[8] Considerable military assistance was also extended to revolutionary groups in Argentina between 1971 and 1977. The People's Liberation Army was helped by the DPRK in 1971-1972 with a donation of $695,000. A guerrilla base at Satta was established in December 1973 with North Korean help, and a cadre of thirty to forty Argentine guerrillas was trained by North Korean agents. In October 1977, the Revolutionary People's Army of Argentina, the Fatherland Safeguarding Movement of Argentina, the Fatherland Safeguarding Movement of Paraguay, and Latin America (a radical leftist group operating in several Latin American countries) shared $1,600,000 in aid from the DPRK. Finally, Bolivian leftists were greatly aided in their antigovernment activities from 1965 to 1973 by $280,000 in North Korean financial support.

In Brazil, North Korea helped establish a guerrilla base in November 1970 in the vicinity of Porto Alegre, where sixteen guerrillas were trained. Additionally, the DPRK forwarded $50,000 to this group, which used the money to purchase arms. Similar activities occurred in Chile. Leftist Revolutionary Chile, an antigovernment guerrilla group, was actively supported in 1973. Two years later, the DPRK supplied communist-oriented leftists there with small arms and other military equipment. In May 1975 four North Korean diplomats were arrested on suspicion of instigating antigovernment student demonstrations. A leftist group in Uruguay also received $343,000 from North Korea from 1965 to 1973.

North Korea has trained revolutionaries both at home and abroad. Guerrilla training inside North Korea has been facilitated by a guerrilla training camp established in 1972 in the vicinity of Pyongyang. (Defectors from North Korea pinpoint Wonhung-ri, Kangdong-gun, South Pyong-an Province, as the location.) Since the establishment of the training camp, more than one huundred members of the Guatemalan People's Liberation Army and fifty members of the Movement for Revolutionary Action (MRA) have gone through training programs varying in duration from six to thirteen months. A large number of Peruvian students were also trained in guerrilla warfare in North Korea in early 1977. Cuba, too, had a small number of its guerrilla warfare instructors trained in January 1978 in assembly of new weapons and techniques of guerrilla warfare. Nicaraguan Foreign Minister Thomas Boggs made a secret visit to Pyongyang in April 1980 to seek North Korean aid. As a result, North Korea sent several dozen military advisers to Nicaragua in March 1981 to help train the Sandinistas.

Twenty Peruvian women were trained within the compound of the North Korean trade mission in Peru in antigovernment subversive activities in April 1977. During the July 1977 general strike in Peru,

North Koreans provided military training to members of an antigovernment organization at a guerrilla base near Lima.

North Korea has also been active as a purveyor of military equipment and training elsewhere in Africa and Asia. In Algeria and Chad, North Korean agents trained guerrillas in 1976 and 1979 respectively. From January 1972 to January 1976, thirty to forty guerrillas from the PLO, Zaire, Angola, and Mexico participated in three-to-five-month training courses at the guerrilla training camp near Pyongyang. Arab terrorists were also provided with weapons: and thirty PLO guerrillas were trained in North Korea in August 1972. In the following year, Palestinian guerrillas were trained by seventy to eighty North Korean instructors. The training of Palestinian guerrillas continued to at least 1975.

Black guerrillas from Zimbabwe-Rhodesia benefited from North Korean military advisory groups in 1976, and even after the demise of white minority rule, North Korea continued to support Robert Mugabe's forces. In July 1981 it was disclosed that two North Korean mechanized infantry battalions and one company of North Korean combat engineers were in Zimbabwe. Guerrilla groups from Somalia trained in the DPRK in 1976, and North Korean experts have trained revolutionaries at the revolutionary school at Tabora, Tanzania since August 1971. In April 1976 North Koreans working in concert with the Japanese Red Army and leftists from Somalia and Pakistan lent active support to Lebanese Muslims. In November 1979 four Lebanese college students were sent to Pyongyang to be trained in espionage.

Asian and European groups have also used North Korean training facilities. All eighteen North Korean diplomats in Colombo, Sri Lanka were ousted for giving financial support to the People's Liberation Front which tried to topple the Sri Lankan government in April 1971. Twenty-five members of the Thai Communist Party received guerrilla training in North Korea in April 1976. As of the beginning of 1981, North Korean training centers had reportedly turned out at least 2,500 operatives.

Interestingly enough, even the United States and West Germany were not totally excluded from the touch of the North Korean revolutionary fervor. North Korea allegedly furnished the Black Panthers with booklets on revolution and guerrilla warfare. The West German Baader-Meinhof gang also received North Korean military training and political cooperation.

In some instances, North Korean advisers have personally operated military equipment for foreign beneficiaries. According to U.S. intelligence reports, more than 100 North Korean pilots have recently been in Libya flying advanced Soviet-built fighters. The pilots began arriving in January 1979 and participated in training exercises with MiG-23 fighters shipped from the Soviet Union to Libya between 1977 and 1978.[9] The North Korean venture in Libya was not unprecedented, for DPRK pilots flew Egyptian aircraft during the 1973 war in the Middle East.[10] North Koreans are also said to have operated Libyan tanks during the 1977 Egyptian-Libyan conflict.[11] More recently, Syria is reported to have had North

Korean military advisers.[12] And in late 1978 Madagascar had North Korean advisers carrying out training missions there.[13]

LIMITATIONS ON NORTH KOREAN CAPABILITIES

North Korea's financial situation does not permit it to lavish its scarce resources on foreign adventures that have little prospect for success. In the early 1970s, the DPRK was able to generate far too little export earnings, with the result that in its effort to modernize its industrial plant it accumulated large foreign debts and was unable to meet payments. North Korea thus became the first communist state ever to default involuntarily on its international obligations.[14] In 1975 the country defaulted on payments due on an estimated $1.7 billion of external debt.[15] Again in 1976 North Korea defaulted on a foreign debt of approximatey $100 million. Japanese companies, to which Pyongyang owed $500 million, were among the creditors affected by the default.[16] In June 1981 North Korea defaulted for the third time on foreign debts amounting to $280 million, this time to two groups consisting of seventy-three European banks. Western European nations and Japan arranged a rescheduling of debt.[17]

To alleviate these financial difficulties, North Korea has engaged in drug trafficking, black market activities, and limited small arms sales. In 1976, for example, the North Korean ambassador to Denmark and two of his aides were expelled for smuggling liquor and cigarettes.[18] More recently, reports have regularly surfaced that North Korea was selling small arms and spare parts to Iran for use in its war with Iraq.

With these sorts of financial problems and with no major arms industries of its own, it is not surprising that the DPRK has concentrated its foreign military assistance programs on training revolutionary cadres. It should also be noted, however, that despite the country's precarious international financial position Kim Il-sung considers it necessary for the DPRK to extend some monetary assistance and small arms aid to revolutionary movements and governments. The rationale for this support is both ideological and a product of Pyongyang's desire to maximize international support for its objective of reunifying Korea.

CONCLUSIONS

For the future, North Korea undoubtedly will continue to maintain its revolutionary relations and to use military assistance on a modest but selective basis to further its foreign policy objectives abroad. Naitional energies, however, will be devoted largely to economic development. A rather drastic change took place during the 1970s in the general direction of public policy, a change that appeared to signal that a new generation of technicians and officials in the Korean Workers party had prevailed over the older generation of militant leaders. From this time the battle between the two

Koreas may be one of gross national product, with the North trying to show that is is a match for the South.[19]

This fact, together with the facts that North Korea consistently commits a much greater percentage of its GNP to defense outlays than does South Korea[20] and that North Korea's international financial status is tenuous at best, argues strongly that in areas other than military training, North Korea's participation in the spheres of international military assistance and arms transfers will remain limited during the 1980s. As long as North Korea remains preoccupied with the pursuits of economic development and Korean unification, what resources it does have or receives from external sources will remain concentrated on those objectives. Thus, while the DPRK will continue to espouse its "revolutionary relations" and train those whose views are similarly revolutionary, it must of necessity remain a minor actor in the military assistance field.

176

NOTES

1.   Glenn D. Paige, The Korean People's Democratic Republic (Stanford, Calif.: Stanford University Press, 1968), pp. 41-43.

2.   For an extensive discussion of this development, refer especially to Samuel S. Kim, "Pyongyang, the Third World," Korea and World Affairs, Vol. 3, No. 4 (Winter 1979), pp. 439-462.

3.   Ilpyong J. Kim, Communist Politics in North Korea (New York: Praeger Publishers, 1975), pp. 42-46.

4.   Kim Il-sung, On Juche in our Revolution, Volume I (New York: Weekly Guardian Associates, 1977), p. 136.

5.   Cited in Kim Il-sung, On the Juche Idea: Excerpts (Pyongyang, n.d.), p. 281.

6.   Ibid.

7.   For an excellent discussion of this subject, see Byung Chul Koh, The Foreign Policy of North Korea (New York: Praeger Publishers, 1969); and Wayne S. Kiyosaki, North Korea's Foreign Relations: The Politics of Accommodation, 1945-75 (New York: Praeger Publishers, 1976).

8.   Much of the information provided in the following pages comes from Vantage Point, Vol 1, No. 6 (October 1978), pp. 18-20 and unpublished data compiled in July 1981 for this author by Naehoe Press (Seoul, Korea). These data were gleaned from various sources, but due to the security considerations, individual sources cannot be divulged by Naehoe Press.

9.   New York Times, February 12, 1979.

10.   Ibid.

11.   Ibid.

12.   Ibid.

13.   "The Report on North Korean Activities in Support of Revolutionary Movements Since 1978," unpublished data, compiled July 7, 1981 by Naehoe Press.

14.   Robert Scalapino, The United States and Korea: Looking Ahead, The Washington Papers No. 69 (Beverly Hills, Calif.: Sage, 1979), p. 40.

15.   New York Times, February 26, 1976.

16.   Ibid., August 11, 1980.

17.   Korea Herald, June 19, 1981.

18.   New York Times, February 26, 1976.

19.   Ibid., August 11, 1980.

20.   North Korean military outlays skyrocketed during the mid-1960s from a figure of 5.8 percent of GNP in 1964 to an estimated 30 percent by 1971. Since 1976 Pyongyang has continuously allotted between 23 and 25 percent of its GNP for defense, although Western sources put the figure somewhat lower, at approximatey 15 percent for 1980. See John Lewis, "The Threat: The North's Behavior Is Not All Reassuring," Far Eastern Economic Review, 108 (May 30, 1980), pp. 44-45. South Korea, meanwhile, spent approximately 4 percent of its GNP on military outlays until 1975, when the percentage jumped to 5 percent; it continued to increase to 6 percent in 1976. In 1971 Seoul spent little more than half the amount of money Pyongyang did on the military ($440 million compared to $749 million) but by mid-decade the trend had reversed; by 1976 the South spent $1.38 billion compared with the north's $1 billion. See Tong Whan Park, "The Korean Arms Race: Implications in the International Politics of Northeast Asia," Asian Survey, Vol. 20, No. 6 (June 1980):650. The National Unification Board recently announced that in 1979 the GNP of South Korea was $61 billion, compared with $12.5 billion for the North; thus per capita GNP of South Korea was $1,624, while that of North Korea was $719.

9
Conclusion

John F. Copper
Daniel S. Papp

One of the most salient points that can be drawn from this study is that the military assistance given by communist nations is almost as diverse and varied as the number of countries in the arms assistance game. Clearly the military assistance programs of communist countries, like those of Western countries, reflect varying capabilities, intentions, and experiences in the military assistance game.

This is not to say, however, that communist nations can be seen by Western decision makers as simply additional nations in the contest for giving arms assistance. As the Soviet Union is by far the largest purveyor of weapons among communist countries, there should be concern about the fact that in 1980 the Soviet Union surpassed the United States in total military assistance. This point must, in fact, be underscored when it is realized that among communist nations only China is pursuing policies in giving military assistance that are at odds with those of the Soviet Union, and China's military assistance program has declined markedly since the mid 1970s. Thus, in the sense that the West must react to communist weapons in Third World countries, it is crucial that the Soviet Union has vastly increased its weapons giving, that most of the Eastern European nations support Soviet policy or are neutral, and that both Cuba and Vietnam are new in the game and are generally supporting the Kremlin in its arms assistance policies.

These factors may suggest that Western countries and particularly the United States must once again increase their weapon's aid and sales abroad. Alternatively, they must seek some means to persuade communist nations to reduce the volume of weapons and other forms of military assistance they have been extending in recent years. A third alternative is to supply China with some of the weapons it needs in return for a stepping-up of its military assistance to Third World countries. This alternative assumes that China's military assistance program has been broadly successful and that Chinese interests necessarily coincide with those of the West. The analysis of China's military assistance program, however, does not necessarily warrant such a conclusion.

If an effort is made to categorize communist nations' military assistance, one simple way to do so would be to note pro-Soviet, neutral, and anti-Soviet programs. It then becomes evident that most of the communist nations' military assistance programs fit into one of the first two categories. Only China's military assistance efforts are anti-Soviet. Moreover, the most important nations of Eastern Europe in terms of giving military assistance belong in the first category -- the pro-Soviet group -- as do Cuba and Vietnam. And, inasmuch as the Eastern European communist countries are very dependent upon the Soviet Union for weapons, this pattern seems unlikely to change. In fact, most of the Eastern European countries will probably be more reliant on the Soviet Union for arms in the future and will thus probably be more pro-Soviet in their own military assistance policies to Third World countries in coming years. The same may even be said about the neutrals among the Eastern European countries discussed.

Similarly, Cuba and Vietnam are highly dependent upon the Soviet Union for military assistance, not to mention economic aid. These bonds could, in the future, be broken; but in the case of Cuba at least it seems unlikely, unless the Soviet Union chooses to take the initiative in severing the ties. Cuba appears too committed to its present policies and has other independent reasons for sending soldiers and weapons to Third World countries. These factors may well determine that it remains a Soviet ally in most crisis situations. This prospect seems even more likely when it is recognized that Moscow has to a large extent taken over Beijing's role as the supporter of wars of national liberation in the Third World -- a role China has sacrificed in recent years to promote better relations with the West, especially the United States, and in order to devote more energy and financial resources to its own development.

Vietnam, however, may be quite a different case. Its economy is in dire straits. It has also changed from a weapons-rich nation, as a consequence of the huge stores of weapons captured at the close of the Vietnam War to a nation that may now be weapons-poor due to the rapid deterioration of its arms, the need for military supplies to defend against China, and the requirement to maintain military control over Kampuchea and Laos and battle guerrillas in both countries. Hanoi needs at least certain kinds of weapons and military assistance from the Soviet Union. Whether Moscow will want to continue to use Vietnam as a go-between in sending arms assistance to Laos and Kampuchea is unknown. So is another question; will Moscow give Vietnam the economic assistance it needs to promote economic development and to counter offers from the West.

North Korea should be seen as a neutral, even though it is receiving much more military assistance from the Soviet Union than from China. While Korea owes a debt to China from the Korean War period and has steadfastly remained neutral in the Sino-Soviet split, it may be expected to tilt toward Moscow at times while remaining in its neutral posture.

All the nations in the pro-Soviet category to some extent can be justifiably labeled Soviet surrogates. Nevertheless, in many cases they pursue aims that reflect their own revolutionary ideologies, and they espouse global objectives that may be derived from their own particular national goals or their own political systems. Thus one should be cautious in using the term "surrogate" pejoratively. However, in the sense that the Soviet Union can count on a number of its bloc allies to act on its behalf or in cooperation with the Kremlin in crisis situations in the Third World, their loyalty must indeed be taken seriously. Not only are they loyal and their policies similar, but in many cases these countries are more effective than the Soviet Union in supporting leftist, procommunist factions in the Third World. The Soviet Union as a purveyor of military assistance suffers from being a white nation and a large power. Consequently, for one or both of these reasons it is often viewed with apprehension by Third World leaders or revolutionary groups. Soviet leaders seem fully cognizant of this and thus have enlisted the cooperation of "fraternal" communist nations in extending Soviet influence in the Third World. Presumably Moscow will continue to do this.

Similarity in the military assistance programs of communist states is seen in the large percentage of assistance goes to nations that are perceived as important for geopolitical reasons, to procommunist or leftist governments, and to anti-South African and anti-Israeli groups -- though Moscow and Beijing do not agree on specific policies. The real point of disparity is Soviet and Chinese arms assistance to leftist revolutionary or insurgency groups and to terrorist organizations, and to a large extent their discords here are based on their perceptions of each other. Both Moscow and Beijing claim to support leftist causes and wars of national liberation. They disagree on style and on leadership. In fact, in recent years almost as a rule they have not supported the same groups. Beijing has more often supported groups independent observers define as something other than left-wing and has generally refrained from aiding terrorist groups. Moscow claims that it is aiding true revolutionary leftist causes, and does not provide arms assistance to terrorist organizations.

The Soviet Union and China clearly give priority to nations in geopolitically strategic areas. Geopolitical thinking and strategic perceptions seem to influence the military assistance of other communist nations as well. Otherwise it is difficult to explain the unusually large amount of arms assistance that goes to nations near the Horn of Africa, for example. Other strategically important areas of the world likewise seem to attract the attention of the Soviet Union, China, and the other communist arms-giving nations: the Middle East in general, nations on the Indian Ocean, Southeast Asia, and Central America.

All communist countries in the arms assistance business have consistently given arms assistance to groups that opposed the white regimes of southern Africa or are anti-Israel. China has not supported the same groups as the Soviet Union. Because of its anti-Soviet stance it found itself aligned with South Africa during the Angola crisis, which sullied its reputation to some extent in this region. But it has had the upper hand nearby -- in its relations with the victor in the struggle in Zimbabwe-Rhodesia. China, in aligning with the United States against the Soviet Union can argue that the Soviet Union's arms efforts are self-serving and destabilizing. Beijing also preaches about the ungenerous nature of Soviet economic assistance to African nations. Although China's attacks on Soviet aid are often patently motivated by its anti-Soviet feelings, it is true that Moscow is not giving much economic aid to Third World countries and can be accused of overreliance upon its military power and assistance in weapons.

Both Moscow and Beijing pursue anti-Israeli policies in their arms assistance programs in the Middle East. Both have and continue to render assistance to the PLO. But China suffers from a lack of transshipment areas and an inability to give sophisticated weapons. It is able to compensate for this -- although the Soviet Union remains the more important supplier of weapons to the PLO -- because of Moscow's legacy of support for the creation of Isreal and its frequent failures in Middle East policies.

The geopolitical emphasis in communist nations' military assistance seems explainable in two ways. First, communist theory lends itself to a geopolitical perspective more than do other political belief systems. The second factor is the policy of containment implemented by the West soon after World War II. To the Soviet Union this policy harked back to the postrevolution period when the West tried to "surround and strangle" the Soviet Union. China had this same experience after the Korean War. Recently, it has often spoken of the Soviet military buildup, especially the growth of the Soviet navy, as an effort by the Kremlin to contain China.

Thus both Moscow and Beijing have given large amounts of aid to nations on or near the so-called "lines of containment." It is clearly no coincidence that the Soviet Union has sent a huge portion of its military assistance to countries in the Middle East, near the Horn of Africa, on the Indian Ocean, and in Southeast Asia. Likewise, it is not surprising that its military assistance seems coordinated with efforts to gain bases or access to ports. Similarly, China has reacted by trying to establish its own bases of operations while seeking to undermine Soviet efforts to establish bases. It is also noteworthy that the Soviet Union's allies in the military assistance game have helped the Kremlin in this effort, or are themselves recipients of Soviet arms for this purpose. These factors certainly help to explain the Soviet arms assistance relationship with Vietnam and to a lesser degree Vietnam's adamancy in holding on to Kampuchea. Moscow has made use of bases and ports in both countries.

Similar generalizations can be made about Soviet and Chinese efforts to maintain regional power balances in certain areas of the world, particularly in South and Southeast Asia. The Soviet Union's large military aid program to India represents an effort to upset the balance of power on the subcontinent in favor of India and to its own advantage. At the same time, it is to China's disadvantage.

Therefore China has aligned itself with most of the other nations of the region. The percceived Soviet effort to upset the regional balance explains why Pakistan is a major recipient of Chinese arms assistance -- the largest among noncommunist countries. Correspondingly this perception helps explain China's arms assistance to the Khmer Rouge and to guerrilla groups in Laos that are fighting the Vietnamese-supported governments in these countries. This is ironic, and indeed for many observers difficult to understand, as Vietnam was previously the largest recipient of Chinese military aid. After the U.S. withdrawal in 1975, China sought to maintain a balance in Southeast Asia in another way, which meant that Hanoi should not have control of the other countries in Indochina. Not only did Vietnam move into Laos and Kampuchea against Beijing's advice and pressure, but it did so with the help and support of the Soviet Union. Therefore, China believed the USSR and Vietnam are colluding to create an anti-Chinese federation in Southeast Asia which served Moscow's containment goals -- thus, China's aid to opposing forces and its efforts to establish friendly relations with other nations in the region.

It seems unlikely that there will be any marked change in Sino-Soviet relations in the near future. That being the case, it appears that the two will continue to be partially motivated in their arms assistance programs by mutual antipathy and opposition. Naturally, the Soviet Union in the past has enlisted the help of the nations with military assistance programs that complement its own; it is likely it will seek to do this even more in the future in order to isolate China or identify China with Western interests and goals in the Third World. The pro-Soviet Eastern European countries, Cuba, and Vietnam have during the late 1970s and 1980s taken a decidedly more anti-Chinese stance in terms of picking recipients of their arms assistance and what they have said about such assistance.

Communist military assistance, similar to Western assistance, tends to build a dependency relationship between provider and client. Certain trends in this realm help make some final assessments or generalizations about communist military assistance possible. Most Eastern European nations have long been client states of the Soviet Union. Cuba and Vietnam (not to mention Mongolia, which has not been discussed in this book) are also Soviet clients. Albania was a client of China's until 1978. During the Korean War, North Korea was a client of both the Soviet Union and China. The same was true of North Vietnam during the Vietnam War.

Among Third World countries, the Soviet Union has had a host of clients. Some have remained in a client relationship with the Kremin for a number of years. Others are clients only temporarily. Many, especially in the Middle East, are client states in the military assistance sense, but not in most other senses. Recently, there is a clear trend for the Soviet Union to have more and more difficulties in maintaining this kind of reationship with Third World countries.

China has not had any client states in the Third World, with the single exception of Tanzania, (Albania, of course, was also a client until 1978) and Tanzania is now receiving arms aid from the West. Thus China has not suffered the loss of clients as has the

Soviet Union. In fact, in the cases of Tanzania and Pakistan, two of the largest recipients among Third World countries, China seems unconcerned about the fact that they are also receiving Western military assistance. It seems that so long as the Soviet Union cannot make inroads Beijing is satisfied.

Cuba, meanwhile, provided extensive military help to Angola and Ethiopia by sending large numbers of soldiers and advisers. In a cerain sense, then, Angola and Ethiopia may be considered Cuban "clients," even though the Cuban assistance effort was and is subsidized by the USSR.

Vietnam is the only other communist nation with clients, Laos and Kampuchea. These relationships are based upon physical proximity and Soviet influence and do not suggest that Hanoi wishes to establish such relationships elsewhere. The Eastern European nations have apparently avoided clients because of the cooperative roles their military aid has assumed vis-a-vis Soviet military assistance and because they cannot compete with either the Soviet Union or the West in terms of the amount or the level of sophistication of military assitance.

Another mode of assessing communist nations' military assistance is to look at the generosity of their arms assistance and the kind of weapons they provide. Clearly there is a range of donors in both realms.

In terms of generosity in giving military assistance China stands at one end of the spectrum with almost all its arms assistance provided gratis or on the basis of no-interest loans. North Korea is at the other extreme, with most of its military assistance motivated by its desperate need for foreign exchange. Other nations fall somewhere in between. Cuba and Vietnam must also be seen as generous. However, as much of their arms assistance depends upon military and economic assistance from the Soviet Union, this generosity must certainly be qualified. The same must be said of the Eastern European nations, although their relationship with the Soviet Union is different and their military aid ties with the Kremlin generally predate their weapons assistance to other countries. Soviet military assistance is generally rendered on the basis of loans with interest. However, the rate of interest is low and a sizable high proportion of the loans are later written off.

China looks philanthropic from another perspective. It is a poor country yet has a sizeable military assistance program. Also, the quality of weapons it provides to other countries and revolutionary groups is similar to what it has at home. In fact, China has on a number of occasions pointed out that it provided others with its best weapons while its own forces were lacking. And this is true. This is generally not true of Soviet military assistance. While there is evidence of new trends, Moscow, like the United States and other Western countries, still disposes of many of its antiquated weapons through its military assistance program. In a number of cases one can argue that the prices charged for these weapons were too high. China cannot be accused of this practice. The Eastern European countries resemble the Soviet Union more than China using this kind of assessment. Cuba, Vietnam, and North Korea have not provided older out-of-date weapons, although Cuba has been a conduit for such Soviet weapons, and it may be argued that Vietnam has sent many U.S. weapons to Laos and Kampuchea that otherwise would have deteriorated.

One factor to keep in mind in measuring the generosity of an arms assistance program is the fact that a number of Third World nations can afford to buy weapons and are willing to do so. Particularly important are the oil-exporting nations. It is clear that the Soviet Union (like the United States and other Western countries) has adopted policies that translate into gaining foreign exchange from weapons sales. Several Eastern European countries have also altered their military assistance policies to take advantage of profits to be made in selling weapons to rich Third World countries. Such policies, which have not been adopted by China, Cuba, or Vietnam, are carried to an extreme by North Korea.

The kind or sophistication of the weapons in each communist nation's military assistance program is also a useful benchmark of analysis. This factor, however, depends to a large extent upon the country's munition industry. Thus, it may be said to reflect capabilities and not policies in most cases. Only the Soviet Union has a large arms industry; therefore it is the only communist nation that is able to supply a broad spectrum of weapons to other countries. China has an impressive munitions industry in some respects, yet in many ways it is lacking. Beijing is able to compensate to some extent in competing with the Soviet Union by a greater willingness to give the best weapons it can produce to allies and friendly countries. Yet, it suffers in trying to compete with the Soviet Union in terms of numbers of aircraft or naval vessels or in their level of sophistication.

It should be noted that the Soviet Union has hesitated to provide its most sophisticated weapons to other countries, including other communist nations and even its close Warsaw Pact allies. It has been less reluctant in several cases when the recipient is able to pay for these weapons. This in part can be explained that unlike the United States, the Soviet Union does not write off much of its research and deveopment expenses by selling its aircraft and other sophisticated weapons systems to other countries.

It should be pointed out that the Soviet Union has never provided any nuclear weapons to any country, guerrilla movement, or terrorist organization, and there is no evidence to suggest that it will. It may, in fact, be said that the Soviet Union has never provided any nuclear weapons know-how to any country and has never seriously considered doing so. After the second offshore island crisis in 1958, during which its ally China was intimidated by U.S. nuclear weapons, Moscow did promise China assistance in building an atomic bomb. But the next year when it came time to fulfill this promise, Soviet leaders argued that they had agreed only to place nuclear weapons in China and that these weapons would be fired only by Soviet military personnel -- at which time China refused the Soviet offer. From the beginning Soviet leaders probably had no intention of helping

China attain nuclear status. In fact, the Kremlin argues that most other nations of the world that have acquired or are about to acquire nuclear weapons, including China, have gotten their help from the U.S.

China on two occasions may have contemplated rendering some kind of nuclear assistance to other nations. But in neither case does substantial evidence exist. In the first instance, China was thought to be considering conducting a test in another country, Indonesia. In the second, the reports of China aiding Pakistan's nuclear weapons program seem only conjecture. All in all, China, in spite of Mao's rather callous attitude toward nuclear weapons, has seemingly not entertained, very seriously at least, making nuclear weapons or technological help a part of its military assistance program. And considering China's present more legitimate role in inernational politics, it seems unlikely that China will do so in the future.

Communist countries also differ in the extent to which they send soldiers, worker-soldiers, and military advisers to recipient countries and provide military training for nationals of recipient countries in the donor state. Of those communist countries studied Cuba has been and remains the most willing to send soldiers into combat abroad. The Soviet Union, and the Eastern European countries are the most reluctant. The determining factors seem to be the effect of public opinion upon policymaking and the reception their forces may expect to receive abroad. The reaction in the West is also a variable. Vietnam has sent soldiers to Laos and Kampuchea, but it is uncertain what it might do if provided an opportunity elsewhere or asked by the Soviet Union to send troops to other countries. North Korea is also an unknown in this respect. China has sent soldiers abroad on a number of occasions. But in the important cases -- the Korean and Vietnam wars -- China's own security was at issue and its troops crossed the border into a neighboring country only at the request of that country's government.

On the other hand, China has sent a sizable number of worker-soldiers overseas. In fact this can be said to constitute a special trait of China's military assistance program. Other communist nations have sent worker-soldiers, but in no case have the numbers been large. And in no instance did this type of aid constitute an important factor in their military assistance programs. Cuba, however, may be in the process of emulating the Chinese model.

All of the communist nations discussed have sent military advisers to other countries and have provided some training for foreign military or guerrilla organizations in their own countries. The Soviet Union, the Eastern European nations, and Cuba have been the most important providers of military advisers. The Soviet Union and the Eastern European nations have been leaders in terms of training foreign military personnel or guerrillas in a communist state. None of the other communist nations has invited large numbers of foreign soldiers or guerrillas, although China is somewhat competitive in this realm. However, Beijing has preferred to support guerrilla training and has generally opted for building training camps in adjacent countries rather than providing such training in China.

It seems likely that most of the important current trends in communist nations' military assistance can be projected into the future. One exception is the marked decline in Chinese military assistance after 1978 resulting from the severing of relations with Albania and Vietnam. It is likely that Chinese military assistance will increase in the near future. But it should be expected that this assistance will be as anti-Soviet as it has been in recent years. Whether China will once again try to establish a reputation as supporter of anti-status quo movements and radical movements is uncertain; it will probably not do so to the extent it did formerly, at least.

Cuba, Vietnam, and Korea in many respects defy efforts to predict their military assistance policies. Many of their arms assistance efforts have been quite ad hoc and to a large extent depend upon factors that can not be anticipated. Much also depends upon their reationships with the Soviet Union.

Eastern European states will undoubtedly continue to pursue diverse military assistance policies. However, given the certainty of continuing Soviet interest in the Third World, one may expect that the military assistance programs of many Eastern European states will grow in the 1980s in direct proportion to their perceived (by the Soviets and Eastern Europeans) usefulness.

The Soviet Union, for its part, has become more and more competitive in the arms assistance field and will probably continue to increase its exports of weapons. Weapons are the only Soviet product that by any standard of quality is considered outstanding. Arms assistance gives Moscow influence in many areas where other instruments of foreign policy do not work or are wanting. The Soviet Union is also now realizing more profits from arms sales; and this trend is likely to continue.

Communist nations, then, are in the military assistance business to stay. While their motivations in extending assistance often differ, many of their programs are surprisingly similar. With the noteable exception of China, a degree of coordination may even be argued to exist. Clearly, for the United States and other Western states, the complications introduced to international affairs by the large-scale entry of communist nations to the military assistance arena during the 1970s will remain into the forseeable future. The challenge to Western policymakers will be to formulate policies that respond adequately to both the similarities and diversities between and among communist nations' military assistance.

Abbreviations

ACDA	Arms Control and Disarmament Agency
ARVN	Army of the Republic of Vietnam
ASEAN	Association of Southeast Asian Nations
AWACS	Airborne Warning and Control System
CIA	Central Intelligence Agency
CPSU	Communist Party of the Soviet Union
DPRK	Democratic People's Republic of Korea
FALN	Forces for National Liberation
FAR	Revolutionary Armed Forces
FNLA	National Front for the Liberation of Angola
FRELIMO	Front for the Liberation of Mozambique
GDR	German Democratic Republic
ICP	Indochinese Communist Party
IISS	International Institute for Strategic Studies
IRA	Irish Republican Army
LDC	less developed country
MPLA	Popular Movement for the Liberation of Angola
MRA	Movement for Revolutionary Action
NSWP	Non-Soviet Warsaw Pact
PAVN	People's Army of Vietnam
PLO	Palestine Liberation Organization
PRC	People's Republic of China
PRK	People's Republic of Kampuchea
SEATO	Southeast Asian Treaty Organization
SIPRI	Stockholm International Peace Research Institute
SRV	Socialist Republic of Vietnam
SWAPO	South West African People's Organization
UNITA	National Union for the Total Independence of Angola
WTO	Warsaw Treaty Organization
ZANU	Zimbabwe African National Union
ZAPU	Zimbabwe African People's Union

Index

advisors (military) 2, 53, 54, 56, 69, 76, 81, 84, 104, 105, 108, 111, 115, 119, 136, 138, 142, 143, 144, 172, 185
Afghanistan 46, 49, 53, 54, 58, 64, 78, 80, 109, 110, 118, 124, 148, 150, 151
Afghan rebels 110, 118
Africa 11, 8, 40, 41, 42, 43, 44, 46, 47, 49, 52, 53, 54, 55, 56, 62, 73, 78, 79, 82, 83, 84, 85, 86, 87, 89, 90, 94, 100, 110, 122, 123, 134, 135, 137, 138, 139, 142, 146, 147, 148, 149, 150, 151, 169, 170, 171, 180   Also see specific countries
   Horn of 57, 62, 111, 119, 179, 180
   North 47, 68, 79
   Sub-Saharan 43, 44, 67, 68, 78, 79, 86, 88, 110, 121
   West 114
African National Congress 55, 84
air bases 56, 57, 59, 105, 110, 111
aircraft 69, 97, 104, 107, 111, 112, 118, 141, 142, 162, 184, Also see specific names and numbers of planes
AK-47 116
Albania 2, 3, 4, 7, 9, 11, 14, 16, 18, 21, 74, 91, 97, 108, 111, 112, 113, 114, 182, 186
Albanian Communist Party 16
al Fatah 119
Algeria 27, 44, 47, 51, 78, 79, 84, 85, 118, 119, 120, 142, 143, 171
Algerian National Liberation Front 118, 119
Allende, Salvador 85, 87, 95, 123
Alouette helicopter 24
AN-26 (aircraft) 140
Angola 4, 44, 46, 49, 53, 54, 55, 57, 58, 59, 62, 68, 78, 79, 81, 82, 84, 85, 86, 87, 88, 90, 92, 94, 114, 119, 121, 124, 133, 135, 136, 137, 139, 140, 142, 143, 145, 146, 147, 148, 152, 171, 180   Also see National Front for the Liberation of Angola, National Union for the Total Independence of Angola and Popular Movement for the Liberation of Angola
antiaircraft guns 104, 105, 107, 108
antitank missiles 17   Also see AT-3 Sagger
Arafat, Yassir 88, 92
Argentina 43, 170, 171
armored forces 19, 20, 31
armored vehicles 20, 22, 27, 47, 51, 69, 83, 112, 141
Arab countries 43, 53, 55, 56, 59, 69, 142
Arab-Israeli conflict 55, 56, 62, 137

Arms Control and Disarmament Agency (U.S.)   5, 8, 10, 11, 23, 24, 50, 58, 67
arms factories,   See munitions factories
arms market (global)   1, 2
arms transfers,   See military assistance
artillery   27, 68, 83, 88, 104, 115, 142, 167
Association of Southeast Asian Nations (ASEAN)   162, 166
Aswan Dam   111
AT-3 Sagger (anti-tank missile)   22
    atomic weapons,   See nuclear weapons
Austria   2, 10
Asia   40, 41, 42, 43, 52, 53, 55, 62, 73, 86, 87, 100, 134, 135, 169, 170, 171, 172
    East   40, 47, 79
    South   42, 43, 44, 46, 47, 49, 54, 64, 78, 80, 123, 181
    Southeast   49, 54, 83, 96, 117, 118, 123, 159, 161, 165, 167, 180, 181,   Also see Indochina
Assad, Hafez   83, 93

Baader-Meinhof Gang   172
balance of payments, and Soviet arms sales   60, 61
Bangladesh   49, 58, 78, 80, 109, 114
Barracked Alert Units   15
barter agreements, in military assistance   5
bases, military   57, 70, 100, 106, 181,   Also see air bases and naval bases
Batista, Fulgencio   136, 146
Belgium   2, 10
Ben Bela   42
Benin   49, 59, 79
Biafra   82, 83
Bishop, Maurice   138, 152
Black Panthers   172
Boggs, Thomas   171
Bolivia   137, 171
Botswana   114
Brazil   2, 10, 76
Brezhnev, Leonid   20, 42
Brezhnev era   13, 19-21, 56
Bulgaria   2, 3, 4, 10, 11, 14, 15, 20, 21, 24, 25, 26, 29, 30, 31, 37, 74, 75, 80-82, 85, 89, 91, 92, 152, 168
Burma   117, 118
Burmese Communist Party (White Flag)   117
Burundi   49, 79, 120

Cam Ranh Bay   161
Cambodia   49, 103, 107, 115, 116,   Also see Kampuchea
Cameroon   79, 114, 120, 121
Caribbean, region   135, 136, 137, 138, 140, 143, 144, 146, 147, 148, 149, 150, 152, 153,   Also see Central America
Carter, Jimmy   2, 146, 156, 182

Cape Verde 50
Castro, Fidel 123, 134, 135, 136, 137, 139, 146, 148, 150
Ceausescu, Nicolae 74, 86, 87, 90, 95
Central African Empire 87, Also see Central African Republic
Central African Republic 50, 121, Also see Central African Empire
Central Amrica 74, 134, 135, 138, 140, 144, 145, 146, 147, 148,
    149, 150, 152, 180
Central Intelligence Agency (U.S.) 5, 8, 11, 26, 45, 46, 58, 67, 76,
    77, 78, 80
Chad 50, 121, 171
Chile 81, 85, 87, 95, 171
China, People's Republic of 2, 3, 4, 5, 6, 7, 8, 9, 11, 15, 21, 54, 56,
    62, 74, 77, 78, 79, 80, 87, 96-133, 162, 163, 165, 168, 169, 177,178,
    179, 180, 181, 182, 183, 184, 185, 186, Also see Sino-Soviet
    Alliance, Sino-Soiet dispute, Sino-Vietnamese War
Chen Yi 104
Christian Science Monitor 82
Columbia 149
Congo 50, 57, 59, 79, 84, 85, 87, 110, 120, 121, 137, Also see Zaire
Congolese rebels 119
construction, as a form of military assistance 1, 2, 5, 46, 51, 56,
    105, 139, 150
Cooley, John 82
coups, military assistance and 8, 119, 120
credits, as a means of giving military assistance 5, 47, 51, 103
Cuba 2, 3, 4, 8, 9, 11, 46, 51, 53, 55, 57, 68, 78, 83, 84, 88, 89,
    114, 121, 123, 134-158, 163, 171, 177, 178, 180, 182, 183, 185, 186
Cultural Revolution (China) 100, 102, 106, 121
Cyprus 82
Czechoslovakia 2, 3, 4, 11, 14, 15, 20, 21, 22, 24, 25, 26, 29, 30,
    31, 32, 33, 37, 69, 74, 75, 82-83, 85, 89, 93, 94, 112, 152, 168

de Gaulle, Charles 118
defense treaties, and military assistance 15, 104
delivery time for arms, U.S. and Soviet Union compared 47
Deng Xiaoping (Teng Hsiao-ping) 106
Denmark 173
developing countries 1, 49 Also see Third World
Dien Bien Phu 104
Duarte, Jose Napoleon 145

economic assistance 56, 57, 58, 75, 83, 89, 99, 110, 112, 115, 121,
    142, 147, 148, 183, 184
economic burden, of military assistance 59, 60, 101, 103, 142, 150
education, as a form of military assistance 31, 32, Also see training
Egypt 2, 7, 8, 10, 42, 46, 49, 52, 53, 54, 56, 57, 58, 59, 62, 69, 70,
    76, 80, 82, 84, 87, 88, 97, 108, 112, 113, 132, 172, 180
Egypt-Libya War 172
el Nimeiry, Gaafar 157
El Salvador 74, 84, 135, 136, 138, 144, 145, 146, 147, 148, 149,
    151, 156, 183, 186, 197

Equatorial Guinea   50, 59, 78, 79, 143
Eritrea, aid to rebels in   83, 112
Ethiopia   44, 46, 47, 50, 51, 53, 55, 57, 58, 59, 62, 64, 68, 78, 79,
    81, 82, 83, 84, 85, 86, 92, 135, 139, 140, 142, 143, 145, 146,
    147, 148, 152, 180
Europe   40, 59
    Eastern   4, 8, 9, 13-38, 40, 53, 55, 62, 66, 72-95, 96, 178, 182,
        183, 184, 185, 186
    Western   123, 147, 173
European wars   30
exchange rates, as a problem in quantifying military assistance   5

F-6 (Shenyang fighter plane)   109, 113, 114
F-7   113
F-9   102
F-14   1
Fantan (Chinese jet fighter)   109
Fatherland Safeguarding Movement (Argentina)   171
Fatherland Safeguarding Movement (Paraguay)   171
Federation of Indochina   160
Forces for National Liberation (Venezuela)   170
Ford, Gerald   161
Fourth World   163
France   2, 24, 44, 82, 105, 118
French Somaliland   120
FROG missile   8
Front for the Liberation of Mozambique   (FRELIMO)   84, 87, 93, 121
FUG-70 (scout car)   22

Gairy, Eric   138
Geneva Conference   105, 107
Germany   15
    East (German Democratic Republic)   2, 3, 4, 10, 11, 17, 20, 21,
        22, 24, 25, 26, 29, 31, 32, 37, 46, 51, 54, 74, 75, 82, 83-85, 89,
        152, 168
    National People's Army   16
    West (Federal Republic of Germany)   2, 15, 83, 172
German Frontier Police   15
Ghana   42, 54, 79, 82, 86, 87, 120
grants, as a form of military assistance   5, 47, 51, 183
Granma   152
Great Britain   2, 24, 102
Grechko, A.   14, 18, 19, 22
Grenada   138, 143, 144, 146, 149, 152
Griffiths, Franklin   63
Group of 77   157
Guatemala   138, 151
Guatamalan People's Revolutionary Army   171
guerrilla forces   97, 100, 110, 115, 118, 137, 171, 184,   Also see
    liberation struggles, insurgency groups, wars of national liberation
guerrilla training camps   108, 119, 120, 142, 170, 185, 186

guerrilla wars 8, 14, 164, 165, Also see wars of national liberation
Guevara, Ernesto "Che" 137
Guinea 42, 50, 78, 86, 97, 114, 119, 120, 137, 143
Guinea-Bissau 50, 78, 79, 84, 143
Gulf of Tonkin 105
Guyana 78, 138, 144, 149

Haig, Alexander 147
helicopters 141, 158, 162, Also see Alouette helicopter
Heng Samrin 5, 115, 116
Ho Chi-Minh 104, 105, 160
Holland (See Netherlands)
Honduras 138, 151
Huang Hua 109
human rights 2
Hungary 2, 3, 4, 10, 11, 15, 17, 18, 20, 22, 24, 25, 26, 29, 31, 37,
    74, 75, 85, 89, 94, 152, 168
Hungarian Revolution (1956) 17
Husak, Gustav 83
Hutchings, Raymond 60

India 42, 43, 46, 49, 53, 54, 57, 58, 59, 76, 78, 80, 100, 102, 108,
    109, 110, 117, 181
Indian Ocean 56, 59, 180, 181, Also see Asia, South
Indochina 98, 100, 104, 106, 115, 117, 159, 160, 162, 163, 165
Indochinese Communist Party 160
Indonesia 42, 49, 53, 79, 82, 88, 97, 113, 117, 185
industrial base, and ability to give military assistance 1
insurgency groups 162, 167, 170, 179, Also see liberation struggles,
    wars of national liberation, guerrilla forces, terrorism
intermediate range ballistic missiles (IRBM) 12
international balance of forces 55, Also see international system
International Institute for Strategic Studies (London) 6, 8, 12, 20,
    26, 28, 30, 37, 140
international system 40, 55, 96, 97
international division of labor 42
Iran 1, 42, 44, 46, 49, 57, 58, 64, 76, 80, 110, 163, 173
Iraq 27, 46, 47, 49, 51, 53, 57, 58, 60, 68, 76, 78, 80, 82, 120, 143, 173
Irish Republican Army (IRA) 82
IS-2 (tank) 141
Islander transport 24
Israel 2, 10, 52, 59, 76, 113, 119, 124, 162, 180
Italy 2, 10

Jamaica 138, 144, 149
Japan 2, 10, 83, 166, 173
Japanese Red Army 172
Japanese weapons (World War II) 101, 103
jet aircraft 102, 103, Also see aircraft and specific names and
    numbers of planes
joint military exercises 32

Jordan 76
Jurem aircraft 24

Kampuchea 3, 5, 79, 83, 87, 116, 117, 124, 159, 160, 161, 162, 163,
      165, 178, 181, 183, 185, Also see Cambodia and Khmer Rouge
Kashmir 108
Katanga, rebels in 84
Kaunda, Kenneth 95
Keita, Modibo 42
Kenya 86, 120
Khmer Rouge 5, 83, 87, 107, 115, 160, 161, 181
Khrushchev, Nikita 16, 17, 18, 19, 41, 42, 100
Krushchev "buildup" 13, 17-19
Kim Il-sung 169, 173
Kintex 81
Korea (North, or Democratic People's Republic of Kintex) 2, 3, 4,
      7, 9, 10, 11, 96, 97, 99, 103, 104, 113, 115, 152, 168-76, 178,
      182, 183, 184, 185, 186
      South, or Republic of Korea 2, 10, 76, 172, 176
Korean War 96, 98, 103, 104, 115, 168, 179, 180, 182, 185
Kuwait 49

landing craft 141
Laos 3, 49, 83, 87, 103, 107, 108, 115, 116, 152, 159, 160, 163,
      178, 181, 183, 185, Also see Pathet Lao
Latin America 46, 47, 50, 52, 73, 78, 79, 82, 84, 86, 87, 100, 122,
      123, 134, 137, 138, 140, 148, 149, 151, 157, 169, 170, Also see
      South America
Le Duan 95
Lebanese leftist 172
Lebanon 49, 57, 59, 81, 82, 163, Also see Lebanese leftists
Leftist Revolutionary Chile 171
liberation movements 54, 70, 82, 84, 87, 89, 90, 97, 98, 100, 103,
      110, 112, 113, 115-122, 123, 124, 135, 136, 137, 138, 140, 148,
      150, 159, 163, 170, 178, 186, Also see wars of national liberation,
      guerrilla forces, insurgency groups, terrorism
Libya 8, 27, 43, 44, 46, 47, 50, 51, 57, 58, 60, 69, 76, 78, 79, 81,
      84, 88, 90, 92, 167, 172
licensing agreements for arms production 19, 22, 24, 26, 27, 31, 32
Lin Biao (Lin Piao) 102
Lon Nol 107

Madagascar 50, 172
maintainance, as military assistance 7
Malaya 117, Also see Malaysia
Malaysia 43, 113, 117, 118
Mali 50, 59, 78, 79
Manley, Michael 138, 144
Mao Zedong (Mao Tse-tung) 98, 100, 101, 104, 105, 123, 126, 185
Mengistu, Haile 60
Meo tribes 117

"metal eaters" 18
Mexico 140, 147, 149, 157, 171
Mi-2 helicopter 22
Middle East 1, 8, 40, 42, 3, 44, 46, 47, 49, 53, 56, 59, 60, 65, 71,
    73, 78, 80, 100, 118, 119, 122, 123, 134, 135, 137, 139, 146, 151,
    161, 163, 169, 180, 182
Mig-15 7, 105, 141
Mig-17 7, 17, 105, 113, 141
Mig-19 7, 108, 109, 114, 115
Mig-21 7, 17, 22, 28, 47, 51, 112, 113, 114
Mig-23 1, 28, 51, 140, 141, 172
Mig-23D (Also known as Mig-27) 7, 47, 51, 113
Mig-27 (Also known as Mig-23D) 7, 47, 51, 69
military assistance, Also see sales, grants, credits
    total world's 1
    trends 1, 2
    definition 5
minesweapers 141
missiles 51, 97, 103, Also see SAM missiles and other specific
    names and numbers
Mongolian People's Republic 152, 182
Morocco 50, 58, 76, 78, 83, 119, 142
Movement for Revolutionary Action (MRA) 171
Mozambique 50, 54, 55, 78, 81, 82, 83, 84, 85, 86, 87, 88, 110, 119,
    120, 121, 132, 137, 152
Mugabe, Robert 5, 81, 82, 92, 122, 172
munitions factories 101, 102, 109, 139, 162, 165, 184
multiple rocket launcher 24
Namibia 55, 82, 87, 88

Nasser, Gamal 60, 70
national liberation wars 5, 8, 9, 14, 41, 79, Also see guerrilla wars,
    liberation struggles
National Front for the Liberation of Angola (FNLA) 5
National Liberation Front (Viet Cong) 105, 170
naval bases 57, 59, 111, 112
Netherlands 2, 10
Nicaragua 74, 84, 138, 143, 144, 146, 147, 148, 149, 151, 155, 156,
    158, 171
Nigeria 7, 50, 79, 83, 85, 86, 121, 167
Nixon Doctrine 180
Nkomo, Joshwa 5, 55, 82, 84
Nkruma, Kwame 42, 54, 120
non-aligned movement 74, 108, 148, 150
non-aligned nations 41, 88, 149, 150
Non-Proliferation Treaty 8, 33, 34
Non-Soviet Warsaw Pact forces 16, 17, 18, 19, 20, 22, 23, 24, 25,
    27, 28, 31, 32, 34
North America 59
North Atlantic Treaty Organizaton (NATO) 25, 27
northern tier (Europe) 20, 30, 31, 32, 33

nuclear weapons   8, 12, 17, 18, 97, 100, 101, 110, 184, 185

Obasanjo, Olusegun   157
Ofer, Gur   59
Ogaden   142
Oman   55
Orao aircraft   24
Organization of African Unity (OAU)   157
Organization of Petroleum Exporting Countries (OPEC)   39, 60, 66
Ortega, Humberto   152
OT-64 (armored personel carrier)   22

Pakistan   42, 49, 58, 59, 76, 78, 80, 97, 108, 109, 110, 113, 118,
    167, 181, 182, 185
Palestine Liberation Organization (PLO)   59, 82, 83, 84, 88, 93, 94,
    119, 120, 171, 180
Palestinian guerrillas   172
Pan Africanist Congress (South Africa)   122
Panama   146, 149
Paraguay   171
Pathet Lao   83, 107
Patriotic Front for the People of Zimbabwe   81, 82
patrol boats   109, 111, 112, 113, 114, 141, 160
Pemba Island   121
People's Liberation Army (Argentina)   170
People's Liberation Front (Sri Lanka)   172
Persian Gulf   59
personnel, training of in communist countries   53, 79
Peru   46, 50, 58, 78, 79, 171
Philippines   117, 118
phoenix missile   1
pilot training   51
Pol Pot   115, 116, 161
Poland   2, 3, 4, 11, 14, 17, 18, 20, 22, 24, 25, 26, 29, 30, 31, 33, 37,
    74, 75, 85-86, 89, 94, 152, 168
Polish crisis (1980-82)   37

Radio-Free Europe Research   82
raw materials, concern for   54, 60
Reagan, Ronald (Reagan Administration)   134, 135, 146, 147
research and development   184
Revolutionary Armed Forces (Cuba)   135, 139
revolutionary movements, See liberation struggles, national liberation
    wars
Rhodesia   87, 111, 114, 121,   Also see Zimbabwe
road building   108, 109, 119
Roberto, Holden   5
rocket launchers   47, 51
Rokossovsky, Konstantin   15
Romania   2, 3, 4, 10, 11, 14, 15, 17, 18, 20, 21, 23, 24, 25, 26, 30,
    31, 32, 36, 37, 74, 86-88, 90, 91, 92, 94, 95, 113, 168

Russo-Japanese War   163
Rwanda   120

SA-9 (missile air defense system)   51
Sadat, Anwar   54
sales of weapons   51, 60, 68, 82, 88, 185, 186
Salvadoran guerrillas   145, 147
SAM missiles   109, 113
Sandinistas   84, 138, 143-144, 146, 152, 171
Saudi Arabia   1, 76
Savimbi, Jonas   5, 54, 121
Scud missile   8, 18, 28, 29, 31
Seaga, Edward   138, 144, 157
Seven Day War   53, 54
ships   97, 103, 104, 107, 113, 114, 184,   Also see patrol boats, submarines and specific names and numbers of ships
Sierra Leone   79, 114
Sihanouk, N.   107
Singapore   163
Sino-Soviet Alliance   99
Sino-Soviet border   100
Sino-Soviet dispute   4, 12, 99, 112, 179, 181, 182
Sino-Vietnamese War   5, 54
soldiers, provided as military assistance   53, 83, 105, 107, 108, 109, 135, 140, 142, 178, 185,   Also see volunteers
Somalia   7, 46, 50, 53, 54, 57, 58, 59, 62, 120, 142, 172, 180
Somoza, Anastasio   144, 146, 152
Son Sann   115
South Africa   55, 76, 111, 114, 119, 121, 122, 142, 180
South America   148, 150,   Also see Latin America
Southeast Asia Treaty Organization (SEATO)   107
southern tier (Europe)   23, 30, 31
Southwest Africa People's Organization (SWAPO)   55, 82, 84, 86, 88, 93, 121, 122
Soviet Union   1, 2, 3, 4, 6, 7, 8, 9, 11, 12, 13-72, 74, 75, 76, 77, 78, 79, 80, 81, 86, 89, 91, 94, 96, 97, 99, 100, 101, 102, 103, 106, 108, 109, 111, 112, 114, 115, 116, 117, 118 119, 121, 122, 123, 127, 134, 136, 137, 139, 140, 141, 145, 146, 147, 149, 150, 151, 152, 156, 158, 161, 162, 163, 166, 167, 168, 169, 177, 178, 179, 180, 181, 182, 183, 184, 185, 186,   Also see Sino-Soviet Alliance, Sino-Soviet border, Sino-Soviet dispute
Soviet strategic-rocket force   18
Soviet navy   52, 56, 69, 100, 180, 181
Socialist Commonwealth   15, 32
spare parts, as military assistance   7, 111, 113
Sri Lanka   49, 80, 113, 114, 172
Stalin, Joseph   40, 41, 104
State Department (United States)   45, 46, 138, 145, 156
status of forces agreements   17
Stockholm International Peace Research Institute (SIPRI)   5, 8, 12, 37, 67

Strongal, Lubomir   93
students   81, 84, 85, 86, 88, 140, 171
SU-7   17
Sudan   7, 50, 79, 81, 83, 86, 88, 89, 113, 114
submarines   97, 109, 112, 140, 141
Sudets, V.   36
Suez Crisis   132
Sukarno, Achmed   42
superpowers   99
support services, as military assistance   7, 75
surplus weapons, given as military assistance   52
Sweden   2, 10
Switzerland   2, 10
Syria   27, 42, 46, 47, 49, 51, 53, 57, 58, 59, 60, 69, 76, 78, 80, 82,
    83, 93, 119, 120, 137, 172

Taiwan   76
Tanganyika   110, 121
tanks   7, 12, 27, 28, 47, 97, 109, 111, 112, 114, 115, 125, 141, 142,
    Also see specific names and numbers
Tan-Zam Railroad   111, 121
Tanzania   50, 79, 85, 97, 108, 110, 111, 113, 120, 121, 124, 129,
    172, 182
technical aid, as military assistance   5, 46, 51, 53, 54, 75, 77, 83
technicians   53, 68, 77, 78, 142, 158
terrorism, military assistance to support   8, 9, 83, 84, 90, 115, 162,
    171, 179, 184
Thailand   116, 117, 118, 167
    aid to rebels in   83
Thai Communist Party   172
Third World   4, 7, 9, 13-39, 47, 48, 49, 51, 52, 53, 72, 73, 74, 75, 76,
    77, 84, 85, 86, 88, 89, 90, 91, 96, 97, 98, 100, 101, 115, 134, 136,
    137, 146, 147, 148, 150, 151, 157, 163, 170, 177, 178, 179, 180,
    181, 182, 183, 184,   Also see developing countries
Tito, Josie   22, 88
Todorov, Stanko   80, 92
Togo   79, 87
torpedo boats   140
Toure, Seko   42
training, as a form of military assistance   1, 2, 5, 20, 31, 32, 46,
    47, 51, 53, 79, 81, 82, 84, 104, 105, 110, 112, 114, 117, 170,
    172, 178, 185,   Also see technical aid and technicians
transport planes   141
treaties of friendship   81, 107
T-34 (tank)   87, 108, 141
T-54 (tank)   17, 28, 81, 87, 141
T-55 (tank)   17, 83, 141
T-59 (tank)   108
T-62 (tank)   22, 114, 141
T-64 (tank)   7, 12
T-72 (tank)   7, 12, 27, 28, 37

T-80 (tank) 27
TU-95 (aircraft) 140
Tunisia 114
Turkey 42, 58, 76, 81

Uganda 50, 83, 111
Union for the Total Independence of Angola (UNITA) 54, 121, 122
Union of Soviet Socialist Republics (See Soviet Union)
United Kingdom (See Great Britain)
United Nations 43, 103, 149, 157, 168
United States 1, 2, 8, 10, 16, 22, 39, 47, 51, 53, 55, 56, 62, 64, 68,
    69, 76, 96, 97, 99, 100, 101, 102, 105, 113, 115, 116, 118, 119,
    122, 123, 136, 140, 146, 147, 149, 161, 162, 166, 172, 177, 180,
    182, 183, 184, 185
Uruguay 171
Ussuri River 100

Valona Bay 16
Valasco, Alberto 157
Venezuela 137, 149, 157, 170
Viet Cong (See National Liberation Front)
Vietnam (South or Republic of Vietnam) 115, 161
Vietnam (Socialist Republic of Vietnam) 1, 2, 3, 4, 5, 7, 9, 11, 76,
    80, 81, 83, 85, 87, 88, 93, 96, 97, 100, 103, 105, 106, 115, 117,
    118, 124, 127, 152, 159-67, 177, 178, 181, 182, 183, 185, 186,
    Also see Vietnam War
Vietnam War 84, 87, 96, 99, 100, 103-07, 116, 170, 182, 185
volunteers 96, 103, 118, 132, 170, Also see soldiers
Warsaw Pact 4, 6, 8, 13, 16, 19, 20, 21, 22, 24, 25, 28, 29, 32, 33,
    47, 182, 184
Warsaw Pact's Political Consultative Committees 16, 20, 38
Warsaw Pact's Joint Armed Forces 20, 21
Warsaw Treaty Organization 16, 17, 18, 19, 21, 27, 33, 52
weapons industry 102, Also see munitions factories
Western military assistance 23, 66
Western countries 177, 178, 180, 183, 184, 185
Western Hemisphere 147, 148, 149, 150
workers, as a form of military assistance 106, 107, 185
World War II 101, 103, 160, 180

Yak 18, 22
Yemen 53
    North Yemen or Arab Yemen Republic 49, 58, 59, 78, 80, 81,
    119
    South Yemen or People's Democratic Republic of Yemen 49,
    55, 57, 58, 59, 78, 80, 81, 82, 84, 119, 143
Yugoslavia 2, 3, 4, 7, 8, 10, 11, 14, 16, 18, 21, 22, 24, 25, 26, 74,
    75, 88-89, 90, 91
Yugoslavian People's Liberation Army 16

Zaire 79, 83, 84, 87, 110, 114, 171

Zambia   50, 79, 83, 84, 85, 87, 114, 120, 121
Zanzibar   110, 121
Zhivkou, Todor   80, 81, 92
Zimbabwe   5, 55, 82, 87, 88, 92, 122, 143, 172, 180
Zimbabwe Africa National Union (ZANU)   5, 87, 121, 143
Zimbabwe Africa People's Union (ZAPU)   5, 84, 86, 87, 143
zone of peace concept (Soviet Union)   41

Contributors

JOHN F. COPPER is Associate Professor of International Studies at Southwestern University at Memphis, Tennessee. He received his M.A. from the University of Hawaii, and his Ph.D. from the University of South Carolina. He is the author of China's Foreign Aid: An Instrument of Peking's Foreign Policy (D.C. Heath, 1976); A Matter of Two Chinas: The China-Taiwan Issue in US Foreign Policy (Foreign Policy Research Institute, 1979, with William R. Kintner); China's Global Role: An Analysis of Peking's National Power Capabilities in the Context of an Evolving International System (Hoover Institution, 1980); and numerous other articles on Asian and international affairs in Asian Affairs, Asian Quarterly, Asian Survey, Current Scene, and International Studies.

DANIEL S. PAPP is Associate Professor of International Affairs and Director of the School of Social Sciences at Georgia Institute of Technology. From 1977 to 1978, he served as a research professor with the Strategic Studies Institute. A graduate of Dartmouth College, he received his doctorate in international affairs at the University of Miami's Center for Advanced International Studies. He has published articles in International Journal, Social Science Quarterly, Soviet Union, Resources Policy, Parameters, US Naval War College Review, and Current History. He is the author of Vietnam: The View from Moscow, Peking and Washington (McFarland, 1981); and The Net of International Relations (Macmillan, 1983).

NACK AN received his Ph.D. at the University of Virginia, and is Associate Professor of Political Science at Georgia State University. He has previously taught at Virginia Polytechnic Institute and Trenton State College. He has written a considerable amount on politics and government in Western Europe. His current research interests include politics in developing nations and the role of the military. He spent most of 1981-82 in Korea collecting materials for a text on Korean politics.

ROSE AN is Associate Professor of Political Science at Morris Brown College. She received her Ph.D. from Rutgers. Her current work centers on Far Eastern comparative politics and political socialization processes. She has published widely in Korean political science and international relations journals.

W. RAYMOND DUNCAN is Distinguished Teaching Professor of Political Science and Director of Global Studies, the State University of New York, College at Brockport. His previous publications include

Soviet Policy in Developing Countries (Krieger, 1981, edited), Soviet
Policy in the Third World (Pergamon, 1980, edited), Latin American
Politics: A Developmental Approach (Praeger, 1976); and The Quest
for Change in Latin America (Oxford, 1970, edited with James Nelson
Goodsell); plus numerous articles on Latin American politics and
Soviet-Cuban policy in the Caribbean, Central and South America.

TROND GILBERG is Professor of Political Science and Associate
Director of the Slavic and Soviet Language and Area Center at the
Pennsylvania State University. His previous publications include The
Soviet Communist Party and Scandinavian Communism: The
Norwegian Case (1973); Modernization in Romania Since World War
II, and numerous articles on Eastern Europe in journals such as
Problems of Communism and East Europe Quarterly.

ROGER E. KANET is Professor of Political Science at the University
of Illinois at Urbana-Champaign. He received a Ph.D. from
Berchmanskolleg (Pullach-bei-Munchen, Germany), a bachelor's degree
from Xavier University, master's degrees from Lehigh University and
Princeton University in international relations and political science
respectively, and a doctorate in political science from Princeton
University. He has held research grants from the American Council
of Learned Societies, the NATO faculty Fellowship Program, the US
Department of State, the International Research and Exchanges Board,
and the US Information Agency. His published works include numerous
articles on Soviet and East European foreign policy and the following
edited or co-edited books: The Behavioral Revolution and Communist
Studies(1971); On the Road to Communism, with Ivan Volgyes (1972);
The Soviet Union and the Developing Nations (1974); Soviet and East
European Foreign Policy: A Bibliography (1974); Soviet Economic
and Political Relations with the Developing World, with Donna Bahry
(1974); Policy and Politics in Gierek's Poland, with Maurice D. Simon
(1980); and Soviet Foreign Policy in the 1980s (1982).

DOUGLAS PIKE is currently the Director of the Indochina Studies
Project of the Institute of East Asian Studies at the University of
California, Berkeley. Previously, he was a US Foreign Service
Information Officer who served most of his adult life in Asia. He
was educated at the University of California, Berkeley, American
University, and the Massachusetts Institute of Technology. He has
been professionally concerned with the Communist movements in
Indochina for his entire career, serving in posts in Saigon, Tokyo,
Hong Kong and Taipei. He was a member of the State Department
Policy Planning Council (1974-77) and was later detailed to the
International Security Agency at the Pentagon. Mr. Pike is the
author of Viet Cong: The Organization and Techniques of the National
Liberation Front of South Vietnam (1964), War, Peace and the
Vietcong (1970), History of Vietnamese Communism (1978), and
numerous articles.